SHARING FRIENDSHIP

Drawing on an extraordinary range of sources, Thomson develops an account of friendship to help us better understand how to be church in the world in which we find ourselves. I am humbled by Thomson's use of my work for shaping the argument of this book. But then, that is what friends do, that is, shape one another. I am so fortunate that Thomson claims me as a friend.

Stanley Hauerwas, Professor Emeritus, Duke Divinity School, USA

Sharing Friendship represents a post-liberal approach to ecclesiology and theology generated out of the history, practices and traditions of the Anglican Church. Drawing on the theological ethics of Stanley Hauerwas, this book explores the way friendship for the stranger emerges from contextually grounded reflection and converses with contemporary Anglican theologians within the English tradition, including John Milbank, Oliver O'Donovan, Rowan Williams, Daniel Hardy and Anthony Thiselton.

Dear Dan,

Wishing you God's blessing as you are ordained Deacon along with some thoughts on the Church for you to ponder!

+ John Selby

26/6/21.

Explorations in Practical, Pastoral and Empirical Theology

Series Editors

Leslie J. Francis, University of Warwick, UK
Jeff Astley, St Chad's College, Durham University, UK
Martyn Percy, Ripon College Cuddesdon and The Oxford
Ministry Course, Oxford, UK
Nicola Slee, The Queen's Foundation Birmingham, UK

Theological reflection on the church's practice is now recognized as a significan element in theological studies in the academy and seminary. Ashgate's series in practical, pastoral and empirical theology seeks to foster this resurgence of interest and encourage new developments in practical and applied aspects of theology worldwide. This timely series draws together a wide range of disciplinary approaches and empirical studies to embrace contemporary developments including: the expansion of research in empirical theology, psychological theology, ministry studies, public theology, Christian education and faith development; key issues of contemporary society such as health, ethics and the environment; and more traditional areas of concern such as pastoral care and counselling.

Other titles in the series include:

The Faith Lives of Women and Girls
Qualitative Research Perspectives
Edited by Nicola Slee, Fran Porter and Anne Phillips

Saving Face
Enfacement, Shame, Theology
Stephen Pattison

Using the Bible in Practical Theology
Historical and Contemporary Perspectives
Zoë Bennett

Military Chaplaincy in Contention
Chaplains, Churches and the Morality of Conflict
Edited by Andrew Todd

Sharing Friendship

Exploring Anglican Character, Vocation, Witness and Mission

JOHN B. THOMSON
Bishop of Selby, Diocese of York, UK

LONDON AND NEW YORK

First published 2015 by Ashgate Publishing

2 Park Square, Milton Park, Abingdon, Oxon OX14 4RN
711 Third Avenue, New York, NY 10017, USA

Routledge is an imprint of the Taylor & Francis Group, an informa business

First issued in paperback 2017

British Library Cataloguing in Publication Data
A catalogue record for this book is available from the British Library

The Library of Congress has cataloged the printed edition as follows:
Thomson, John B. (John Bromilow), 1959–
    Sharing Friendship: Exploring Anglican Character, Vocation, Witness and Mission /
by John B. Thomson.
        pages   cm. – (Explorations in Practical, Pastoral, and Empirical Theology)
    Includes bibliographical references and index.
    1. Friendship – Religious aspects – Christianity. 2. Anglican Communion –
Doctrines. I. Title.
    BV4647.F7T46 2015
    241'.6762–dc23   2014041894

ISBN 978-1-4724-5452-2 (hbk)
ISBN 978-1-138-05334-2 (pbk)

Contents

Preface

This book explores the character of Anglican mission as friendship for the stranger in forms of ecclesial life and in conversation with contemporary Anglican theologians and practitioners. Ministry as a vicar, a theological educator and a trainer, in England and abroad over the past 25 years has convinced me of two things. First, that Anglicans have something distinctive to contribute to the character of Christian mission. Second, that Anglicans have lost confidence in their distinctive charism or gift. For many, certainly in England, there is diffidence about being Anglican and also a lack of historical awareness about what has made us the church we are. In the more assertive and activist parts of the Church of England there can also be a diminishment of the value of the historic Anglican project in favour of more immediately engaging ways of sharing the faith. Yet without a sense of who we are there can be no faithful way of recognising the character of our vocation in mission. So this book represents a post-liberal approach to ecclesiology and theology generated out of the history, practices and traditions of the Anglican Church with particular reference to England but including insights from life and work in Africa and Latin America. It avoids abstract definitions of mission or friendship and instead explores the way friendship for the stranger emerges from contextually grounded reflection. This is a particular sort of friendship rooted in the way of Jesus, the origins of the English Church and the shape and practices of the Church of England since the Reformation. The stranger is the *paroikos*, the parishioner, who is literally the neighbour or wanderer we do not yet know or who has become estranged from us through past enmity, circumstance, culture or illness. The stranger is also reality which is yet to be disclosed to us in the human and non-human worlds. The stranger is both intimate and cosmic. At a time when English Anglicans feel on the back foot, when internal conflicts can seem overwhelming and when new ways of being church are being explored, I believe that Anglicans in England need a clear sense of their character as a community called to love the stranger that England now represents if they are to remain faithful to their distinctive calling. Anglicans cannot simply be instrumental or pragmatic about their vocation, since this would be to sell their soul for a mess of potage.[1] Their witness must flow from their character, which is disclosed by their practices and story as

---

[1]   Genesis 25: 29–34.

an *ecclesia* or church committed to its *paroikoi* or neighbours in every dimension of their lives.

The book is divided into three parts. The first part is about the practice of Christian friendship and is rooted in a conversation with the work of the theological ethicist Stanley Hauerwas. The focus here is on how Anglican mission, past, present and overseas, represents God's self-giving friendship particularly through its flexible understanding of mission as parochial. This self-giving friendship is rooted in the discipleship of the New Testament and is formed through the practices of worship, community and tradition. I argue that this vision of friendship with the stranger was embodied by early African mission to the British Isles and, though not exclusive to Anglicans, is at the heart of Anglican witness. The second part is about reflection. It is a conversation with some of the creative and challenging thinking going on in English Anglicanism and how this helps us *see* the context and possibilities of Anglican mission today. Consequently the section ranges over many themes showing how Anglicans engage with creation, society, history, politics, grace, hermeneutics, culture and wisdom. My intention is to show a range of ways in which contemporary Anglican thinkers expand our vision of Anglican vocation. My hope is that readers will be challenged and encouraged by the quality and extent of this intellectual work and recover confidence in their Anglican calling. The third part looks at the challenge of mission and witness today with particular attention to secularisation, fresh expressions of church and the witness of Anglican churches in England and overseas. It argues that friendship with the stranger is rooted in the DNA of Anglican congregational life but that this can only be sustained today if Anglicans are prepared for the sort of self-giving which characterised the mission of Jesus as recalled in Philippians 2: 5–11. This witness keeps alive the story of Anglican mission as well as embodying it, advocating and improvising upon it in today's world.

What makes this book distinctive is that it looks at witness, mission and vocation through the lens of Anglican character particularly as it has emerged and is practised in the English context. It encourages a conversation between practitioners and scholars and is therefore about bridge-building and openness which are key aspects of Anglican character. As someone who has studied and written on the work of Stanley Hauerwas, I have also made an attempt in this book to explore how Anglican churches, particularly the Church of England, are communities of character and to see what this might look like for Anglicans reimagining their contemporary vocation. It is the fifth of a series of books responding to his challenge and its fruitfulness within the English context. The first argued that his project enables the church to recover a proper freedom for faith grounded in its story and practice rather than relevance to contemporary cultures.[2] The second explored the possibilities for witness in a church on edge, feeling increasingly marginalised by its host society.[3] The third was a liturgically shaped discipleship development course which privileged practice rather than ideas as the vehicle for Christian formation.[4] The fourth improvised upon Hauerwas's work to explore embodied apologetics or living holiness.[5] This book is a meditation on Anglican character, particularly within England, and its suggestiveness for distinctively Anglican mission. In theological terms it is a post-liberal exploration of Anglican ecclesial ethics by a ministry practitioner situated within this church's mission in England. As such it seeks to display the theme of Anglican friendship rather than defining it in advance in an essentialist way or by comparing Anglican friendship with other traditions beyond noting the way Christian friendship emerged in contrast to views of friendship practised in the ancient Greco-Roman world. My intention is to show how Anglican witness in practice is best captured by the notion of friendship for the stranger and the strange or friendship with the other rather than simply with the familiar. Furthermore to speak of this sort of friendship as central to the character of Anglican witness is not to fantasise about a naïve utopian and idealistic view of the church which can easily be deconstructed by the ambiguous performance of the church throughout history. Rather to begin with the church is to begin with the actual existence of this fragile, practising and performing historic community within which the Bible is seen as Scripture, the story of God's activity in life, confident that the Holy Spirit will guide that fallible church into God's truthfulness in God's good time.[6] This is not confidence rooted in abstract, philosophical truth but is grounded in relational truth which continually refuses to allow the church to see itself as complete or self-referential. Instead the Scriptures and the story act as critical checks on any pretentions of the church to see itself as a sufficient theological resource. However this reserve does not mean that the community which seeks to be formed through worship and discipleship is irrelevant to the witness of the Gospel. Its social life is a public manifestation

---

2   John B. Thomson, *The Ecclesiology of Stanley Hauerwas: A Christian Theology of Liberation* (Aldershot: Ashgate, 2003).

3   John B. Thomson, *Church on Edge? Practising Christian Ministry Today* (London: Darton, Longman and Todd, 2004).

4   John B. Thomson, *DOXA: A Discipleship Course* (London: Darton, Longman and Todd, 2007).

5   John B. Thomson, *Living Holiness: Stanley Hauerwas and the Church* (London: Epworth, 2010).

6   John 16: 13.

of something of the impact of the life of Jesus today in a way that is plausible and easier for many people to 'read' than the Scriptures or theology.

Mission, evangelism, fresh expressions and emerging church are all front-page items on the agendas of Anglicans today. Statistics raise questions about survival as the media regularly report declining and aging congregations, apparently empty churches and a general carelessness about Christian practice in society at large. To commentators, such as Callum Brown, it seems that Christianity is rapidly disappearing from the public square.[7] Yet there are surprising things happening in unexpected places, such as South Yorkshire, which do not attract the headlines but perhaps indicate the way Anglican witness and mission are developing. These convince me that the Anglican way remains fruitful and one which we need to recover and re-imagine for the new challenges we face.

Synopsis

Chapter 1: Friendship as Character

In this chapter I situate my exploration of Anglican character in a conversation with the theological ethicist, Stanley Hauerwas. Hauerwas recovered the centrality of character for Christian ethics and his work helps to illuminate the distinctive character of Anglican mission within the contemporary world. In particular his discussions on Christian friendship with the stranger, the formation of Christian identity through performance and practice and the peaceable catholicity of the church are very fruitful here.

Part I: Practice

Chapter 2: Friendship as Love

This chapter argues that early mission in England was an expression of Christian friendship. This entailed missionaries rooted in North African spirituality reaching out to the strange and wild islands on the fringes of the Roman Empire. I also expose the distinctiveness of Christian love as friendship and how it differs

---

[7]   Callum Brown, *The Death of Christian Britain: Understanding Secularism 1800–2000*, 2nd edn, (Abingdon: Routledge, 2009) and *Religion and Society in Twentieth Century Britain* (London: Pearson Longman, 2006).

from other contemporary and ancient views of friendship using the work of Liz Carmichael along with insights from Elizabeth Moltmann-Wendel and Paul Avis. I conclude the chapter with a case study looking at the way the East African Revival and the anti-apartheid struggle in South Africa flag up key elements of Anglican character.

Chapter 3: Friendship as Discipleship

This chapter explores discipleship in the New Testament and uses apprenticeship as a way of integrating formation of character with friendship. It traces this discipleship formation through the practices of Jesus, of the early church and in the genre of the Gospels. The chapter looks at character formation and performance as fruitful elements of mission today and also argues that the church is properly to be a school of Jesus' apprentices. It argues that for Anglicans discipleship development is fundamentally about formation rather than information and emerges through the disciplines of discipleship practices focused in common worship.

Chapter 4: Friendship as Worship

This chapter looks at witness and sign as evidence of character. For Anglicans, Christians are formed, through worship, into signs of God's transforming love in the world and as meaningful flesh which invites interpretation. Worship represents a form of character training for the performance of situated or incarnational discipleship, discipleship which is characterised by a hospitable conversation with the world in which the church shares the Gospel and repents over its past failures. Living God's story is part of God's slow saving revolution.

Chapter 5: Friendship as Church

This chapter looks at the character of the Church of England, its origins as a form of practical holiness, wisdom and outward facing mission. The significance of common worship, gathered community, parish, story and pastoral mission are explored and rooted in the core vocation of the Church in England, a vocation which continues today.

Part II: Reflection

Chapter 6: Radical Friendship

In this chapter I discuss Radical Orthodoxy as a robust expression of Anglican friendship which seeks, through sharp conversation, to engage therapeutically with society and church. The work of John Milbank is given particular attention with its challenge to the secular, its historical analysis of the failure of the church and its commitment to recovering Christian discourse and narrative. I raise questions about elements of this project but see it as an important expression of Anglican character today.

Chapter 7: Gospel Friendship

This chapter focuses upon the work of Oliver O'Donovan in the areas of ethics, politics and justice. I show how he challenges many contemporary ways of telling the story of how English and North Atlantic societies were formed by arguing that this story requires a clear attention to Christian practice. This is an exercise in confidence building among Christians, particularly Anglicans, as they face revisionist accounts. It shows that, for Anglicans, truthful historiography is central to their understanding of Christian character.

Chapter 8: Graceful Friendship

This chapter engages with the work of Rowan Williams and integrates his wide-ranging writing within the concept of gift. Gift or grace lies at the heart of Christian friendship since all is held in the loving gaze of God. The church is therefore an icon of this graceful friendship in its multi-faceted character as a community embodying and committed to living life within the horizon of this graceful love. The history of Anglicanism offers a distinctive example of this sign particularly within English society and therefore has resources for challenging elements of contemporary English society which corrupt and subvert this vision. Yet equally this vision talks back to the Church on issues of peace, sexuality and cultural collusion.

Chapter 9: Listening Friendship

In this chapter I look at Anglican hermeneutics as an expression of self-giving friendship focused on the other using the work of Anthony Thiselton, Jeff

Astley, Malcolm Grundy, Richard Impey and Sam Wells. Thiselton shows us that careful listening to texts is about listening to the voice of the other which cannot be conflated into my voice. Astley challenges the church to pay attention to ordinary as well as academic theologians, whilst Grundy and Impey invite us to listen to congregations as resources for mission insight. Wells picks up themes of worship, liturgy and formation to show how Christians become aware of the particular mission vocation they are called into.

Chapter 10: Wise Friendship

This chapter looks at the work of Dan Hardy and David Ford, who have rehabilitated wisdom as the most fruitful way of learning about the magnificent complexity of life and of the way the story of faith fits within this. Both show that Anglicans see mission in cosmic terms and that worship and mission belong together. They use expressions such as abduction, attraction and fullness to speak of the way the church expresses and opens up the way of God. In addition Ford's work emphasises the importance of the face, of listening to the cries of the struggling and the importance of the church as a school of desire and of wisdom seeking to discern a way for today.

Part III: Challenge

Chapter 11: Social Friendship

This chapter situates the above in a discussion about the context within which contemporary English Anglican mission is lived. Using Charles Taylor's work I look at the character of the secular age and its impact on Anglican mission. I then turn to the insights of Grace Davie, Robin Gill, David Martin and Martyn Percy to see how their reflections suggest ways for the Church of England to continue its mission faithful to its character. Contextual approaches, such as those of Nigel Rooms on Englishness, Pete Ward on celebrity and Graham Ward on urbanism are also discussed.

Chapter 12: Fresh Friendship

This chapter discusses the 'Fresh Expressions of Church' initiative of Anglicans and Methodists. It listens to its advocates and critics before suggesting that, for Anglicans, 'Fresh Expressions' are compatible with Anglican mission so long as they cohere with Anglican character. The work of 'Fresh Expressions' advocates, such as Steven Croft, Steve Hollinghurst, Paul Bayes et al. and critics such as Alison Milbank, Andrew Davison and Alan Billings are engaged with. In addition Ann Morisy, Kenneth Leech and Luke Bretherton further enrich the conversation.

Conclusion

Using stories from three representative parishes from the Diocese of Sheffield, experience of diocesan ministry and links with an Anglican partner church in Argentina, this chapter tries to show how *kenosis*, or self-emptying, is essential for a mission of self-giving friendship with the stranger which reflects the Gospel embodied in the story of Jesus. It argues that such self-giving friendship is both attractive to those beyond the gathered church and yet deeply challenging to those within it, particularly to the more comfortable parts of the church. Anglican mission, if it is to be faithful to its character, requires Christians to see mission as engaging with those people and contexts which are different, strange and unknown to us. This is about embodying a Gospel in which, through Christ, the stranger becomes our friend, the unknown community becomes a familiar community and in which difference is celebrated peaceably.

***

Christianity is always Christianity with an adjective which locates the particular expression of this way of following God within a distinctive story. The Anglican way is rooted in a complex story of how English people sought to understand the Gospel within their culture and context, a way which migrated and mutated through the admittedly ambiguous legacy of English imperialism across the globe. That migration and mutation is itself leading to improvisations upon the inherited Anglican way that need further adjectives. However what each shows is that there is no abstract ideological Christianity which floats above the contingencies of history, community and context and that the drift towards dispensing with such adjectives actually colludes with the worst of the Enlightenment project's dislocating of human identity. It is my contention that Anglican discipleship locates this way in the mundane rather than in the extraordinary in contrast to secularist and some other Christian approaches which conspire to represent 'religion' as eccentric and abnormal. Both collude with the view that God is another object within the created cosmos who has to demonstrate assertive presence in a manner persuasive to 'normal' human rationality. In contrast an Anglican way regards God as that loving other-focused reality giving and sustaining all that exists who 'does not guarantee for himself a place in the created world, a place alongside other agents, and so is visible only when a human life gives place, offers hospitality to God, so that this place, this identity becomes a testimony'.[8] In this sense the God whom Anglicans worship is eccentric, that is not imposing and central but present particularly in the ordinary on the margins where those with power can be blind. Anglicanism is therefore at its best when it is a church of and for ordinary people rather than when it is seduced by power, elitism and celebrity.

The aim of this book, therefore, is to help Anglican Christians in England recover confidence in their distinctive character, calling and mission within England. As a parish priest in inner urban Doncaster, I found that hospitable friendship was fruitful in an area sceptical of more aggressive engagement. Equally in my present role, I detect a hunger among Anglicans of all backgrounds for a deeper grasp of our story which provides a positive and generous account of its character and makes more explicit its influence upon English society. I write as one formed in a variety of Christian contexts. My Ugandan childhood exposed me to a vibrant, young, adventurous, African-Anglican vision of mission which was mediated by local people. Time in Scotland with Presbyterians and Episcopalians showed me the value of congregations and shared leadership in mission. A move to England brought me into contact with Anglican evangelicalism in parish and university which was energetic, outward looking, charismatic and committed to building up the church. During ordination training and as a lecturer, I spent time in the South African Anglo-Catholic tradition which exposed me to liberation and contextual theology and flagged up the importance of the church in Anglican discipleship, mission and social engagement. Parish ministry in northern England in suburban and inner urban areas convinced me that the parish remains fruitful and fundamental to Anglican mission in England, particularly in its more demanding areas. Yet present mission imperatives, together with staffing and funding challenges, mean that congregations must work in partnership if Anglican mission is to flourish. Indeed as parishes of all traditions are forced by circumstance to be more collaborative they are discovering that they can appreciate and indeed learn from one another in mission. Tradition bearers are building bridges with those of different convictions. These conversations enable Anglicans to improvise upon their inheritance in imaginative and inspiring mission. They are ways of sharing friendship in church which enables sharing friendship beyond church. They display the character of Anglican community.

---

8   Rowan Williams, *Faith in the Public Square* (London: Bloomsbury, 2012), p. 319.

***

There are many people whom I must thank for teaching me about Anglican character. The congregations of St Mary, Wheatley and St Peter, Warmsworth, both in Doncaster, have shown me the meaning of this friendship in one of the more challenging ecclesial contexts of England. I recall those Ugandans and South Africans whose hospitality and generosity embodied the sort of character I have been exploring and enabled me as a stranger to be welcomed into their communities. I am grateful to former colleagues in the Diocese of Sheffield and to the many parishes I visited who continually surprised me with their warmth and commitment in reaching out to others as God's friends often in very challenging circumstances. I am indebted to Graham Pigott, my spiritual director for the past decade, whose wise insights and challenges have turned my confused ideas into clearer thoughts. Likewise I am obliged to Anthony Thiselton, Vernon White, Alan Billings and Sam Wells for their comments on my ideas. I have tried to listen to their insights but take full responsibility for what follows. I am also grateful to Stanley Hauerwas for the stimulation of his thinking over the past 18 years. It was he, after all, who challenged Christians to focus first upon their character before engaging in any activities, a challenge with particular force for a ministry practitioner like myself. Above all I am grateful to my parents and to my wife, Sue, and daughters Anya (with son-in-law Jonny) and Emily who have embodied the friendship and venturesome love of God over many years.

Finally I acknowledge the permission of Wm. B. Eerdmans Publishing Company for using material from John B. Thomson, 'Let us cook you your tea vicar!' in Stanley E. Porter and Matthew R. Malcolm, *Horizons in Hermeneutics: A Festschrift in Honor of Anthony C. Thiselton* (Cambridge, UK: Eerdmans, 2013), pp. 268–85 and Ashgate Publishing Ltd for using material from John B. Thomson, 'Sharing Friendship: God's Love in Ordinary Church Life' in Jeff Astley and Leslie J. Francis, *Exploring Ordinary Theology: Everyday Christian Believing and the Church* (Farnham: Ashgate, 2013), pp. 189–97.

JOHN B. THOMSON
Feast of St Bartholomew
25 August 2014

PART I
Practice

Chapter 1
Friendship as Character[1]

In *Approaching the End: Eschatological Reflections on Church, Politics and Life*, Stanley Hauerwas asserts that

> the very grammar of Christian speech presumes that those who use the language have a character commensurate with it. This is the key reason why theology and ethics cannot be separated; indeed theology is first and foremost an exercise in practical reason.[2]

Character, the mark or stamp of a person's or community's identity, forms a central theme in Hauerwas's work, which has involved a re-articulation of the place of the church as a distinctive community of Christological witness. For Hauerwas the central feature of this witness is political and Christological, peaceableness expressed through friendship for the stranger whether encountered in the special needs community, the sick, the unborn or indeed the world beyond the church. This is not a pacifism which seeks to justify itself as a strategy based on a calculation but is a witness to the social agenda of Christ's life and passion.[3] It is an experiment with truth through sharing in God's justice since 'to do justice is to be a part of the community whose life is centred on and ordered by Jesus, God's justice'. It is a justice seen especially in the giving and receiving of friendship in a 'Spirit blown mobile community' with those estranged from us such as Alzheimer's sufferers.[4] Friendship for the stranger identifies a community as Christian and it is my contention that such friendship for the stranger is central to the worship, polity and performance of Anglicans which, as Hauerwas suggests, reflects the fact that 'Anglicanism is a holiness movement'

---

[1]   John B. Thomson, 'Let us cook you your tea vicar!' in Stanley E. Porter and Matthew R. Malcolm, *Horizons in Hermeneutics: A Festschrift in Honor of Anthony C. Thiselton* (Cambridge, UK: Eerdmans, 2013), pp. 268–85.

[2]   Stanley Hauerwas, *Approaching the End: Eschatological Reflections on Church, Politics and Life* (Grand Rapids MI/Cambridge UK: Eerdmans, 2013), p. 42.

[3]   Stanley Hauerwas, *War and the American Difference: Theological Reflections on Violence and National Identity* (Grand Rapids MI: Baker Academic, 2011), pp. 75–80.

[4]   Hauerwas, *War and the American Difference*, pp. 86, 104–16.

in which 'what we do with our bodies is more indicative of who we are than what we say we believe'.[5] Hauerwas's work, therefore, forms the backdrop to the rest of this book which is an implicit conversation with his challenge to focus on churches as communities of character. It is therefore an attempt to tease out the character of Anglican mission through its practice, reflection and ongoing performance. To situate this exploration and to show why clarifying character is vital for the mission of the church, this chapter will outline key themes from Hauerwas's work. These will not determine the remainder of the book so much as contextualise it as part of an ongoing conversation about how contemporary Christians seek to share in God's mission within late modern societies in ways which are faithful to their historic vocation and yet able to engage creatively with new challenges.

Stanley Hauerwas, Character and the Church

Stanley Hauerwas's theological ethics is an attempt to articulate a distinctively Christian character embodied as the church. This is not simply about recognising the corporate character of Christian discipleship but is about recognising the hermeneutical implications of ecclesial identity. How we see or interpret the world is relative to the communities we are formed by. There is no abstract spectator perspective divorced from the contingencies of time and place. Consequently the effect of participating within the Christian community is to understand God, the Scriptures, the Christian story and the world in a distinctive manner. Hauerwas's understanding of the place of the Church in Christian character emerges most clearly in his 1981 collection of essays entitled *A Community of Character*. In these essays he sought 'to reassert the social significance of the church as a distinctive society with an integrity peculiar to itself ... the truth of whose convictions cannot be divorced from the sort of community the church is and should be'.[6] He thereby attempted to generate a specific politics of the church by asking 'what kind of community the church must be to rightly tell the stories of God?'[7] *A Community of Character* begins with 10 Theses which Hauerwas uses to articulate the architecture of his theology. Immediately evident in each thesis is the social and narrative character of Christian ethics consequent upon its fundamentally ecclesial nature. The primary vocation of the church is to live

---

[5]   Stanley Hauerwas, *Learning to Speak Christian* (London: SCM, 2011) pp. 15–22.

[6]   Stanley Hauerwas, *A Community of Character: Towards a Constructive Christian Social Ethic*, 4th edn, (Notre Dame: University of Notre Dame Press, 1986), p. 1.

[7]   Hauerwas, *A Community of Character*, p. 4.

its story as a people on a journey convinced of the lordship of God in the world and serving the world on the terms implied by this cross-informed story. Jesus is known today through this social ethic and the Scriptures are interpreted within the politics of the church.[8] Furthermore the canon of Scripture are those stories which express the forgiving life of God experienced by God's people and the tradition called church is an ongoing argument about the way these should be interpreted.[9] Appealing to Scripture for Hauerwas is appealing not to texts but to a narrative community called church.[10]

Hauerwas's hermeneutics flags up the importance of tradition and community in the Christian story. The church is a school of virtue rooted in an apprentice model of education, whose authorities, the saints, are those who have more fully appropriated and displayed the faith and are thereby able to educate other disciples in living and dying in ways appropriate to the story. The truthfulness of the Christian tradition is witnessed to in its capacity to sustain hope and patience in the face of the tragic, since tragedy subverts the possibility of self-deception.[11] Yet it is definitively established by the peaceable performance of the church as the contemporary story of the peaceable Christ.[12] In his work on Bonhoeffer he argues that there is a necessary connection between peaceableness, non-violence and the quest for a truthful politics.[13] Peaceableness, therefore, is not an abstract ideal which judges the church but a hermeneutical way of living in which the church continues to embody the way of Jesus witnessed to in the cross.[14] It is a form of life which challenges the liberal pragmatism of Reinhold Niebuhr and is indebted to the Anabaptist tradition of John Howard Yoder. It is this awareness of the significance of the history of Jesus for Christology that Hauerwas believes to be at the core of a recovery of a church of integrity. This is in contrast to other accounts which in their concentration upon the teaching of the Kingdom

---

[8]   Hauerwas, *A Community of Character*, p. 37.

[9]   Stanley Hauerwas, "Forgiveness and Political Community", *Worldview* 23/1–2 (January–February 1980), pp. 15–16.

[10]   Stanley Hauerwas, *In Good Company: The Church as Polis* (Notre Dame: University of Notre Dame Press, 1995), pp. 9, 20 footnote 4.

[11]   Hauerwas, *A Community of Character*, pp. 60, 91 and Stanley Hauerwas, 'The Church's One Foundation is Jesus Christ her Lord' in Stanley Hauerwas, Nancy Murphy and Mark Nation, eds, *Theology without Foundations, Religious Practice and the Future of Theological Truth* (Nashville: Abingdon, 1994), pp. 143–62.

[12]   Stanley Hauerwas, *The Peaceable Kingdom: A Primer in Christian Ethics*, 3rd edn, (Notre Dame: University of Notre Dame Press, 1986).

[13]   Stanley Hauerwas, *Performing the Faith: Bonhoeffer and the Practice of Nonviolence* (London: SPCK, 2004), p. 19.

[14]   Hauerwas, *Performing the Faith*, p. 16.

lost sight of the whole of Jesus' life as a resource for imitation by the church. For Hauerwas, Jesus' life was a recapitulation of God's way with Israel, which discloses the sort of God Christians and Jews worship. For Christians, the cross is the supreme illustration of this peaceful trust in the ways of God, whose virtues are renunciation, humility and service. Hence his ecclesiology, rooted in Christological peaceableness, is intrinsically eschatological, since the victory of Christ witnessed to in the resurrection, gives the church the confidence to risk living peaceably in a world as yet uncommitted to peaceful living since this is to live with the grain of the universe.[15] This is what living the kingdom means for it reflects what Jesus showed, namely that this sort of peaceable life is possible now since God is sovereign since this is reality.[16] Friendship of the outcast, peaceful resistance to the evil one, forgiveness all illustrate kingdom-living informed by this eschatology.

Ecclesial formation, character and virtue therefore dispose Christians to inhabit the world in a distinctive way thereby enabling them to 'gain the experience to negotiate and make positive contributions in whatever society we may find ourselves'.[17] In particular this will enable Christians in America to recognise that liberalism forms them to interpret the world in a manner that conflicts with the Christian story, particularly in the latter's assumptions about the right to life and happiness, individualism and freedom of choice. Indeed 'the story that liberalism teaches us is that we have no story and as a result we fail to notice how deeply that story determines our lives'.[18] The church therefore serves the world by being a contrast community and thereby supplies the world with a truthful story about its own identity. It acts as a hermeneutic for the world as well as for itself since the world has no integrating narrative that makes sense of its constituent parts without the story of God witnessed to in the church. Yet at the same time Hauerwas believes that ethical demands such as the Decalogue are community-specific and contextual. They cannot be understood apart from the story of God's covenant with Israel. Rather than abstracting them and setting them up as transcendent universals, such stories supply the church with a tradition and history through which to see how the same God works at different

---

[15]   Stanley Hauerwas, *With the Grain of the Universe: The Church's Witness and Natural Theology* (London: SCM, 2001).

[16]   Stanley Hauerwas, *War and the American Difference*, p. xii.

[17]   Hauerwas, *A Community of Character*, p. 74.

[18]   Hauerwas, *A Community of Character*, p. 84. This is particularly evident in the modern university. See Hauerwas, *With the Grain of the Universe*, p. 231 and Stanley M. Hauerwas, *The State of the University: Academic Knowledges and the Knowledge of God* (Oxford: Blackwell, 2007), pp. 3–8.

times and in different places and thereby suggests how the church might rightly envision God's ways with the world in the present context. Likewise there is a plurality of discipleship stories which are embraced in God's story. Indeed part of the church's character is to be able to listen to the 'otherness' of these stories with respect and attentiveness.

Hauerwas does not equate the church with the kingdom. Instead the life of the kingdom is broader than the church. For 'the church does not possess Christ; his presence is not confined to the church. Rather it is in the church that we learn to recognise Christ's presence outside the church'.[19] The church is therefore a foretaste of this kingdom, a community whose training enables it to identify the presence of the kingdom beyond itself and whose presence also identifies the world as that community that as yet does not believe. The church therefore 'tries to develop the resources to stand within the world witnessing to the peaceable kingdom and thus rightly understanding the world'.[20] The virtues required for this involve trust, hope and love and as an empirical reality, the marks of this church, which represent the social witness of this church, are the resources of its sacraments, preaching and distinctive living.

In stressing the communal character of hermeneutics, Hauerwas is not implying that there is only one horizon within the interpretative dynamic. Agreeing with Iris Murdoch's criticism of the narcissistic implications of Cartesian thinking and her work on attention and art, Hauerwas believes that we need to be trained to see the 'other' as beyond our own self consciousness.[21] Indeed the 'other' is to be regarded as a gift and someone to be befriended.[22] Christians need to be formed and trained to see life and its challenges in a way analogous to 'an artist engaged in his work rather than a critic making a judgment about a finished product'.[23] Since no-one is an abstract spectator, such training involves inhabiting and employing the wisdom of the Christian community. Such communal wisdom provides a distinctively Christian way of 'seeing' or describing issues such as abortion, the care of children and the elderly, euthanasia and disability. For example, Christians believe that a good death (euthanasia), is one which leaves a good memory and trustfully locates that death in the ongoing story of the grace of God embodied in the church. In liberal ethics autonomy disconnects people from this communal story, subverts

---

[19] Hauerwas, *The Peaceable Kingdom*, p. 97.
[20] Hauerwas, *The Peaceable Kingdom*, p. 102.
[21] Stanley Hauerwas, *Vision and Virtue: Essays in Christian Ethical Reflection* (Notre Dame: University of Notre Dame Press, 1981), p. 34.
[22] Hauerwas, *The State of the University*, pp. 64–70.
[23] Hauerwas, *Vision and Virtue*, pp. 14, 30–36.

any sense of history and undermines the capacity of a community to celebrate the lives of the elderly by caring for them. Furthermore caring for children, the disabled and the elderly reflects the Christian commitment to welcome the new and strange which self-centred liberal ethics finds increasingly conflictual with its autonomous convictions. Hauerwas is therefore particularly concerned with focusing upon the character of the church, the 'who', in order to make possible a faithful and truthful Christian hermeneutical engagement with the 'what' or 'other'. His concern is that the post-Enlightenment liberal tradition has ignored the social and communal character of human identity in its epistemology and in the process fails to recognise that this 'other' is 'seen' by different communities in different ways relative to the languages they speak. Indeed he regards the church itself as God's new language, a community whose way of life not only speaks of God but interprets life from within the divine story its life narrates.[24] In this he rejects the notion of the spectator, since all are embedded in embodied communities, whether this is a conscious belonging or one unreflectively taken for granted. He is also concerned that the church has been colonised by the subtle subversion of liberal thinking and capitalist consumerism which combine to strip Christians of the resources to interpret the world as Christians. In taking this stand he represents part of a wider debate about the legacy of the Enlightenment with its confidence in the singular and abstract subject able to grasp the meaning of the world as a sort of spectator. For Hauerwas the thinking subject is always embedded in contexts and communities which both dispose and form that subject to interpret the world and human living within it in ways related to that embeddedness. Consequently there is no neutrality in human thought. Hauerwas argues that Christians ought to articulate their own distinctive vision of human living without embarrassment in public discussion. They should not be reduced to silence by a self-deceptively confident way of thinking rooted in a false notion of spectator objectivity.

Given Hauerwas's commitment to Christian formation and truthful interpretation, the role of liturgy emerges as central to his thinking. As Augustine indicated, the worship of God, the character of Christian lives and politics belong together.[25] Worship happens when the church gathers to be exposed as a community to the transforming grace of God. This is necessarily a corporate activity and consciously situates the church within the narrative of God's salvation. It is akin to a training session in which Christians are equipped

---

[24]   Stanley Hauerwas, *Christian Existence Today: Essays on Church, World and Living in Between* (North Carolina: The Labyrinth Press, 1988), pp. 47–65.

[25]   Hauerwas, *Learning to Speak Christian*, p. 80.

to perform their faith in the world. Consequently Hauerwas teaches ethics through liturgy and also focuses his attention upon particular churches, such as Broadway Methodist Church, as resources for seeing the effect of training upon performance.[26] Worship also situates biblical hermeneutics since it ensures that the texts of the Bible are recognised as Scripture by locating them within the community which 'knows that its life depends on faithfully remembering of God's care of his creation through the calling of Israel and the life of Jesus'.[27] Such a political reading of Scripture has been hidden in liberal hermeneutics with the consequence that Scripture has lost its authority and revelatory power. Hauerwas notes that theologians rarely learn their texts in a liturgical context which properly contextualises them, so there is no connection made between the politics of the community which identifies these texts as their Scriptures and the work of most theologians.[28] This leaves the Scriptures prey to deconstruction by those who seek to understand them principally by fitting them into alien patterns of thought. For Hauerwas, such a failure to fit our world into the world the Scriptures open up represents an apolitical reading of these Scriptures.[29] Hermeneutics is therefore fundamentally a political and temporal process and has linguistic and social dimensions that distinguish the church from the world. Hence Hauerwas applauds the strangeness evident in William Stringfellow's determination to practise the language of the apocalyptic rather than feeling obliged to translate this into the deceptive language of liberalism.[30] Through keeping Christian language pure a truthful reading of life can be had. He also sees martyrdom is a particular hermeneutical challenge to the world since martyrdom trusts the true interpretation of its meaning to God.[31]

All this gives new meaning to local Christian practice. For example sermons emerge as the contingent ongoing interpretation of the divine ethos for a particular Christian community. They are the *parole* or speech of theology rather than the *langue* or formal language of the discipline. It is the way a community articulates its faith in time. Hauerwas's sermons reflect his conviction that Christian hermeneutics requires the church if it is to avoid a narcissistic

---

[26] Hauerwas, *In Good Company: The Church as Polis*, pp. 153–63. On Broadway Methodist Church see Hauerwas, *Christian Existence Today*, pp. 111–31.

[27] Hauerwas, *A Community of Character*, p. 53.

[28] Hauerwas, *A Community of Character*, p. 56, footnote 9.

[29] Hauerwas, *A Community of Character*, p. 55.

[30] Stanley Hauerwas, *Dispatches from the Front: Theological Engagements with the Secular* (Durham: Duke University Press, 1994), pp. 107–13.

[31] Stanley Hauerwas, *Against the Nations: War and Survival in a Liberal Society* (Notre Dame: University of Notre Dame Press, 1992), pp. 62–90, 91–108.

concentration upon texts.[32] Discussing the thought of Hans Frei, he argues that 'realistic narrative' must reflect the authority of a community's tradition rather than being seen simply in terms of literary intelligibility. This is why liturgy is so important to Hauerwas as mentioned above since the 'plain sense' of the story is illuminated through the corporate life of the Christian community. The church itself is both the subject and agent of the narrative and hence it is the people, rather than the words or sentences that exhibit these narratives.[33] The sermon is therefore a communal action of the church articulated through the office of the preacher which seeks to be faithful to Scripture and to attend to the revelation which follows upon the existent tradition.[34] As he comments, 'our stories become part of the story of the kingdom' making 'Jesus' story a many-sided tale'.[35]

Friendship and the Church

In this story friendship emerges as a critical way of understanding the relationship between God and God's people, the church.[36] Friendship is fundamentally a gift, which establishes a relationship with God who is a name rather than a concept and is rooted in the opening invocation of the Lord's Prayer, 'our Father'.[37] Hence friendship is about exploring an identity through story and therefore across time. Friendship with God through Christ entails exploring this communally since God's friendship is with his people. As Augustine argued, there is no love of God without love of neighbour.[38] This exploration is therefore very material; it involves being transformed through worship to follow this God. Hauerwas distinguishes Christian friendship from classical friendship by stressing the former's commitment to the integrity of the other person.[39] Friendship is not simply for usefulness or pleasure. It is not based on common virtue or character which is effectively self-love and controlling power. Instead it is open to the other,

---

[32]   Garrett Green, *Theology, Hermeneutics and Imagination: The Crisis of Interpretation at the End of Modernity* (Cambridge: Cambridge University Press, 2000), p. 187.

[33]   Green, *Theology, Hermeneutics and Imagination*, p. 192.

[34]   Green, *Theology, Hermeneutics and Imagination*, p. 193.

[35]   Hauerwas, *A Community of Character*, pp. 51–2.

[36]   See Thomson, *The Ecclesiology of Stanley Hauerwas* and *Living Holiness*.

[37]   William H. Willimon and Stanley Hauerwas, with Scott C. Sage, *Lord Teach Us: The Lord's Prayer and the Christian Life* (Nashville: Abingdon Press, 1996).

[38]   Hauerwas, *Learning to Speak Christian*, p. 64.

[39]   See Stanley Hauerwas and Charles Pinches, *Christians Among the Virtues: Theological Conversations with Ancient and Modern Ethics* (Notre Dame: University of Notre Dame Press, 1997).

particularly to the tragic, since tragedy challenges any sense that a relationship is based upon self-interest.[40] Since Christ has released us from the need to control our own story we can join in God's story, whose character is not fundamentally dependent upon us. The love of this story spoken of in John 15:13 involves compassion, friends sharing suffering and entering into suffering for friends. Hauerwas argues that Christian friendship is about being incorporated into the church as a community which participates in God's story. Indeed we get to know God in this way since God is known in communion. Christian friendship depends upon God rather than upon us and is eschatologically orientated to the fullness of friendship with God. Similarly friendship shows us who we are since we learn of ourselves through others. Jesus teaches 'that Jews and Christians might well often learn the very meaning of the word and practice of neighbourliness from the outsider.'[41] Christians therefore seek to love selflessly, a love most evident when we love strangers and when we preserve friendship by forgiving one another. This is why Hauerwas believes peaceableness to be so central to Christian discipleship. Peaceableness enables us to befriend our enemy without abusing that act of friendship through violence. It also enables us to discover the stranger speaking to us as a friend.[42]

Furthermore friendship is necessary to do good since we need each other to name both virtue and vice.[43] This has particular force for Hauerwas in debates about homosexuality. If early Christians discovered that friendship in Christ with Gentiles opened up new theological horizons and consequently asked them to re-configure the boundaries of salvation, so the fact of finding friendship with gays and lesbians raises similar implications for him. This is especially so given the theological implications of baptismal practices which indicate that the primary calling of the whole church is to be baptismally reproductive rather than biologically so. As Aelred of Rievaulx argued the core priority of Christians is to build up the body of Christ.[44] Similarly friendship with the disabled illuminates friendship since they ask of us openness, attention, hospitality and time.[45] We are

[40] Thomson, *Living Holiness*, p. 53.

[41] Hauerwas, *Learning to Speak Christian*, p. 185.

[42] Thomson, *Living Holiness*, pp. 13–14.

[43] Stanley M. Hauerwas, *Sanctify Them in the Truth: Holiness Exemplified* (Edinburgh: T&T Clark, 1998).

[44] See 'Resisting Capitalism: On Marriage and Homosexuality', and 'Time: Friendship and Aging' in Stanley Hauerwas, *A Better Hope: Resources for a Church Confronting Capitalism, Democracy and Postmodernity* (Michigan: Brazos Press, 2000), pp. 47–51 and pp. 179–80. See also Stanley Hauerwas, 'Gay Friendship: A Thought Experiment in Catholic Moral Theology', in *Sanctify Them*, pp. 117–18.

[45] See 'Timeful Friends: Living with the Handicapped' in *Sanctify Them*, pp. 143–56.

to become the kind of friend God is and this entails personal transformation and a common quest for what is good and fruitful. Friendship generates new insights as the experience of friendship opens up new ways of conceiving of moral or ethical issues. In the peaceableness of God's reign, within which Christians live, friendship can embrace those who are different from us. This friendship is not simply about being nice to people. It is about befriending people as Christians, that is those who represent Christ, rather than simply about being friendly people. Thus this friendship can be robust as well as peaceable in its character.

Hauerwas believes that friendship is a particularly definitive practice for the church since it respects the other person in a non-manipulative manner; it depends upon truthfulness to succeed and in the process challenges self-deception by such truthful speaking. Furthermore the church is not threatened by the stranger but in the practices of reconciliation such as confession, forgiveness and absolution it fosters the bonds of community as strangers become friends with God and with one another. Thus an inner urban church refusing to desert a challenging area and offering an open Sunday meal to its neighbourhood as a continuation of the Eucharist symbolises the tenacity of Christian friendship and hospitality.

Character, Friendship and the Contemporary

Hauerwas seeks to understand the character of the church within the contemporary context of postmodernity. Postmodernity represents a mood as much as a movement, an approach to understanding characterised by suspicion and anxieties about power.[46] The 'post-moderns' are particularly hostile to any sense that the 'other's' particularity and consequent irreducibility should be compromised. The present is all, the subject is unstable and all teleology and humanism are deceptive. The effect of postmodernity has been to contest meta-narratives and mega-solutions with a consequent 'shattering of innocent confidence in the capacity of the self to control its destiny'.[47] The outcome is that truth is reduced to rhetoric and claims to truth seen as manipulative bids for power.[48] For Hauerwas these challenges demand a fresh understanding of the church and, more importantly, of faithful performance. This led him to

---

[46]   Jean-François Lyotard, *The Postmodern Condition: A Report on Knowledge*, trans. G. Bennington and B. Massumi (Minneapolis: University of Minnesota Press, 1984), p. xxiii.

[47]   Anthony C. Thiselton, *Interpreting God and the Postmodern Self: On Meaning, Manipulation and Promise* (Edinburgh: T&T Clarke, 1995), p. 11.

[48]   Thiselton, *Interpreting God and the Postmodern Self*, pp. 11–16.

establish and demonstrate the importance of a substantive communal tradition or culture whose claims to plausibility can be observed in a form of life.[49] Such an interpersonal enfleshed tradition stabilises the social self and prevents it disappearing into an arbitrary flux of rhetorical signs. It also ensures the preservation and subversive influence of memory which Hauerwas believes both modernism and post-modernism actively subvert in the service of the economic drives of capitalism.[50] Indeed Hauerwas regards the university as 'the great institution of legitimization in modernity' whose fundamental driver is no longer truth seeking but money making and which promotes an abstract rather than contextual interpretation of knowledge.[51]

For Hauerwas the life and passion of Christ displays God's peaceableness. Christological peaceableness is the end of sacrifice as well as the end of the church. It enables the church to interpret history doxologically as it worships the reigning Lamb which was slain in his rejection of instrumental violence. Together these secularise the modern state with its pretentions to total power sustained by the sacrifices of war.[52] Consequently the self and truth are found in this divine narrative as the church becomes the community which explicitly lives in this story, especially at the local level where it is public, visible and accountable. Commenting on the tragedy in Rwanda, he argues that this commitment to a truthful and exhaustive story which includes all parties is vital if reconciliation is to be possible.[53] Furthermore, for Hauerwas, the Christian self is no longer the abstract stable subject of modernity or the fluid instability of postmodernity, but rather the baptised self, whose identity is rooted in the Christian community and its embodiment through time.[54] Consequently the communal character of the Church and the materiality of spirituality re-emerge surprisingly as fundamental to witness through the performance of local Christian communities, such as Broadway and Aldersgate Methodist Churches.[55] These act as embodied embryonic signs of the truthfulness of the Christian story and prevent it from dissolving into ideas or rhetoric.[56] Here Christians are formed through the liturgy to display practices such as forgiveness, peacemaking, praise, enduring friendship and caring for the sick and dying which offer a text for wider society

---

[49]   Hauerwas, *A Better Hope*, p. 17.
[50]   Hauerwas, *A Better Hope,* pp. 146–8.
[51]   Hauerwas, *The State of the University*, pp. 5–8.
[52]   Hauerwas, *Approaching the End*, pp. 22–7.
[53]   Hauerwas, *Learning to Speak Christian*, p. 29.
[54]   Hauerwas, *Sanctify Them*, p. 78.
[55]   Hauerwas, *Sanctify Them*, p. xi.
[56]   Hauerwas, *With the Grain of the Universe*, pp. 217–8.

to interpret and an ecclesial hermeneutic about God.[57] This is where Christians learn to see.[58] This is where Christian imagination is formed which contests other forms of liturgical formation such as war and its demands for sacrifice.[59] Yet these particular instantiations of Christian performance are located within the greater story of the church and Israel whose significance is carried in the theological memory of the whole church. The local church is always part of the catholic church and ensures that the latter does not become an abstraction.

The church as tradition and embodied communities is therefore central to Hauerwas's project within the ethos of contemporary life. The tangibility of the church, expressed in its embodiment, practices and performance, communal identity, training and formation, language, tradition, contingency, embeddedness, practical wisdom, narrative, attention, discipleship as an ethic rather than an idea, worship and character contest the instabilities and fluidities of postmodern thinking. They thereby flag up the remarkable value and significant witness of mundane congregations whose life exhibits these practical and material realities. Here testimony becomes enfleshed. Here is where the contemporary story of Christ's character is written on the bodies of his disciples.[60] Hauerwas's project seeks to display a distinctive Christian ethic or way of life in which Christians embody the story of God in the world and thereby indicate the interpretative significance of the life of the church as it practises and performs its life in contemporary North Atlantic societies. In so doing Hauerwas's approach runs the danger of equating theology with ecclesiology or theology with ethnography, and thereby be effectively a form of socio-pragmatism. This could lead to a Durkheimian view of the Church and strip it of any transcendental 'other' as Nigel Biggar once asserted.[61] I have argued elsewhere that Hauerwas regards his work as theology rather than simply ethnography.[62] However, as Hauerwas comments, 'I have steadfastly tried to let my own so-called doctrine of God emerge from within my presentation of issues as basic as why we continue to have children or how we are to account for our care of the mentally handicapped'.[63] In this way Hauerwas argues that training and habits condition the Church to perform its faith in ways which display its claims that this is the way God acts in the world.

---

[57]   Hauerwas, *A Better Hope*, p. 18.

[58]   Hauerwas, *Learning to Speak Christian*, p. 34.

[59]   Hauerwas, *War and the American Difference*, p. xv, pp. 56–68.

[60]   Hauerwas, *Learning to Speak Christian*, p. 52.

[61]   Hauerwas, *Sanctify Them*, p. 37.

[62]   Thomson, *Living Holiness*, pp. 75–6.

[63]   Stanley M. Hauerwas, 'Many Hands Working: A Response to Charles Mathewes', *Anglican Theological Review* 82/2 (Spring 2000), p. 362.

Certainly Hauerwas's theological ethics, with his interest in the character, friendship and contemporary performance of Christian living, appear confident about the influence of Christian pragmatics upon doctrine and its interpretation. Hauerwas's worry is that the church can easily become an abstract church, an idea of church rather than a flesh and blood baptised community. This was his critique even of his mentor, Karl Barth. Barth, for all his stress on the witness of the church, still felt able in the *Dogmatics*, to represent the significance and ethos of the church in a way that was not intrinsically bound up with the performance of the church.[64] Thus, for Hauerwas, the embodiment of the church in its micro performances is critical to its mission and witness. This is where sanctification is visible, a redeemed baptismal anthropology which acts as the primary witness of the pilgrim church. Theology is therefore displayed through the 'texts' of trained church living rather than imagined through reflection simply upon literary texts. Thus, as Brad Kallenberg has argued, Hauerwas's theology involves interpreting the embodied apologetic of the church rather than articulating a rhetorical apologetic for God in the world.[65] For Hauerwas such ecclesial forms of life act as a language making claims to truth about God and the world which is not self-contained or watertight but is inhabited by God and therefore open to change.[66] It is a language of peaceable friendship which attends to those beyond its community in ways which cohere with this ethos. Indeed, 'God's dominion is not limited or confined to the church ... rather ... its "origin", its most concentrated expression is there displayed'. The church is not a closed language.[67] Indeed the church is to be a church for the world.[68]

Hauerwas and the Anglican Way

Hauerwas might be expected to be critical of Anglicanism as a Constantinian church, particularly in its English expression. Indeed his Christological peaceableness and commitment to distinctive witness ask questions of English Anglican faithfulness. Nevertheless later writing indicates an appreciation by

---

[64] Hauerwas, *With the Grain of the Universe*, pp. 34–53. See also Hauerwas's interpretation of Bonhoeffer's political theology as reclaiming the visibility of the Church as the necessary condition for the proclamation of the Gospel, in Hauerwas, *Performing the Faith*, p. 34.

[65] Brad J. Kallenberg, *Ethics as Grammar: Changing the Postmodern Subject* (Notre Dame IND: University of Notre Dame Press, 2001), p. 156.

[66] Hauerwas, *Christian Existence Today*, p. 10.

[67] Stanley Hauerwas, *Wilderness Wanderings: Probing Twentieth Century Theology and Philosophy* (Colorado: Westview, 1997), p. 6.

[68] Hauerwas, *A Better Hope*, p. 157. See also Hauerwas, *The State of the University*, pp. 55–6.

Hauerwas of this ecclesial experiment which is sympathetic to its character and attentive to its theological fruitfulness as an exercise in practical reasoning congruent with his own theological commitments.[69] Anglicanism is rooted in a commitment to locality which ensures that its witness is fundamentally embodied, storied and traceable. Yet it is also catholic without seeking to be totalitarian.[70] As such 'Anglicanism can be understood as an ecclesial expression of Alasdair MacIntyre's account of tradition-constituted rationality.'[71] Its way of discerning truth necessarily requires argument and politics, a unity of love in which 'what matters ... is the reality of the interdependence that gives visibility to our catholicity.'[72] This is about friendship found in the interplay of difference rather than premised on a singular sense of common identity. As we shall argue in Chapter 5, the English Anglican experiment is rooted in the post-Reformation Elizabethan settlement which sought to embody an approximation of harmonious difference within a common worshipping and ordered community focused upon mission among the English peoples. This end or goal, though at one level a pragmatic response to the chaos of Europe and the impossibility of ideological agreement even within the English Church, was also a theologically motivated vision. It recognised the goal of the church to be an approximation of the End of the church itself, namely a community of harmonious difference held together in God's grace and love as the body of the glorified Christ. In this way the means become the ends in the making since seeking provisional unity in difference, befriending those within and beyond the identified boundaries of the public church and representing diversity in performance within broad but flexible notions of common identity all contribute to the generation of a sign which embodies the character of Christian discipleship. Living at a time when Christendom is waning, it will be the character of Anglican mission which will need to be central if this vocation is to remain faithful and the Anglican way is not to be co-opted by other powers which subvert its character. This character is expressed in sharing Christ's friendship with those estranged from God and from one another. In this context Hauerwas's work invites Anglicans to explore more thoroughly their own character as a Christian community.

---

[69]   Hauerwas, *Approaching the End*, p. 42.
[70]   Hauerwas, *Approaching the End*, pp. 113–14.
[71]   Hauerwas, *Approaching the End*, p. 115.
[72]   Hauerwas, *Approaching the End*, p. 117.

Chapter 2

Friendship as Love

English Christianity: An Expression of African Friendship

Christianity arrived in the islands we now call Britain during the Roman period, probably from the south through Gaul and then through what we now call England as soldiers and merchants moved around.[1] Indeed the presence of British Bishops at the Council of Arles in 314 testifies to a structured diocesan church in this part of the Roman Empire as do many place names, the ROTAS cryptogram at Cirencester and even the contested theology of the Briton Pelagius.[2] However with the departure of Roman administration and invasions by the Anglo-Saxons, British Christianity was forced onto the back foot and was associated with defeat. The renaissance and recovery of Christianity came in the first instance from the north-west as a form of Celtic or Irish mission focused around Iona, which re-engaged with northern 'England' through the south-west of 'Scotland'. The English tribes, we might say, were converted first from the north, before a second recovery mission from Rome led by Augustine began in Kent.[3]

What distinguished this northern mission movement was its indebtedness to North African Christianity and especially to its monasticism.[4] The eighth-century English historian and monk, Bede, identifies Ninian as a key figure in the northern mission during the fifth century with his base at Candida Casa in Whithorn, Galloway. Ninian had spent some of his formative years under the monastic discipline bequeathed to Gaul by Martin of Tours and Martin himself

---

[1]   Tertullian and Origen, both North African Christians, show awareness of Christianity in the northern Isles in the third century. See N. Chadwick and M. Dillon, *The Celtic Realms*, 3rd edn (London 1974), pp. 159–60.

[2]   Henry Mayr-Harting, *The Coming of Christianity to Anglo-Saxon England* (London: Batsford, 1972), pp. 34–9.

[3]   Mayr-Harting, *The Coming of Christianity*, pp. 51–93.

[4]   Mayr-Harting, *The Coming of Christianity*, pp. 79–85. See also Diarmaid MacCulloch, *A History of Christianity* (London: Allen Lane, 2009) pp. 315, 330–33; John Finney, *Recovering the Past: Celtic and Roman Mission* (London: DLT, 1996) pp. 52–3; and Margaret Deanesly, *A History of the Medieval Church 590–1500* (Oxford: OUP, 1972) pp. 36–7.

followed monastic practices generated by the Desert Fathers in Egypt, Tunisia and Algeria. Bede refers to Ninian as 'a most reverend bishop and holy man of the British nation ... whose episcopal see, named after St Martin the bishop ... is still in existence among the English nation'.[5] Ninian was most probably not the founder of the church at Candida Casa, since a letter of Pope Celestine indicates that it was the practice to appoint bishops only to existing Christian communities.[6] A similar point can be made about Ireland when Palladius was appointed bishop to the Scots there.[7] Nevertheless the energy and impetus for the renaissance of Christianity within the British Isles came from Ireland. Columba would make a similar journey to Iona over a hundred years later thereby reinforcing the mission from Iona to the Scots and Picts and drawing upon the monastic strengths which were themselves rooted in the traditions and practices of the Egyptian Desert Fathers. The fervent and competitive asceticism reflected in reciting psalms in icy water, the hermitic tendencies of missionary settlements like Iona and later Lindisfarne and the cohesion of the monastic movement can all be traced to this legacy. Indeed it is not surprising that North Africa made such an impact on the British Isles when trade routes around the western coastline of Brittany, Cornwall, Ireland and Cumbria all reveal archaeological evidence linking them to Gaul and through Gaul to the Mediterranean world.[8] Indeed the *djellaba* or traditional garment worn in much of North Africa has many affinities with the monastic habit.

Friendship: Interpreting Christian Love

The English Church, therefore, is indebted to the friendship of North African Christians, expressed by missionary monks, merchants and other travellers willing to share the Gospel with the wild and strange tribes of the inhospitable isles to the north-west of their known world. In so doing they embodied the sort of friendship exhibited by Jesus and the early church, showing us that Christian friendship particularly for the stranger is at the heart of Christianity and integral to mission and, according to Liz Carmichael, is in sharp contrast to ancient classical understandings of friendship. The latter presumed that

---

    5   Bede, *Ecclesiastical History of the English Speaking People*, III/ 4 (London: J.M.Dent & Sons, 1912) pp. 108–9.
    6   E.A. Thompson, 'The Origin of Christianity in Scotland', *Scottish Historical Review* 37, (1958), pp. 18–19.
    7   Bede, *Ecclesiastical History*, I/ 3.
    8   Mayr-Harting, *The Coming of Christianity*, pp. 35–6, 83–5.

only morally good people of similar character and status could be friends.[9] For the ancients, friendship was about like attracting and relating to like thereby enabling a harmonious binding of persons. For Plato, friendship involves *eros* or desire since it is about seeking our true beloved, whilst Aristotle believed that friendship exists where each wishes the other well and is willing to act on that good will. In this way community, or sharing in common, was possible.[10] Thus friendship is about character rather than about utility. It is about mutuality rather than usefulness and is rooted in self-love, since the friend is seen as another self. As such friendship is grounded in a common character, involves the mutual attractiveness of good character and embodies virtue. Only good people can be friends, though potentially, as the Stoics believed, this was possible for all human beings.[11] In contrast Christian friendship finds its roots in the biblical narratives which speak of God's love for the world as a reality which is other than God. Whilst this was articulated in the Old Testament, it was particularly in the New Testament that Christian friendship took on a distinctive characteristic which distinguished it from the classical tradition. Jesus befriended those who were not like him, whether they were a different gender, social class or simply morally ambiguous, for example in Luke 7: 34.[12] He represented an understanding of divine friendship as that which was between those who are not alike and challenged his hearers to embody this in their relationships. John 15: 14–15 is a critical text here, since it speaks of Jesus transforming his followers from the equivalent of slaves or servants into friends and thereby reveals all his followers to be both friends of God and friends together in his *koinonia* or communion.[13]

Christian friendship, therefore, departed from the classical norms by treating all, irrespective of social or gender status, as friends in the love of God. Indeed, rather than demanding that the vulnerable and poor raise themselves up to a status whereby friendship with their betters was possible, Christian practice took its agenda from the self-giving example of Christ. He emptied himself in order to reach out and enable the lowest to discover the friendship of God. Consequently renunciation of wealth and power in favour of vowed poverty rapidly became a virtue in early Christian practice. The critical friendship was with God, *charitas* as *amor dei*, charity as divine love whereby, in Augustine's terms, all our virtues

---

[9] Liz Carmichael, *Friendship: Interpreting Christian Love* (T & T Clark: London, 2004), p. 7.
[10] Carmichael, *Friendship*, pp. 12–22.
[11] Carmichael, *Friendship*, p. 23.
[12] Carmichael, *Friendship*, p. 38.
[13] Carmichael, *Friendship*, pp. 105–8.

are functions of our love for God.[14] Indeed the monastic movement was an attempt to give space for this sort of love. Monasteries in the Benedictine and then Cistercian tradition were to be schools of love within which Christians were to learn to love others in the love of God. For some, such as Abelard and Heloise, this entailed self-renunciation, a disinterested love which sought nothing from the one befriended and in the process deified or sanctified those involved. For Aquinas, God is subsistent love; he is friendship and therefore all are potential friends of God.[15] Consequently Christian friendship is characterised by four objects; friendship with God, friendship with our own body as God's gift and the object of God's friendship; friendship with our neighbour as the one God loves and who is God's gift to us and finally, friendship with our enemy or stranger who is loved by God and therefore to be loved by us.[16] The Jesuits took this latter notion to heart as they moved beyond the securities of the stable gathered community to befriend the stranger, expressing friendship which is turned outwards rather than inwards.

Following the Reformation, theologians in the Church of England continued to explore the notion of friendship. For seventeenth-century thinkers, Jeremy Taylor and Katherine Philips, Christian love is friendship and entails loving others more than ourselves, even to death. Thomas Traherne and Richard Baxter believed that Christ's love transformed the limitations of natural friendship, whilst nineteenth-century theologian John Henry Newman used 1 John 4: 7 to argue that Christians should cultivate friendship with those around them.[17] More recently, C.S. Lewis popularised Christian love with his book *The Four Loves*, whilst Bishop Stephen Neill argued that Jesus is the friend through whom bad friends become good friends. Other thinkers enriched this understanding of friendship.[18] John Burnaby explored the parable of the Good Samaritan in a way which saw this not as an invocation to general philanthropy but as particular love governed by a special cause. He believed that love grows intensively rather than extensively.[19] Simon Weil spoke of love as paying attention to the other, whilst Jürgen Moltmann regarded friendship as open and specific. Soulless bureaucracy was socialism without friendship.[20] For feminists, friendship was

[14]   Carmichael, *Friendship*, p. 65.
[15]   Carmichael, *Friendship*, pp. 70–75.
[16]   Carmichael, *Friendship*, pp. 117–21.
[17]   Carmichael, *Friendship*, pp. 136–50.
[18]   Carmichael, *Friendship*, p. 155.
[19]   Carmichael, *Friendship*, pp. 163–74.
[20]   Carmichael, *Friendship*, pp. 178–83.

a valuable concept since it was neither authoritarian nor gendered, whilst some gay theologians also saw friendship as a way of characterising their relationships.[21]

For Carmichael friendship in the Christian tradition involves imitating the friendship of God in ways that focus on the other and what they can become in the love of God. It requires formation of character, mediated through prayer and participation in the Christian community and it is neither exclusive nor abstract.[22]

Friendship and the Other

As Carmichael indicates, a number of female theologians have argued that friendship offers a more fruitful theological category for women than the ambiguous language of family or politics. For example Elizabeth Moltmann-Wendel draws upon the work of Virginia Woolf, Sally McFague, Carter Heyward and Mary Hunt to argue that seeing 'God as friend is a healing image for our day'.[23] Friendship entails intimacy, trust, closeness and yet detachment and respect for the other. It is about well-being and, for Christians, finds its opposite in the stranger we are challenged to include, rather than the enemy we are to contest.[24] She also sees the theme of friendship as having a particular contribution to the debate around same-sex relationships and in engaging with new social realities which are increasingly configured around friends rather than the biological family.[25] Nevertheless friendship is culturally conditioned and is therefore also gender conditioned. Much of the language about Jesus' friendship has become tied up with male notions of sacrifice and human centred views of reality. In contrast she wants to focus on his table fellowship with its sense of a sharing of life in an ordinary community, of a life-giving and life-orientated way of inhabiting the world which can engage the ecological challenges we face.[26] Here the language of self-surrender takes the place of a sacrifice to death where 'this is my body' refers not to a sacrificed body but to the healing, life-giving body of Jesus for all. She therefore uses the term *theogusty* (literally tasting God) to speak of our tasting this life-giving body as we receive Holy Communion.[27] Moltmann-Wendel believes that women like Mary Magdalene are the most

---

21   Carmichael, *Friendship*, pp. 184–93.
22   Carmichael, *Friendship*, pp. 198–9.
23   Elizabeth Moltmann-Wendel, *Rediscovering Friendship* (London: SCM, 2000), p. 5.
24   Moltman-Wendel, *Rediscovering Friendship*, p. 8.
25   Moltman-Wendel, *Rediscovering Friendship*, p. 3.
26   Moltman-Wendel, *Rediscovering Friendship*, pp. 23–40.
27   Moltman-Wendel, *Rediscovering Friendship*, p. 50.

faithful friends of Jesus and furthermore that the life-giving intimate and open friendship seen in the story of Jesus can liberate women from oppressive stereotypes and offer a more fruitful and tactile way of practising Christian discipleship in the contemporary world.[28]

Friendship and Difference: Two Case Studies in Recent African Anglicanism

Friendship has also been a key catalyst in two distinct yet remarkably similar movements within twentieth-century African Anglicanism which have impacted on my own understanding of Christian friendship: the East African Revival and the anti-apartheid struggle in South Africa. The East African Revival was a renewal movement within East African Protestantism, particularly within its Anglican form. The *Balokole* movement, ('the saved people') was a unique blend of African spirituality and the Anglican conservative evangelicalism of the Ruanda Mission. It began in the 1930s in Gahini, Ruanda and spread like wild fire throughout Ruanda, Burundi and the southern areas of Uganda. The *Balokole*, who called themselves the Brethren using the inter-gender term *Ab'oluganda* (the brethren), practised a strict holiness code, particularly regarding sexual and economic ethics, stressing the importance of repentance, forgiveness, living in the light with Christ and one another and the centrality of the cross and atonement. Its radical message was the basic equality of all Christians, black and white, female and male, lay and clergy within the love of God.[29] In short it represented an experiment in inter-racial, inter-gender and inter-ecclesial friendship sustained by an ongoing commitment to openness expressed in repentance, confession of sin and mutual forgiveness and sharing. The Brethren's commitment to '*Yesu Yakka*' or 'Jesus Only' entailed 'seeing themselves as modelling a non-racial, non-tribal, non-ethnic solidarity with those who were saved'[30] This was a new clan or tribe which rejected nationalism in favour of a universal solidarity which embraced all participants in a 'democratic inter-gendered, inter-racial fellowship' which challenged traditional African as well as contemporary European assumptions.[31]

---

[28]   Moltman-Wendel, *Rediscovering Friendship*, pp. 72, 88–102.

[29]   Kevin Ward, *A History of Global Anglicanism* (Cambridge: CUP, 2007), pp. 175–88; and Adrian Hastings (ed.), *A World History of Christianity* (London: Cassell, 1999), pp. 224–25.

[30]   Kevin Ward and Emma Wild-Wood, *The East African Revival: History and Legacies* (Farnham: Ashgate, 2012), p. 5.

[31]   Ward and Wild-Wood, *The East African Revival*, p. 18.

At a time when, in order to resist the latter, the nativists were attempting to re-traditionalise African identity by restricting women's public role and stressing the distinctiveness of African over and against European culture, the 'revivalists created a cosmopolitan sphere of discourse that subverted African patriots' localised definition of community'.[32] This set them at odds with such nativists who saw in their behaviour undisciplined libertarianism, sectarianism and poor 'civic virtue'.[33] In particular the revivalists' openness to female agency, their privileging of salvation over biological reproduction and the men's refusal to beat their wives set them at odds with traditional cultural norms.[34] Furthermore many *Balokole* rejected the violent methods of, for example, the *Mau Mau* Kikuyu uprising in 1950s Kenya for pacifist and fellowship reasons and were therefore seen as disloyal and colluding with colonialism.[35] Equally they were reserved about clericalism, being predominantly a lay movement with egalitarian convictions.[36] In a disrupted society where traditional forms of belonging and identity were being put under pressure, they found in the friendship of Christ a unity and friendship with different others across African tribal divisions and with foreign Europeans. As Ubaya Uchiki of Congo asserted, 'all of us are the same tribe … I love all tribes … I have fellowship and love with all tribes'.[37] In addition Europeans, through brokenness, the confession of sin and the mutual seeking of forgiveness, found a unity and depth of relationship with Africans which was quite unusual for the time and was embodied in inter-racial mission team work.[38] An example of this was my mother who arrived as a single woman in 1953 to teach with the Ruanda Mission in Kigezi in the South-West of the country. Living in a more rural and isolated area, she became fluent in Ruchiga, the language of the region. Later she became proficient in Luganda when, after marrying my father in 1958, she moved to Kampala. However whilst in Kigezi, she was drawn into the revival fellowship and was amazed that such discipleship enabled Africans to confess wrongdoing in a culture traditionally hostile to any loss of face, enabled ex-patriots to transcend their English reserve and perceived haughtiness, promoted African leadership in the Church and fostered practices such as the sharing of money through the 'brethren's bag' (common purse). As part of the *Balokole* she gained access to African Christianity and

---

[32]   Ward and Wild-Wood, *The East African Revival*, p. 108.
[33]   Ward and Wild-Wood, *The East African Revival*, p. 113.
[34]   Ward and Wild-Wood, *The East African Revival*, pp. 120–25, 156–60.
[35]   Ward and Wild-Wood, *The East African Revival*, p. 39.
[36]   Ward and Wild-Wood, *The East African Revival*, p. 17.
[37]   Quoted in Ward and Wild-Wood, *The East African Revival*, p. 130.
[38]   Ward and Wild-Wood, *The East African Revival*, p. 191.

society through friendship with her African sisters. Here was a social form of Anglican discipleship with affinities to early Methodism which challenged the individualism and dualism of English evangelicalism. It embodied a community of friends whose life together expressed a democratised Christianity and challenged hierarchical attitudes among some missionaries. It represented a 'Christocentric universalism' in which all were siblings.[39]

South Africa was a particularly stressful country in which to live during the second half of the twentieth century. On the surface it was an explicitly Christian society with over 70 per cent claiming to share this faith. Yet Afrikaaner racist politics and social order were in sharp contrast to the norms of Christian practice across the rest of the globe.[40] The ruling Afrikaaners and their Dutch Reformed Church believed apartheid (or the separation of the races) to be biblical and therefore God-designed. To support this Afrikaaner Calvinist ethnic '*volk*' or people separatism they drew on a particular reading of Kuyperian theology which stressed distinctive orders within creation and also on the conviction that different societies and cultures had their own character which, within Christian believing, should not be contaminated by others. Whilst fear of difference, anxiety about poverty and a literalist approach to Scripture played their part, it was this sense of a divinely mandated structure which drove its ideologies despite the impossibility of such segregated life.[41] Many English-speaking whites effectively supported this even if they were less vocal. However the global church contested this interpretation and the Anglican Church of the Province of Southern Africa, with other churches, was at the forefront of this resistance, particularly during the time of Archbishop Desmond Tutu. For Tutu and others like him, prophecy was indeed a word spoken to God's people, within and beyond the Anglican community. Thus their message was to fellow Christians such as the Afrikaaners and drew predominantly on internal Christian discourse rather than external ideology. In particular they used the language of Liberation Theology to stress the social location of Jesus as among the poor which, in South Africa, meant predominantly the majority black community. They and other protagonists also drew upon African notions of *Ubuntu* or community to

---

[39]   Ward and Wild-Wood, *The East African Revival*, pp. 208, 210.

[40]   Alan Boesak, *Black and Reformed: Apartheid, Liberation and the Calvinist Tradition* (Johannesburg: Skotaville, 1986), pp. 108–19.

[41]   See John B. Thomson, 'Protestant Theology: South Africa' in Alister E.McGrath (ed.), *The Blackwell Encyclopedia of Modern Christian Thought* (Oxford: Basil Blackwell, 1993), p. 521.

subvert segregationalist ideologies.[42] Indeed some argued that Jesus belonged to the oppressed and was therefore himself 'black' and that it was in relationship with the black community and its interests that God's concerns and friendship were to be found.[43] Indeed Bonganjalo Goba argued that 'reconciliation ... cannot take place without liberation ... the black/white conflict can be resolved by a clear commitment to the liberation movement in which blacks have a primary responsibility of leading whites, who by virtue of supporting the existing political system, have completely denied themselves such an opportunity'.[44] This was a radical message which became focused in *The Kairos Document* published in 1986 and its sequel, *The Road to Damascus*, published in 1989.[45] Together these documents set the churches in sharp conflict with the rulers of South Africa. They deconstructed the ideology of apartheid, advocated a theology of resistance and transformation and in particular presented this as a prophetic *kairos* word, a word for a critical time, to Christians in that country challenging them to identify practically with the interests of the majority community oppressed by apartheid.[46] They also critiqued other Christian responses, which they labelled 'state' and 'church' theology since they believed that these either explicitly (state) or effectively (church) supported apartheid. Such responses were idolatrous and apartheid itself was a heresy.[47] God, for these prophets, was one who demanded active love rather than simply contemplation, a love willing to confront.[48] Faith had to be interpreted from the perspective of those suffering

---

[42]   Gabriel M. Setiloane, *African Theology: An Introduction* (Johannesburg: Skotaville, 1986), pp. 9–15.

[43]   See Basil Moore (ed.), *Black Theology: The South African Voice* (London: Hurst & Co, 1973), pp. ix, 8; Alan Boesak, *Farewell to Innocence: A Social-Ethical Study of Black Theology and Black Power* (Johannesburg: Ravan Press, 1977), p. 9; Itumaleng J. Mosala and Buti Thlagale, *The Unquestionable Right to be Free: Essays in Black Theology* (Johannesburg: Skotaville, 1986), pp. 45; Simon Maimela, *Proclaim Freedom to My People: Essays in Religion and Politics* (Johannesburg: Skotaville, 1987), pp. 71, 99, 143; and Itumaleng J. Mosala, *Biblical Hermeneutics and Black Theology in South Africa* (Michigan: Eerdmans, 1989), pp. 4–10.

[44]   Bonganjalo Goba, *An Agenda for Black Theology* (Johannesburg: Skotaville, 1988), p.5.

[45]   *The Kairos Document: Challenge to the Church*, 2nd edn., (Johannesburg: Skotaville, 1986) and its follow up, *The Road to Damascus: Kairos and Conversion* (Johannesburg: Skotaville, 1989).

[46]   See John W. de Gruchy, 'South African Theology Comes of Age', *Religious Studies Review* 17/3 (July 1991), pp. 197–229.

[47]   See John de Gruchy and C. Villa Vicencio (eds), *Apartheid is a Heresy* (Cape Town: David Philip, 1983).

[48]   *Kairos*, pp. 17–18, 25–6.

rather than from the perspective of the powerful.[49] Love as a form of friendship sought the well-being of the oppressor through liberating them from this role.[50] In this way *The Kairos Document* and *The Road to Damascus* represented a radical expression of Christian friendship, since they sought to expose the true roots of the problems Christians were facing in South Africa in order to foster the conditions within which that society and its churches could be healed and flourish. As Tutu commented, the premise of the good life, for Christians, is shalom for all, a view which apartheid contradicts in its undermining of a Christian vision of creation and redemption.[51]

The East African Revival and the Christian Anti-Apartheid prophetic movement in South Africa, whilst not singularly Anglican, represent an interesting coincidence of vision which coheres, I believe, with an Anglican disposition towards friendship for the stranger. In East Africa, this involved finding in Christ a point of congruence with different others, represented in different tribes and ethnicities in a way with significant affinities to the later experience of Christians in South Africa. Both involved disturbing challenges to those with power and although the East African Revival was atonement focused and the Christian Anti-Apartheid movement, creation focused, both were about redemption and about realising symbolically an eschatological vision of peaceableness. To achieve this Christ, in both views, had to break down the powerful and raise up the poor into a common fellowship whose character and form embodied Jesus the self-emptying poor agent of divine reconciliation.

Conclusion

Friendship for the stranger exemplifies the love of God. This love, often called agape or self-less love, is at the heart of the practice of Jesus, who describes his core community as friends (John 15:12–15) yet ironically only calls one person friend or companion in the Gospels, the estranged Judas (Matthew 26: 50). It is very different from ancient Greek notions of friendships focused on pleasure, utility or indeed virtue since these were all fundamentally self-referential and about self-love.[52] Consequently whilst Christians, like Jews, see friendship with God as the goal of life this quest is sought in a way that desires all to share in

---

49   *Kairos*, pp. 18–20.
50   *Kairos*, p. 24.
51   de Gruchy and Villa Vicencio, *Apartheid is a Heresy*, p. 39.
52   Samuel Wells and Ben Quash, *Introducing Christian Ethics* (Oxford: Wiley-Blackwell, 2010), pp. 276–7.

God's friendship.[53] Ironically this stranger-seeking friendship fostered much stronger *koinonia* or fellowship than the ancient Greeks managed since all were now common neighbours of equal status rather than simply those in the particular polis or city. Equally the challenge of Christ was to love, or will good for others whilst self-love was not selfishness but about developing a character which would emulate the boundless love of God.[54] Hence practices which foster friendship are vital to the life of the church.

Such practices are central to Anglican mission and as I have argued infuse Anglican ways both within the English context and beyond. Common worship and intentional congregating for that worship train Anglicans in the virtues which sustain godly friendship with their neighbours or parishioners even when, as in the East African Revival, there was a degree of tension between revivalists and existing church structures. The public sociability of Anglicanism disposes Anglicans to be hospitable and compassionate. Even when exclusive covenanted relationships, such as marriage, include friendship, this is not in order to seal the relationship but to ensure its robustness so that this friendship can appropriately make space for difference in its openness to new strangers such as children. The liturgical blessing of marriage positions and relativises marriage as something within the church rather than simply of itself. This speaks of marriage as one vocation among many which the friends of Jesus can respond to within the deeper friendship embodied by the church. This prevents marital friendship from becoming exclusive since those in the church are not chosen by one another but are simply there by the grace of God.

English Anglicans are friendship people. They owe their faith to acts of African friendship and these expressions of Anglican friendship continue to remind all Anglicans that this disposition is intrinsic to their discipleship.[55] It is not a unique vocation, nor one Anglicans have or continue to excel in, but it is why they are as they are.

---

[53] Wells and Quash, *Introducing Christian Ethics*, p. 275.

[54] Wells and Quash, *Introducing Christian Ethics*, pp. 278–81.

[55] For contemporary reflections upon the challenges that this represents in contemporary England see Duncan Dormor, Jack McDonald and Jeremy Caddick, *Anglicanism: The Answer to Modernity* (London: Continuum, 2003) and Samuel Wells and Sarah Coakley (eds), *Praying for England: Priestly Presence in Contemporary Culture* (London: Continuum, 2008).

Chapter 3
Friendship as Discipleship

According to L. Gregory Jones and Kevin Armstrong discipleship is about being apprenticed into a form of life which reflects the shape of Christ's self-giving love. It is about calling, educating and shaping human life into a movement which reflects God's life in the world today.[1] Discipleship therefore transforms Christians so that they can perform the faith. In this sense discipleship, friendship and mission all require apprenticeship. Apprenticeship is the way we learn a form of life from wiser and more mature practitioners. We are immersed in the mundane practices of the church in order to be transformed into a cross-shaped community of holy friends.[2] It is necessarily an unequal relationship, since the trainer and the apprentice are in a different relationship to what is being learned. Yet it is also about sharing and giving friendship, since the apprentice gains practical knowledge about how to perform their craft from another in a way that is relational before it is commercial or contractual. It is fundamentally an exercise in giving and cultivating grace in another which may only secondarily involve payment. Historically apprenticeship involved being inducted into a form of practical wisdom which took time to learn and involved the development of character as well as skill. It is therefore about becoming a certain sort of people whose capacities enable them to perform and improvise upon their craft in ways faithful to its traditions.

This understanding of discipleship challenges many contemporary assumptions about human flourishing. As the sociologist, Anthony Giddens comments, 'modern institutions differ from all preceding forms of social order in respect of their dynamism, the degree to which they undercut traditional habits and customs and their global impact'.[3] Indeed even among Christians there are those who believe that it is possible to skip over the past and read the texts of Scripture without any sense of the historical thread which connects us to their original world or the tradition within which these Scriptures have

---

[1]   L. Gregory Jones and Kevin R. Armstrong, *Resurrecting Excellence: Shaping Faithful Christian Ministry* (Michigan: Eerdmans, 2006), pp. 51–2.

[2]   Jones and Armstrong, *Resurrecting Excellence*, pp. 55–71.

[3]   Anthony Giddens, *Modernity and Self-Identity: Self and Society in the Late Modern Age* (Cambridge: Polity Press, 1991), p. 1.

been interpreted. Such Christians do not see themselves as part of an ongoing story whose truthfulness is tested and deepened in the crucible of history. They view Christianity as a cluster of abstract timeless ideas. In contrast I will argue that apprenticeship connects people with a past that is living and embodied in their practice. It reminds us that 'temporal distance ... is not a yawning abyss, but is filled with the continuity of custom and tradition, in the light of which everything handed down to us presents itself'.[4] To talk about Jesus and the practice of apprenticeship is therefore to speak about a way of discipleship which is contemporary and yet historical, a sharing of his friendship across time. It is to speak about the contemporary church, the public community of the Jesus movement, which carries the memory of Jesus in its body and believes itself to be infused with his risen life.[5] Jesus' story and its formative character have been transmitted in the testimony of Scripture, the practices of discipleship and in forms of worship. Anglicans believe that the contemporary Jesus movement has emerged through forms of discipleship apprenticed through the reiterative, corporate reading of Scripture within the practice of worship. This ensures that contemporary discipleship is congruent with the Jesus story. Indeed contemporary performances of discipleship help us to understand and learn the stories of Jesus by showing their formative impact in contemporary lives. This is particularly the case when we meet disciples witnessing in demanding circumstances since these contexts provide less opportunity for self deception. The challenges are too raw and the discipleship costs too significant. Indeed these 'shaken' disciples testify to the reliable friendship of Jesus since, as Andrew Shanks points out, being shaken opens up space for the transcendent.[6] Christian communities therefore represent the ongoing impact of the Scriptures. They are the contemporary Jesus communities which continue to learn from the risen Jesus in their midst.

Apprenticing Friendship in the New Testament

To grasp the distinctive nature of apprenticeship in the New Testament we need to look at discipleship and learning in the classic stories of the Jesus movement. At one level the earthly Jesus does not seem to have apprenticed his disciples in ways

---

4   Hans Georg Gadamer, *Truth and Method*, 2nd edn (London: Sheed & Ward, 1993), p. 292.

5   See Matthew 28: 20, Luke 24: 49, John 20: 22–3 and Acts 2: 1–13.

6   Andrew Shanks, *God and Modernity: A New and Better Way to do Theology* (London: Routledge, 2000), pp. 3 and 75.

recognisable to the Jewish or Hellenistic cultures of the time. He did not follow the *talmid* traditions of rabbinic Judaism which focused around intense textual exegesis and Torah schools. The Greek understanding of *mimesis* or imitation is absent from the teaching of Jesus in the Gospels. Instead disciples are called as individuals to follow after Jesus in a way which has little time for abstract study and is characterised by a break with the past rather than an induction into it.[7] As Hengel points out, a key text which demonstrates the uniqueness of Jesus' approach to discipleship is Matthew 8: 21–22. This invites would-be disciples to break with Torah and custom 'on the basis of his (Jesus') unique authority as the proclaimer of the imminent kingdom of God'.[8] Implicitly taking the role of God, Jesus personally and directly calls his followers and invites them into a relationship with himself which is like the relationship of the prophets to God in the Old Testament. The disciples' relationship is centred upon friendship with Jesus and his disclosure of the reign of God, rather than obedience to Torah texts or the acquisition of philosophical ideas or knowledge.[9] It is a charismatic interpersonal relationship rather than an intellectually driven movement. Indeed the role of the disciple is to witness to Jesus and his messianic mission which proclaims the imminent reign of God over Israel.[10] It is not primarily about banking beliefs or being a pupil. Jesus invites individuals, male and female, to join him in a way of life which embodies the reign of God present on earth. It is about being with him, being formed through this relationship and therefore is more about practical wisdom than intellectual capacity, friendship rather than exegetical expertise. It is a way of life which Ian Wallis argues, is so embedded in the characters of the early church that it enables them to recognise that Jesus is risen as they continue to practise his way.[11]

Jesus therefore roots his teaching in his own sense of vocation rather than in an exegesis of the Torah. His authority is not like that of the scribes. Consequently discipleship is about obedience. It involves following Jesus (*akolouthein*) and being formed into someone who is part of his community, rather than engaging in the sort of exegetical or intellectual learning (*mathetein*) characteristic of

---

[7]   Martin Hengel, *The Charismatic Leader and His Followers* (Edinburgh: T&T Clark, 1981), p.32. See also Mark 1: 16ff, Matt. 4:18–22 and Luke 5: 1–11.

[8]   Hengel, *The Charismatic Leader*, p. 15.

[9]   Hengel, *The Charismatic Leader*, p. 15. See also David Brown, *Discipleship and Imagination: Christian Tradition and Truth* (Oxford: Oxford University Press, 2000), p. 483.

[10]   Henry Wansbrough (ed.), *Jesus and the Oral Gospel* (Sheffield. JSOT Press, 1991), p. 200.

[11]   Ian Wallis, *Holy Saturday Faith: Rediscovering the Legacy of Jesus* (London: SPCK, 2000).

rabbinic Judaism or Greek philosophy. Jesus' followers are to be witnesses to the reign of God present in Jesus rather than pupils learning a philosophy of life.[12] It is interesting that the concept of following after and of being a disciple are both virtually absent from the Septuagint (LXX), disciple being mentioned three times and following (*akolouthein*) being virtually absent.[13] The verb to learn (*mathanein*) is mentioned 55 times in the LXX and is linked to the revelation of God and his will through the Torah. It expresses a whole life obedience rather than merely intellectual assent. Although the word disciple (*mathetes*) is used 261 times in the Gospels and Acts, its meaning is determined by Jesus rather than by contemporary rabbinic or Hellenistic parallels and unlike these, there is no end to the learning of the disciple since it is a ceaseless following after Jesus through life, rather than the mastery of a body of knowledge. Friendship with Jesus is ongoing and develops throughout the course of the disciple's life. Discipleship is not transitory but the fulfilment of the disciple's destiny and is an ongoing experience of listening to Jesus.[14] Like Jesus this is a life with suffering and service at its core.[15] Consequently after Easter the followers of Jesus are first called 'those of the way' (*te odos*).[16] They were a community on a life-transforming journey with the risen Jesus rather than an intellectual school or exegetical tradition. They were being apprenticed in the practical wisdom of Jesus rather than becoming students.

Interestingly the word disciple (*mathetes*) is virtually absent beyond the Gospels and Acts. Discipleship in this sense appears to be about associating with the earthly Jesus, a relationship which continues but in a different way after Easter. Yet although the relationship of Jesus with his disciples before Easter is distinctive and its imitative character relatively underplayed, there is evidence of Jesus providing the basis for the post-Easter church's ongoing relationship with him which would become more apprenticeship like in its character. For example, Jesus teaches using *meshalim* or pithy memorable narrative sayings which seek to explain who and what he is about. Many of these belong to the Q material of the Synoptic Gospels whose character suggests the existence of blocks of teaching material which were circulating independent of the birth, passion

---

12   Wansbrough, *Jesus and the Oral Gospel*, p. 200.

13   Richard N. Longenecker (ed.), *Patterns of Discipleship in the New Testament* (Eerdmans, Cambridge, 1996), pp. 2–3.

14   K. Rengstorf, 'manqanw ktl', in G. Kittel and G. Friedrich, *Theological Dictionary of the New Testament* vol. 4 (Grand Rapids: Eerdmans, 1967), pp. 390–461, 448. See Matthew 3: 1–14.

15   David Brown, *Discipleship and Imagination*, p. 488.

16   Acts 9: 2.

and resurrection narratives. [17] These often follow the wisdom tradition in their use of rustic material and expound life rather than texts.[18] In addition whilst not inviting imitation, the call to follow implies a formative journey however imperfect the discipleship band is. In particular it is a call to experience the friendship of Jesus rather than a demand to be a servant in the manner of rabbinic schools.[19] Disciples are the friends of Jesus, 'sharing with him his uncertain and indeed perilous destiny and becoming his pupils only in a derivative sense'.[20]

After Easter there is a change in the mode of discipleship formation for the authors of the Gospels and New Testament letters. In Paul's writing imitation becomes a significant concept. In 1 Corinthians 4: 16 the Corinthians are invited to imitate Paul in the norms of Christian practice, whilst chapter 11: 1 locates this challenge within the pattern of Paul's imitation of Christ himself. Furthermore 2 Corinthians 5: 14, 8: 9, directs the church to imitate the example of Christ expressed in his grace, love, gentleness, forbearance and suffering and also to follow Paul's own example and that of fellow Christians such as the generous Macedonian churches.[21] Romans portrays discipleship as the way we are conformed to or become like God through Paul's exploration of the theme of the righteousness of God (*dikaiosune theo*). In the Christ Hymn of Philippians 2 imitation is central to discipleship.[22] Here Paul delineates the shape of discipleship by modelling it on the story of Jesus which he wishes the Philippians to practise (*phronein*). He thereby integrates both rabbinic and Greek traditions so that discipleship becomes a form of practical wisdom and faith becomes more reflective, traditioned and demonstrably rooted in Scripture. A similar theme can be found in Hebrews which represents a sermon on the cost of discipleship expressed through the exegesis of five Old Testament texts.

This change is also evident in the literary form of the Gospels which were written to encourage imitation. According to Richard Burridge their genre is closest to Greco-Roman *Ancient Lives* which were quasi biographical accounts telling the story of a hero whose combined words and deeds offered an example for their followers to imitate.[23] These were instruction stories, each with a

---

[17] Wansbrough, *Jesus and the Oral Gospel*, p. 270.

[18] Hengel, *The Charismatic Leader*, p. 47. See also Wansbrough, *Jesus and the Oral Gospel*, pp. 192, 270.

[19] Hengel, *The Charismatic Leader*, p. 51.

[20] Hengel, *The Charismatic Leader*, p. 54.

[21] Longenecker, *Patterns of Discipleship*, pp. 127–39.

[22] Longenecker, *Patterns of Discipleship*, pp. 151, 155–6.

[23] Richard A. Burridge, *Imitating Jesus: An Inclusive Approach to New Testament Ethics* (Grand Rapids, Michigan: Eerdmans, 2007), pp. 19–30.

particular focus, which encouraged followers 'to imitate the central character in his deeds and words ... for the gospels this becomes the call to discipleship, keeping Jesus' teaching and following his example in a new mixed community of all who respond'.[24] For Mark this was about living the self-denying ethic of Jesus; for Matthew it was about living real righteousness following Jesus as the true interpreter of the Torah; for Luke it was about embodying the universal concern of Jesus particularly for the marginalised and outcasts, whilst for John it was about sharing a story about cosmic reality.[25] Imitation involves Christian disciples improvising upon the stories of Jesus which they receive in ways that are faithful and yet appropriate to the conditions of life they are part of. Consequently the existence of the Gospels as discipleship manuals reflects the need for stable, trustworthy remembering. Mark, as Philip Davis has suggested, may well be shaped for discipleship development, since it begins with baptism and has an open ending which invites the church to take on the story in their discipleship. [26] Matthew's concluding challenge to his readers in chapter 28: 19 is the imperative 'to make disciples' (*matheteusate*), whilst the Luke-Acts material explores discipleship before and after Easter, showing a literary structure designed to show their correspondence.[27] The Johannine tradition aims to unite contemporary readers with the founding disciples as those who together are related to and believe in Jesus. The stories of Jesus and the movement which emerged after his passion therefore indicate that the disciples were apprenticed into the life of Jesus, the embodiment of the friendship of God, as they reflected upon the stories and deeds of Jesus, orally and then in writing. The corporate character of the church, the liturgical shape of the Gospel material and the talk about imitation and exemplars suggests that discipleship remained a way of embodying the story of Jesus and its distinctive characteristics of self-giving love, forgiveness and service in ever new mission situations.

Discipleship: Sharing the Friendship of the Risen Jesus Today

The Philosopher of History, Benedetto Croce argued that all history is contemporary since the past is inaccessible and so accounts of the past represent

---

24   Burridge, *Imitating Jesus*, p. 348.
25   Burridge, *Imitating Jesus*, p. 408.
26   Longenecker, *Patterns of Discipleship*, p. 26.
27   Longenecker, *Patterns of Discipleship*, pp. 52–3.

imaginative but contemporary reconstructions of the evidence of that past.[28] For Christians, however, the memory of Jesus is not simply about contemporary reconstruction. As the risen Lord, the historical Jesus is the contemporary Jesus present in the community which continues his story. Consequently the character of this community has revelatory significance. Indeed, as we have seen, Stanley Hauerwas coined the phrase 'a community of character' to describe the church as the social life of Jesus today.[29] This character takes the form of a living tradition into which new disciples are apprenticed as they learn how to follow and embody the practices of Jesus in their own contexts in a way that acts as a proto-universal sign of God's friendship for all. Such contextual performances apprentice the next generation of disciples in the story of Jesus and demonstrate that discipleship is about doing rather than speculating, it is about walking the way of Jesus in order to talk the story of God's friendship in Jesus. Disciples learn the language of Jesus in order to interpret the world as his followers and improvise upon the way of Jesus. In Charles Taylor's words such apprenticeship represents an incarnational rather than an excarnational faith.[30] It is embedded rather than abstract, a social rather than an individualistic way. As such it is a charismatic performance since the way cannot be abstracted but has to be found in the conversation of the church with the Spirit of the risen Jesus. This conversation generates a practical wisdom distilled in the crucible of life's challenges rather than an abstract theory or technique. As such apprenticeship involves handing on the wisdom of discipleship rather than holding onto it.

Conclusion

If apprenticeship is about learning in practical ways how to be Jesus' friends and to share his friendship then the school of such friendship is communal worship as we shall explore further in the next chapter. Worship is the ongoing tradition of concentrated reflective practice which connects with and continues the risen life of Jesus. Worship situates the classical texts of Scripture within an attentive community whose reading of them is disciplined by the continuous practice of reading by the church and before them, by Israel. Worship displays those practices and the manner of formation and learning which the community

---

28 See R.G. Collingwood, *The Idea of History* (Oxford: Oxford University Press, 1978), p. 202.

29 Stanley Hauerwas, *A Community of Character. Toward a Constructive Christian Social Ethic*, 4th edn (Notre Dame: University of Notre Dame Press, 1986).

30 Charles Taylor, *A Secular Age* (London: Belknap Harvard, 2007), pp. 288 and 740.

of Jesus recognise are crucial for their formation as they have reiteratively read
the stories of Jesus in the light of the story of Israel for the past two millennia.
Communal worship has affinities with a musical score which shapes the sound
but does not determine it, or a rugby practice which trains players in the rules
of the game. The well-trained and experienced player improvises as the music or
game is being played just as in worship, Christians learn how to improvise upon
the story of Jesus in the range of contexts they find themselves in. This can be an
argumentative experience but it is always rooted in the inherited story and its
sustaining discipleship practices. Context informs but does not control the way
the story develops. Instead there is a conversation with Scripture and the history
of Christian practice which tests the faithfulness of contemporary discipleship
as it responds to new challenges. This conversation crafts disciples into people
who can improvise upon the Jesus way as reflective disciples.[31] It reminds us
that there is no ideal form of discipleship but a number of faithful ways which
become apparent as these conversations develop.

For Anglicans liturgy apprentices disciples through the practices of gathering
together, confession and forgiveness, listening to and reflecting upon Scripture
and the telling of Scriptural stories, prayer, the sacraments, vocation and service
and so on as we shall see in the next chapter.[32] These practices take their cue
from the stories of Jesus and train his friends to share that friendship with the
world. Anglican communities are very diverse and reflect Richard Burridge's
insight that Jesus' rigorous teaching was shared with a very inclusive and
mixed community.[33] Common worship holds this mixed community together
in a creative conversation about the Gospel. To reverse Grace Davie's famous
aphorism, apprenticeship indicates that we must belong if we are to believe.[34] It
represents a journey of discovery as we take part in the contemporary drama of
God's story. For Anglicans, therefore, to share in the friendship of Jesus means
becoming his apprentices, apprentices who draw their wisdom from the history
and practice of the church, the company of Jesus' friends improvising upon the
stories of Scripture. As they participate in this formative movement, which
involves learning the practical wisdom of discipleship rather than achieving
exegetical expertise or intellectual prowess, they become witnesses of the reign
of God embodied in Jesus. It is about 'formational wisdom rooted in tactical

---

[31]   See Roger Walton, *The Reflective Disciple* (London: Epworth, 2009), pp. 23–4.

[32]   John B. Thomson, *Doxa: A Discipleship Course* (London: Darton, Longman and
Todd, 2007).

[33]   Burridge, *Imitating Jesus*, pp. 71–2, 152, 388–91 & 409.

[34]   Grace Davie, *Religion in Britain since 1945: Believing without Belonging* (Oxford:
Blackwell, 1994), p. 4.

savity, emotional intelligence, reflexivity, responsiveness'.[35] For this reason paying attention to communities of ordinary disciples worshipping God and listening to Scripture is vital if we are to grasp what it means to be apprentices of Jesus today.

---

[35] Martyn Percy, *Anglicanism: Confidence, Commitment and Communion* (Farnham: Ashgate, 2013), p. 15.

Chapter 4
Friendship as Worship

Many congregations in England today appear small, relatively marginal and uncertain about their mission in contemporary society. According to the sociologist, Grace Davie, English society, like most of Europe, is characterised by a 'take it for granted' view of public religion.[1] Like other public utilities, it is there to be used when wanted, but otherwise not engaged with. It is a sort of National Spiritual Service.[2] Hence, as Lynda Barley has shown, whilst 86 per cent of the population visited churches each year and 72 per cent claimed to be Christians in the 2001 census, only 8 per cent attended regularly.[3] According to Davie, the committed core, therefore, act vicariously for those who believe but don't actively belong. Such a casual approach to public faith combined with the fragility of many congregations raises sharp questions about mission. The Church of England's *Mission Shaped Church Report* and the *Fresh Expressions* movement seek to engage with such questions, as we shall see in Chapter 12.[4] Yet what are these small gatherings of Christians for? How can they make a difference amidst an apparently indifferent community?[5] In particular, if the Christian way or journey is fundamentally about embodying the grace of God, how can they be divine gifts to those among whom they are set?[6] How can such small and relatively impotent communities witness to the great mission of God to redeem, restore and renew the world in the face of large scale indifference?

---

[1]   Grace Davie, *Religion in Modern Europe: A Memory Mutates* (Oxford: Oxford University Press, 2000), pp. 55–61.

[2]   Martyn Percy, *Anglicanism: Confidence, Commitment and Communion* (Farnham: Ashgate, 2013), p. 112.

[3]   Lynda Barley, *Churchgoing Today* (London: CHP, 2006), p. 2. The most recent census (2011) indicates that only 60 per cent of the population now self-designate as Christians though there are wide regional variations.

[4]   Graham Cray et al., *Mission Shaped Church* (London: CHP, 2004).

[5]   John B. Thomson, *Church on Edge? Practising Christian Ministry Today* (London: Darton, Longman and Todd, 2004).

[6]   John Milbank, *Being Reconciled: Ontology and Pardon* (London: Routledge, 2003), pp. ix–xi.

Signing Friendship as Christian Communities

As we have noted it was Stanley Hauerwas who made the surprising assertion that the first task of the church in mission is to be itself since 'the truthfulness of Jesus creates and is known by the kind of community his story should form'.[7] What he meant by this was that the church is the community which represents the effect of God's grace in lives open to that grace. Hence it represents a sign of salvation, an expression of the living holiness of God active in the world. The church does not therefore have to do anything in the first instance to indicate the friendship of God for the world. Its very existence is evidence of that, even taking account of its fragility and failures. Certainly the church is not the kingdom of God and hence is not everything God is about. Nevertheless the church embodies and expresses the Gospel which is for all. To play with Karl Barth's phrase, the church is the crater left behind by the explosion of God's salvation in Christ. In consequence as Christians gather and allow God to transform them, they become able to see the particular mission challenges before them. As gift and givers, they are trained to see how they are to be expressions of divine friendship in diverse contexts.[8]

Anxiety about being relevant and effective can therefore give way to the assurance that as effects of God's grace, simply being who they are is a major sign of God's compassion for the world. Their gift is to be signs, which, though not exhaustive or finished expressions of God's love, are still significant witness to that grace. God is the principle agent in mission rather than human beings. Focusing first and foremost on what God is about rather than upon what we can do for God does not imply passivity or complacency. As will become apparent below, the transformation of sinful Christians is a major enterprise of God and discipleship is about co-operating with God's grace. However focusing upon God gives hope that human fallibility and fragility do not determine the effectiveness of grace. Christians are gifts of grace for the world's blessing precisely as those who know ourselves to be forgiven sinners. The church, therefore, acts as a sign of what God is bringing about through the slow time of transformation. It is a form of exemplary politics as a new society emerges configured around the grace of God expressed in Christ. As such what the church is becoming enables the mission of God provisionally to be seen and gives faith an empirical bite. A particular example of such a tangible sign of material grace is an Anglican

---

[7]   Stanley Hauerwas, *A Community of Character, Toward a Constructive Christian Social Ethic*, 4th edn (Notre Dame: University of Notre Dame Press, 1986), p. 37.

[8]   Ann Morisy, *Journeying Out: A New Approach to Christian Mission* (Moorhouse: Harnsbury, 2004), pp. 30–31.

congregation located on a rough Barnsley estate. Until recently the whole area had an air of dilapidation and depression, with most buildings boarded up and local teenagers looking bored. Yet this little community of 25–30 adults with a handful of youngsters has managed to renovate their building, maintain an active Christian presence in the area and remain committed to serving that community despite the absence of a vicar. They embody the Anglican mission of the church in this deprived area of Barnsley as a sign of salvation.

Sharing Friendship as Transformed People

Although being the church is the first way Anglicans share God's friendship, this actually involves being transformed in order to co-operate more faithfully with the agenda of God. In Eucharistic language God takes, blesses, breaks and gives. In order to be gifts which speak of divine friendship disciples need to experience the blessing and breaking of transformation as God takes what they are and forms them into witnesses of grace. Whilst creation is a gift and reflects the glory of God, the work of transformation, mediated through Eucharistic worship in particular, is about intensifying this glory and gift by transforming lives so that they speak of the love of God for the world. It is therefore through ongoing transformation that people become gifts signifying saving grace for the world effective on God's terms and within God's mission. Worship, particularly Eucharistic worship, therefore, forms Christians into signs and agents of God's reign and mission in the world. It shows people what God does in lives openly offered to grace and regularly trained in the practices of discipleship.

Anglicans believe that such transformation is rooted in the public worship of the gathered community. As they gather in common worship Anglicans believe that they imbibe the transforming grace of God eucharistically through word and sacrament in a way that affects who and what they are. Indeed, as Rowan Williams has pointed out, Anglican divines Richard Hooker and George Herbert believed that transubstantiation was fundamentally about human lives rather than arguments about the status of bread and wine post consecration.[9] Transformation into an icon of God's love is not primarily about the condition of the bread and wine so much as about the condition of the community which has received the gift of God into itself in order to embody that gift in the bread and wine of ordinary living. Worship, therefore is a missional gift since it forms people whose lives are marked by the effects of God so that they display the

---

[9]   Rowan Williams, *Anglican Identities* (London: DLT, 2004), pp. 24–45.

welcome of God available to all. They are thereby being made Christians since righteousness is not simply imputed to them but also imparted to them. In consequence participating in regular church worship is vital since, through participating in the transforming effects of worship, disciples become revelations of God and God's love for the world. Their lives begin to display something of the world God is bringing about through Christ in contrast to that given over to sin. Indeed, as Michael Ramsay argued, worship forms Christians into meaningful flesh, epiphanic flesh that signifies what God is about and signifies God's compassion for the world.[10] The gift of meaningful flesh offers the world a challenge. The challenge is to make sense of this flesh, even when it can appear odd to common sense analysis. Indeed sometimes being odd in a sinful world is one of the gifts of the church to that world. It indicates that this gathering is on God's terms rather than being determined by human choice. As such it witnesses to God's effect upon the church. Worship, therefore, forms people into evidence for the saving impact of God in the world. Being made distinctive through worship is simply another way of becoming holy witnesses. It is how Christians continue as part of the ongoing revelation of God to the world.

Gathering to worship, therefore, is akin to participating in a training session. As Anglicans participate in the liturgy and its spiritual exercises such as praise, confession, attention to Scripture, intercession, taking the sacraments and so on they not only hear the word of God but are trained in the virtues of Christian practice and learn the habits of life which reflect and express the grace of God. In short they become Christians, or in Augustine and Aquinas's terms, people of charity.[11] Such training or formation means that as they share in God's mission they do not need rules to know what to do. Instead, like competent athletes, they can improvise in diverse situations confident that their training has equipped them to make good judgements that enable them to participate faithfully in God's mission.[12] Such improvisation means that new situations require fresh expressions of faithful Christian practice. In one ex-mining village near Doncaster a congregation has set up a cinema in part of the church as a way of re-engaging with its local community, most of whom find it too expensive to travel to Doncaster. In addition local children help the vicar and members of the congregation prepare meals, which they share together. In

---

[10]   Williams, *Anglican Identities*, pp. 87–101.

[11]   Wells and Quash, *Introducing Christian Ethics* (Oxford: Wiley-Blackwell, 2010), pp. 278–9.

[12]   Samuel Wells, *Improvisation: The Drama of Christian Ethics* (London: SPCK, 2004), p. 78.

worship, trusting that through this and in the light of the journey they and other Christian communities have made, they will learn how to speak faithfully as God's language for today. The gift of the church to the world, therefore, is to live and speak as Christians so that the world may see and hear the Gospel story of God's friendship embodied by the church.[18] The character, plausibility and nature of that language will therefore be seen in the way the language enables Christians to live faithfully with God in that world. Living conscious that we are dependent creatures rather than autonomous agents relieves Christians of the need to be in control with all the pressure and anxiety that this generates. Christians live not as independent self-interested consumers out to maximise their own well-being at the expense of everyone else and hence in structural conflict with everyone else. Rather Christians recognise that even their enemies are made in the image of God and to befriend them as fellow neighbours in God's world is to offer a different vision of society in a fractious and divided world. Forgiving those who have offended them and asking forgiveness of those they have offended speaks of a redeemed creation in which peaceableness rather than violence is most fundamental. Undertaking lifelong vows such as those of celibacy, marriage or ordination speaks of trust in the promise-keeping character of God, in and through the vicissitudes of life. All these gifts contrast with much in contemporary society where tabloid moralism, the therapy culture of self-preoccupation, and the destructiveness of serial relationships undermine human flourishing.

Yet Christians also need to face the pain caused where their language has broken down or been abusive of others, for example in the history of the Crusades or the slave trade. Similarly Anglicans recognise that worship must be common if it is to be truthful and so this language has to be learned with other Christians rather than independently of them. This means that when new or unexpected ways of speaking the language emerge, such as over sexuality or usury, it is important to listen to all members of the community, particularly where disagreement exists.[19] Only thus can the language develop faithfully and speak to the world about God's love. Furthermore such reflection upon past practice helps participants appreciate how the Christian language has developed through history and locates contemporary speakers in a broad community of culturally and historically diverse people. In more fragile congregations this can

---

[18]   For a rich discussion of this, albeit from an Anabaptist perspective, see Bryan Stone, *Evangelism after Christendom: The Theology and Practice of Christian Witness* (Grand Rapids, Michigan: Brazos Press, 2010).

[19]   See the Indaba process of facilitated listening invited by *The House of Bishops Working Group on Human Sexuality* (London: Church House Publishing, 2013).

be a great encouragement and enable people to take heart in the sharing of their faith. In larger congregations it can act as a check upon triumphalism and self-confidence.

Sharing Friendship through Living God's Story

The presence of a community being transformed through worship to be God's language in the world represents a story about God and the cosmos which discloses the identity and meaning of that world before God. Evangelism is how the story is shared, the story of creation, reconciliation and eternal friendship with God made possible by the action of God in Jesus Christ. It is also about sharing testimony to the friendship of God so that these little stories are set within this great divine drama. Indeed, as these stories are shared, it becomes clear that other people's stories have equal place in this complex drama and that the mission of the church is to invite all people to locate their stories within God's great epic. Indeed the truth of Jesus' story is revealed in its capacity to embrace and redeem all other human stories. Such stories are taken, blessed, broken and, through this transformation, offered as narratives of grace. This story also indicates that creation belongs to God and should be respected as such rather than treated as a disposable human instrument or utility.

Furthermore since this story is about God's friendship, it is capable of offering space to all people without diminishing their diversity. This surely is what Jesus displayed as he actively engaged with the marginalised or poor of his society. The story speaks of hospitality for all who repent and in the process lifts up the lowly and puts down the mighty from their thrones. Monarchs and minions mix in God's story. Yet, as liberation theologians and South American Pentecostal pastors have reminded the church, this story is not a consolation for the poor and powerless but an energising gift restoring dignity and giving hope in the struggle for justice in life. Its truthfulness is demonstrated by its capacity to challenge the comfortable to move beyond their comfort zones and serve strangers. In such movement 'down' a counter story is told which contrasts with that most often heard in western societies. If God is friend then Christians can risk themselves in this sort of adventure aware that love for God's sake means love for their neighbour's sake. The offering of Christian lives at the Eucharist is an offering for the sake of the neighbour and flows from the transforming practice of Holy Communion. They are sent out in the power of the Spirit to engage with that world in the light of the story they are a part of and as bearers of that story.

Nevertheless Anglicans believe that being aware of being part of an ongoing story which is not yet complete ensures that they serve the world with humility and aware of their limitations. Stories assume the reality of time and an ending. This is a reminder that today's interpretation of the story is contingent and will be told differently in the future. Furthermore the timeful character of the story points to a future finale when the story will be fully told on God's terms. No-one possesses the Gospel. This is God's privilege. Anglicans believe that their role is to be part of what Timothy Gorringe calls 'the long revolution of remaking by God'.[20] This long and often slow revolution reminds them that there is much of the story that remains unknown and therefore suggests reserve about determining the scope of the Christian community. The hidden work of the Spirit is a reminder that grace operates beyond the knowledge of the church. Hence relationships with other faiths and with those professing no public faith will also be characterised by friendship seeking to discover what can be affirmed rather than looking for conflict and contention. In so doing Christians need not be ashamed of sharing their faith. A respect for plurality means that all should have a voice rather than one ideology policing all others.

Conclusion

For Anglicans Christianity is fundamentally a way rather than an idea, a form of life rather than a philosophy, a participation in the saving activity of God in the world rather than a package of beliefs. Hence worship is the way God forms Christians into witnesses whose lives together and dispersed embody this way. Consequently micro Christian communities, such as the one in Barnsley, are quite remarkable as witnesses to the activity of God in ordinary life. To gather for public worship is therefore of critical importance if such signs are to be formed. In addition through such transformation or transubstantiation, these communities begin to represent a language which describes how God's friendship is expressed in the world for its good and for its life. This form of life is shaped by the template and training of worship enabling this life to speak of the great story of God. Such speaking is not simply rhetoric but the practice of discipleship. It involves reaching out to those who have little time or inclination to be part of this community. It includes patient visiting of those who have links with the church through the occasional offices. It entails welcoming in strangers,

---

[20]   Timothy J. Gorringe, *Furthering Humanity: A Theology of Culture* (Aldershot: Ashgate, 2004), p. 23.

such as drug addicts, prostitutes, the mentally ill, folk from overseas and seeking to express God's embrace of them. It recognises the importance of memory, symbol and place in mission through its careful renovation of the buildings and its encouragement of local people to visit the building and treasure it as theirs rather than simply the congregations. It raises horizons by linking up with the overseas church as a way of ensuring that the catholicity of the church is not simply an idea but a practice of giving, loving and learning from all Christian people. In particular through generous corporate giving it seeks to signify the grace of God across England. To be a community which God is transforming to embody a language of hope and a story of divine friendship is the sign of mission. Like Jeremiah the challenge of living in what can seem like an exilic situation is about seeking the well-being of society in a way that witnesses to the love of God for that society. Such congregational and diocesan gifts are fragile and often ignored, but they are all over England since the God Jesus embodied is always 'God-with-us', never God in isolation from his people. As a patient missional presence in an increasingly frantic world, they are a material gift witnessing to the grace of God focused in Christ and active in that world for its salvation.

Chapter 5

Friendship as Church

The word 'common' is often used as a term of derision rather than as a term of value. Yet, properly understood, common is a word which describes what is shared and precious. It speaks of collaboration, togetherness, community, accessibility, material sharing and belonging which are captured in the Greek word *koinonia* or fellowship, often used to describe the Christian community. In this chapter therefore, I want to explore Christian friendship through the Anglican commitment to common worship, embodied community, a shared story and a pastoral mission, since these represent a template for Anglican witness and express the character of Anglican friendship for God, for one another, for our story and for the world in which we are situated.

Anglican Mission as Friendship in the Flesh

Shared and tangible friendship is at the heart of English Anglican mission.[1] In all their diversity and struggles most Anglicans are committed to an incarnational and communal understanding of discipleship, ministry and mission. Belonging to God, to others, to a shared history and to the world is always a fleshly experience. It is faith in flesh as it is faith in common. Such a view contradicts much popular understanding of faith and indeed some views about church held within the church itself. For most English people churchgoing is regarded as peripheral to belief. English society has taken the Protestant concerns for interiority and freedom of choice to extremes and detached belief from accountability to any communal form of life. Churchgoing is often regarded as something for those who cannot survive on their own. In addition for some in the church churchgoing seems to offer little benefit when commending the faith to outsiders. Impatience with the embodied church exists among radicals who either wish that the church could be transformed into something more relevant

---

[1] For a historical account of the way Anglicanism emerged see Alastair Redfern, *Being Anglican* (London: DLT, 2000) and Mark Chapman, *Anglican Theology* (London: T&T Clark International, 2012).

to contemporary life or believe that the church is now so compromised by its history and tradition that it is best consigned to history. Hence some Christian activists withdraw from church and prefer to build the Kingdom of God through working with other likeminded groups. Yet faith becomes vacuous and dissolves into the unaccountable ideas of diverse people if we seek to know God without knowing one another; in short it represents a new form of idolatry. In particular the very character of Christianity is subverted as the story of God in Jesus becomes an ideal rather than a particular embodiment of God's friendship for the world, re-expressed in the church. What makes Christianity distinctive is destroyed if the Gospel is regarded as a set of abstract and timeless ideas about God's salvation which are chosen by individuals who may or may not decide to belong to a church. I write this as one gratefully formed in the evangelical stream of Anglicanism. However, this vital, energetic and imaginative tradition can give the impression that a personal response to Christ is an individualistic one with little sense of the social character of discipleship. Such a view of discipleship colludes with the broader culture and subverts the essentially social character of discipleship as seen in the New Testament and Church History. If faith is fundamentally about an interior individual choice, then belonging to church is also voluntary. There is little sense of being grafted into a community through baptism and having our identity embedded in the messy richness of the church. Such individualism further underwrites the eighteenth-century Enlightenment myth of autonomy which neglects the social character of human identity and the fact that through baptism we are church and cannot live the life of faith independent of that community.

Anglican Mission as Practical Holiness

Anglican mission is church mission and participating in church is a witness to God's gracious friendship and call to salvation. First and foremost this witness happens as Christian communities embody the story of God's reconciling love. As Christians live within this story God transforms them, or in older language divinises or sanctifies them, so that they become icons of this grace to the world around them. The American theologian Brad Kallenberg calls this 'embodied apologetics'.[2] Embodied apologetics signs the salvation of God. It reflects the divine signature in ordinary lives. Such icons are a visible invitation to friendship

---

[2]   Brad J. Kallenberg, *Ethics as Grammar, Changing the Postmodern Subject* (Notre Dame: University of Notre Dame Press, 2001), p. 156.

permitted to hear'.[19] Anglican worship encourages local entrepreneurial mission in particular contexts and this mission is discovered through a conversation with God and society.[20] Traditionally this has meant interpreting Scripture within the horizon of tradition and in the light of sound learning. Such conversations take place at parish, diocesan, provincial, Anglican Communion and indeed ecumenical levels. To facilitate this Anglicans are committed to 'an open Bible, a pastoral priesthood, common worship, ethical living and truth seeking' (Lambeth 1930).[21] Common worship therefore trains Anglicans to perform their faith and interpret the signs of their times.

Common Life: Friendship Together

According to Paul Avis Anglicans represent a form of social catholicism which is open to all in society.[22] Thus the diocese and parish rather than the congregation are the basic units of Anglican community, since both historically symbolised a mixed and inclusive constituency.[23] It is also why Anglicans, such as Desmond Tutu, were so deeply involved in the struggle in South Africa for an open society. Furthermore Anglicans believe that God baptises us into the church. Baptism rather than race, gender or choice is the mark of God's friendship. Hence the church is not another club of likeminded people we choose to belong to, but a company of diverse people whom God calls together through baptism. It is therefore an untidy and uncomfortable church within which Christians learn the meaning of community, a person-centred ecclesial polity.[24] In consequence Anglican mission involves patient expressions of hospitality, gracious challenge and friendship with all.[25] This mission is reflected in Anglican church structures.

---

[19]   Duncan Dormor, Jack McDonald and Jeremy Caddick, *Anglicanism: The Answer to Modernity* (London: Continuum, 2003), p. viii.

[20]   Dormor et al, *Anglicanism*, p. viii.

[21]   Stephen Sykes *Unashamed Anglicanism* (London: DLT, 1995), p. 111.

[22]   Paul Avis, *Anglicanism and the Christian Church: Theological Resources in Historical Perspective* (Edinburgh: T&T Clark, 1989), p. 7.

[23]   Andrew Davison and Alison Milbank, *For the Parish: A Critique of Fresh Expressions* (London: SCM, 2010), pp. 64–91, 144–69.

[24]   Martyn Percy, *Anglicanism: Confidence, Commitment and Communion* (Farnham: Ashgate, 2013), p. 22.

[25]   Diarmaid MacCulloch, *A History of Christianity* (London: Allen Lane, 2009), p. 955. Here he argues that Anglicans were often at the forefront of the Ecumenical movement in the twentieth century. Percy likewise argues that Anglicanism has emerged as a way of living together in patience. See Percy, *Anglicanism*, p. 15.

For example the diocese is the local church whilst parishes are its mission stations. Indeed the word parish (from the Greek *paroikos* meaning a migrant or neighbour) is a mission concept delineating the locus of the congregation's mission, whilst the 'ecclesia' or congregation (from the Greek, *ecclesia* meaning citizens' assembly) is the community gathered around the Lord's Table to listen to the stories of Scripture, to be nourished in the sacraments and be transformed into mission agents. Likewise self-giving friendship is embedded in the synods and clergy chapters of the church which require those of differing traditions to share together and learn from one another.[26] This can be a clash of fundamentalisms, as Alastair Redfern describes it.[27] However it can become a conversation of friends, whose love and respect for one another is enhanced by mutual appreciation of each other's reasons for faith. This must be the way forward with some of the significant disagreements about gender and ministry and about sexuality. Recognising that unanimity is highly unlikely, there will need to be gracious space for principled difference and an exploration of these issues through a process of testing reception which must be based upon trust.[28] This has been the Anglican way in the past and coheres with the character of Anglican ecclesiology. As Percy comments such an approach is about 'formational wisdom rooted in tactical savity, emotional intelligence, reflexivity and responsiveness'.[29] It tests the robustness of our mutual friendship in Christ and forms us more faithfully into disciples of Jesus as those we feel to be outsiders are recognised as insiders within the love of God. Hence Anglican mission involves inviting outsiders to become insiders in God's community by locating their stories within the great story of God's grace. Historically the English parish was territorial and of a size which enabled its priest to walk to its boundaries in an hour or two at most.[30] However a 'parish' can also be a social group or network. Since the diocese is more extensive than the parish, it can include a variety of 'parishes' and yet also remind each parish that it belongs to the wider church. It therefore prevents the local church being captured by one particular culture or class of people.

---

[26]　George Carey, 'Parties in the Church of England' in *Theology* vol 91 (1988), pp. 266–73.

[27]　Redfern, *Being Anglican*, pp. 1–12.

[28]　For a discussion of reception see Maggie Dawn, *Like the Wideness of the Sea: Women Bishops and the Church of England* (London: Darton, Longman and Todd, 2013).

[29]　Percy, *Anglicanism*, p. 15.

[30]　MacCulloch, *A History of Christianity*, p. 369.

A Shared Story: Friendship with the Past

Stories matter to people, especially stories involving the past, though the dominant élites of contemporary western societies seem to suffer from HADS (Historical Attention Deficit Syndrome). Consequently as Christopher Andrews notes, 'for the first time in recorded history, there has been a widespread assumption that the experience of all previous generations is irrelevant to present policy'.[31] Anglicans however believe that their ambiguous history cannot be ignored even though it brings problems and challenges.[32] They are a storied people who cannot understand their present without attention to their past.[33] The parish, in particular, reminds Anglicans that they are situated within an ongoing and diverse history of mission. This mission is occasional because it happens in particular situations whilst always being part of a story woven together over many centuries.[34] Consequently in England the Church of England remains webbed into most people's lives either actively or in the cultural air they breathe. Indeed, as we have seen, Grace Davie describes congregations as vicarious representatives for the majority of the nation.[35] The Church of England still remains the church of first resort for most of the population. Indeed more people hear the Gospel preached in pit villages around Rotherham and Doncaster than hear it preached at many larger suburban congregations of Sheffield. This is because greater numbers attend occasional offices in these villages than attend services in the suburban areas. In addition the shape of the Church of England today only makes sense in the light of the history of the English Church. The English Reformation church was an early 'ecumenical experiment' seeking to avoid the sort of conflict Europe experienced. Initially it sought peaceable respect and openness to other churches, even though this was not always adhered to by later figures. English Reformers believed that only God could resolve the disputes of their age. Hence latitude, inclusiveness and tolerance should mark the Church of England. As far as possible it should be a friendly church embracing people with

---

[31] Christopher Andrews, *The Defence of the Realm* (London: Penguin, 2010) p. 585.

[32] Andrew Shanks, 'Honesty' in Dormor et al, *Anglicanism*, pp. 125–46.

[33] This is at the heart of 'Engaging with the Past to Shape the Future: The Experience of Building on History: The Church in London' project which seeks to root contemporary debates about mission and ministry in the context of history so that new ways forward can take place in a grounded and reflective way. For further details see www.open.ac.uk/buildingonhistory

[34] Contextual from the Latin *contexere* meaning to weave together.

[35] See Grace Davie, *Religion in Britain since 1945: Believing without Belonging* (Oxford: Oxford University Press, 1994) and The Sociology of Religion (London: Sage, 2007).

different views, for example, on the meaning of the Eucharist. Certainly there are boundaries indicated by the commitment to Scripture, the Catholic Creeds and the Book of Common Prayer. However at the heart of this ecclesial experiment is a recognition of the provisional character of fallen human perspectives and a willingness to let God be judge. This has also enabled Anglicans to work respectfully with other Christian communities and indeed with other faiths and to offer minority faiths in England a sense of security about their own practices.

Pastoral Mission: Friendship with Others

Alan Billings argues that 'the church is there to make God possible'.[36] Consequently mission should engage people where they are just as Jesus did when he dwelt among his own people. Living among the people, therefore, remains central to the Anglican missionary model. The Anglican Church is a polity of presence.[37] It is a way of being church which is committed to face-to-face encounter and is attentive to local communities and nations.[38] This is reflected in the commitment of the Church of England to be present in every community in England. The Gospel is about welcome before it is about challenge. Where spiritual hunger is expressed the call is to find ways to engage sensitively with this. Thus in many areas memorial services are emerging as significant evangelistic occasions, along with Christmas, baptisms and funerals. Likewise major occasions, such as the Millennium Celebrations and the Olympics have given churches particular opportunities to share the Gospel. Pastoral mission was the traditional rationale for the parson, the cleric publicly representing the church in the local community of the parish. However this personal, inclusive and catholic chaplaincy mission has been challenged by the cumulative impact of the welfare state, the decline in church attendance, the rise of professional caring and the cost of stipendiary ministry.[39] Yet its ethos remains more fundamental to the Anglican project than other alternatives such as a more congregationally

---

[36]   Alan Billings, *Making God Possible: The Task of Ordained Ministry Present and Future* (London: SPCK, 2010), p. 8.

[37]   Ben Quash, 'The Anglican Church as a Polity of Presence' in Dormor et al., *Anglicanism*, pp. 38–56.

[38]   For a reflection on the way Anglican establishment is mutating in England see Jeremy Morris, 'The Future of Church and State' in Dormor et al., *Anglicanism*, pp. 161–80.

[39]   For a recent discussion about the relationship of the Church of England and its host society see Michael Turnbull and Donald McFadyen, *The State of the Church and the Church of the State: Re-Imagining the Church of England for our World Today* (London; DLT, 2012). Their view is that the church signs the sacred in every English community as a witness to

focused ministry, tractarian clericalism or liberal social activism.[40] If it is to survive the parson's role will need to be expressed by the congregation as a whole rather than simply focused in a single person. Since half of all adults in contemporary Britain live within 30 minutes drive from their mothers and only ten per cent of households move house each year, we should not underestimate the importance of place and presence for mission today.[41] As John Inge and Philip Sheldrake argue places matter much more than is often appreciated.[42] Places are contexts where people's sense of identity and belonging are explicitly registered, whereas spaces are contexts where memory and significance are very superficial. This has consequences for the mission of the church in particular areas. Much of London, for example, is very cosmopolitan and socially fluid and mission needs to be responsive to this. On the other hand a town like Doncaster has a predominantly stable population with deep place memories. Ministry and mission have to work with these realities rather than against them and follow the example of Pope Gregory the Great when he re-thought mission strategy for sixth-century England. Instead of destroying local shrines and temples, his second letter to Augustine told him to transform them into places of Christian worship. This was culturally sensitive mission rather than riding roughshod over people's history and identity.[43] It set the tone for Anglican mission to work with the grain of local culture wherever possible in ways that surprises people with God's love rather than terrifying people with God's judgement.

Anglican mission is therefore mission in pastoral mode. It is mission rooted and explored in an ongoing commitment to particular people and places, particularly those with special needs, and is focused around worship and the quest for human flourishing.[44] This contrasts with ways of mission which are speculative rather than embedded and resists a standardised approach to mission in favour of appropriate engagement with differing contexts and communities. Consequently its vision of a vibrant and dispersed church needs a diverse and rooted ministry. Anglican ministers are more like rugby players than American

---

the coherent presence of grace infusing creation. The church positions the state without competing with it.

[40]   For a discussion of these different models of ordained ministry and their assumptions about the church and mission see Billings, *Making God Possible*, pp. 55–135.

[41]   Michael Moynagh, *emergingchurch.intro* (Oxford: Monarch Books, 2004) p. 77.

[42]   See John Inge, *A Christian Theology of Place* (Aldershot: Ashgate, 2003) and Philip Sheldrake, *Spaces for the Sacred: Place, Memory and Identity* (Baltimore, Maryland: The John Hopkins University Press, 2001).

[43]   MacCulloch, *A History of Christianity*, pp. 342–3.

[44]   Timothy Jenkins, 'Anglicanism: The Only Answer to Modernity' in Dormor et al., *Anglicanism*, pp. 194, 98, 202.

footballers, who must be able to improvise rather than being specialists with one key role. It will involve dynamic, flexible, and imaginative approaches to mission, particularly since English society has undergone major changes in the past century. For example we are now predominantly urban rather than rural; we travel more; we consume rather than produce; most are materially rich but time poor; we are overwhelmed with media and choice; we see ourselves as individuals rather than community people; we stress equality. A changed society needs an improvising rather than a reactionary church. [45] Like good jazz players, Anglicans are invited to improvise upon the music of the Gospel whose tune is expressed in the event of Jesus but whose impact is discovered in the contingencies of life and its diverse contexts. [46]

Conclusion

'Anglicanism is something that is formed by worship, praying the Scriptures and through an ecclesial practice that is, at once, local and catholic'. [47] It faces many challenges yet at its best it has much to offer. God's friendship expressed through the practices of common worship, common life, a common story and common mission remains crucial to the ongoing Anglican project, certainly in England. Rowan Williams has suggested that English Anglicanism will need to become a mixed economy church, with fresh expressions of church as well as continuing expressions of church living side by side and intersecting. Nevertheless to be true to its historic calling, Anglicanism needs to retain a practical rather than speculative way of sharing in God's mission. Anglicanism is a way of discerning the challenge of following Christ through a conversation between disciples, their contexts and the church catholic. It is a political rather than an ideological way, found through debate and engagement with its core texts and story within the embrace of public mutually accountable worship. It listens and pays attention to the tapestry of contemporary society rather than being tempted to take an abstract speculative view. Fundamentally, then, it is a church for the common people rather than a church for the powerful élite. In this it rejects modes of mission which advocate a single model of mission since this dis-embeds the church from its context, privileges a minority view as the

---

[45]   Wells, *Improvisation*.

[46]   See Daniel W. Hardy and David F. Ford, *Jubilate, Theology in Praise* (London: Darton, Longman & Todd, 1984), pp 21–3. They see jazz as a metaphor for Pentecostal worship. I see it as a metaphor for Anglican discipleship.

[47]   Percy, *Anglicanism*, p. 20.

total view, diminishes the value of local practice and performance and assumes that everywhere is basically the same.[48] Anglicans have an exciting, though slow vision as Christians committed to reaching out to those estranged from God with an invitation to share in that divine friendship.

[48]   See Davison and Milbank, *For the Parish*.

PART II
Reflection

Chapter 6

Radical Friendship

Healing Friendship

Radical Orthodoxy is a movement within English Anglicanism purporting to offer an equivalent Christian therapy for contemporary western societies which have become estranged from their core religious story. A confederation of Anglican theologians associated with Cambridge University in the 1980s and early 1990s, John Milbank, Catherine Pickstock and Graham Ward, are its best known representatives although I shall concentrate on the work of John Milbank in this chapter.[1] Radical Orthodoxy is not about re-imposing a traditionalist view of Christianity based upon rules or propositions. Instead it re-engages Christian tradition in order to liberate its potential for fruitful and creative discipleship today.[2] It argues that many contemporary theological approaches are captive to assumptions which are corrosive of Christian practice. In contrast Radical Orthodoxy claims to offer a more robust and fruitful theology rooted in a richer exploration of the Christian tradition. It suggests how the church can be healed in order to live as a holy community and thereby engage in its mission to witness to the grace of God in life. As such it is an example of sharing friendship in a robust yet Anglican way.

Radical Orthodoxy argues that we find the truth about God and thus reality through worship.[3] We discover truth as we are drawn by our desire for the infinite, for God, above all things. This reflects the Anglican conviction that we learn of God through participating in worship. Such worship explores Christian identity as it is embodied in the Scriptures and in the church. Hence the liturgical life of the Christian community resources theological reflection since human identity is fundamentally constituted by worship. We are *homo*

---

[1]   John Milbank, Catherine Pickstock and Graham Ward (eds), *Radical Orthodoxy* (London: Routledge, 1999).

[2]   Jeremy Morris (ed.), *Faith and Freedom: Exploring Radical Orthodoxy* (Affirming Catholicism; Third Millennium, 2003), pp. 5–15.

[3]   See Catherine Pickstock, *After Writing: On the Liturgical Consummation of Philosophy* (Oxford: Blackwell, 1998), p. xii where she argues that philosophy finds its meaning not in metaphysics but in the practice of liturgy and worship.

liturgicus before we can become *homo sapiens*, worshipping creatures before we can become wise. Radical Orthodoxy therefore seeks to free the church from colonisation by modernity with its belief in human autonomy and rationality.[4] To do this it aims to re-invigorate the catholic dimension of Anglicanism using the doctrine of participation associated with the fourth-century African theologian, Augustine of Hippo. Augustine held that all creation participates in and desires God the infinite and therefore bears the marks of the creator in its identity and life. Bodies and their relationships are inscribed with the signature of God who is never known in the abstract but always in and through creation. The particulars of life therefore are theologically significant and should not be subsumed within abstract ideals or generalisations. Similarly the church as the initial site of the restored community in God is a focal sign of this participation. As the true society it embodies the beginnings of the emerging Kingdom of God and represents the continuing story of God in the world.[5] Hence by paying careful attention to the church and its story theologians can get a richer and more rigorous insight into the character of God's ways with creation.

Since the Bible suggests how Christians are to live with God and is itself made plausible by the way Christians live, practical holiness is crucial for evangelism and mission. In addition since the ongoing story of the church continues the Scriptural story, the Bible represents a series of under-determined texts. These require the worshipping church, past and present, to act as an interpreting community whose corporate witness exhibits the dynamic and open meaning of these texts. Conservative readings of Scripture are over-determinative because they regard the text as fixed and final. On the other hand liberal readings are too fluid because they regard the text as capable of wide-ranging interpretations. Radical Orthodoxy, in contrast, sees the practice of the church's life as filling out the meaning of Scripture. This is not about adding to Scripture so much as reading it faithfully and truthfully in the present. Hence to interpret Scripture and discipleship truthfully depends upon faithful Christian character. Consequently worship forms Christians into practitioners of the faith and thereby faithful readers or interpreters of Scripture.

---

[4]   See Chapter 2 above for an exploration of modernity as the Enlightenment era.

[5]   See John Milbank, 'The Church is the Site of the True Society', *The Church Times* (16 December 2011), pp. 12, 14.

Critical Friendship

John Milbank therefore believes that the church must reflect deeply upon its history if it is to grasp the character of its contemporary mission and he rejects the popular view that the social sciences can give us an objective account of social reality, including theology, based on a secure foundation of human reason. Contemporary social science is based on a false interpretation of Christian theology which emerged in the work of the medieval philosophers Duns Scotus and William Occam. These philosophers sought to preserve God's freedom to act, or God's free will and power. To be free, they argued, God must not be bound to creation in any way. In so doing they lost sight of the doctrine of participation advocated by Augustine of Hippo and Thomas Aquinas, which saw the co-inherence of God and creation in the Incarnation and the activity of the Trinity.[6] God's love manifests divine freedom in the very action of loving and sharing in creation. God's love is about giving space to the other and sharing in the life of the other. In contrast Scotian and Occamist views led to an arbitrary view of God's freedom. No longer was God's freedom constrained by God's character. Instead God can do whatever he wants since he is bound by nothing except his own will. This arbitrary view of the divine gradually influenced the way the human will was seen. It led to the notion that the human will was only accountable to itself, a secularising move which led to the divorce of faith and reason in the eighteenth-century Enlightenment. God and the world are now segregated and God is regarded as marginal to human understanding of that world.

Failed Friendship

For Milbank the roots of this error lie in the politics of the twelfth-century western church. The clerical authorities conflated the two distinct expressions of Christian polity, the clerical dimension or '*sacerdotium*' and the lay dimension or 'regnum', into one by subsuming 'regnum' within '*sacerdotium*'.[7] This caused a reaction by lay politicians, first in the medieval monarchy and its Reformation successors and then in the social politics of the Enlightenment. As a result politics became divorced from the formative practices of worship giving the impression that a Christian society did not require virtuous Christian leaders.

---

[6]   John Milbank, *Theology and Social Theory: Beyond Secular Reason* (Oxford: Blackwell, 1990), p. 15.

[7]   Milbank, *Theology and Social Theory*, pp. 15, 290.

Politics and sanctification were divorced and this contributed to a de-sacralising of the world. The worship of God was no longer critical to the shaping of a good human society. The triumph of 'secularism' is thus the failure of church politics and this has allowed a more ancient paganism to emerge with a different understanding of politics, power and violence. Yet this secularism is based upon the idea that there is nothing at the heart of reality. It therefore cannot sustain society. The contemporary mission of the church must therefore begin by exposing the vacuum of secularism and re-engaging with the older and richer theological tradition which Scotus and Occam subverted.[8] This involves reading the Bible critically within the history of Christian practice, diagnosing what has made the Christian body ill and finding appropriate therapeutic resources to encourage its healing.[9] For example, healing the English body politic requires that the two political dimensions of society represented by sacramental ordination and anointed monarchy be reconnected.[10] It includes recovering Augustine of Hippo's view of the church as a community which witnesses to God's peaceable polity and Aquinas's view of the church as a community of charity and friendship.[11] Both of these theologians saw the church as a social and trans-mortal community of pilgrims whose charity and friendship are not derived from ancient virtue ethics but from the social holiness integral to the Christian story.[12] Ancient virtue ethics emerged from societies whose fundamental vision of reality was violent. These societies promoted as their heroic ideal a powerful champion who could temporarily check the destructiveness of the world using controlled violence. In contrast Augustinian Christianity, with its doctrine of the Fall, assumed an original peace, which, though corrupted into violence, nevertheless remains more fundamental than violence. This peace is God's destiny for creation and underwrites the peaceable and charitable practices advocated by Augustine and Aquinas, since 'the church is nothing other than the continuing event of charity'.[13]

---

[8]   Milbank, *Theology and Social Theory*, p. 17.

[9]   C.C. Pecknold, *Transforming Postliberal Theology: George Lindbeck, Pragmatism and Scripture* (London: T & T Clark, 2005).

[10]   John Milbank, *The Future of Love: Essays in Political Theology* (London: SCM, 2009), p. xiii.

[11]   Milbank, *The Future of Love*, p. 155.

[12]   Milbank, *Theology and Social Theory*, pp. 231, 242, 389–98.

[13]   Milbank, *The Future of Love*, p. 155.

Restoring Friendship

Augustine sought to contest the violence of ancient paganism and its dialectical approach to truth in a way faithful to the peaceable vocation of the church. Hence, in the *City of God* he told a story that contrasted a community of peaceable friendship with a community living in sin. This narrative strategy is pertinent when engaging with modernity as the offspring of paganism. Modernity cannot be dislodged using dialectical argument, since dialectic is a form of ancient conflict resolution which is rooted in a violent view of reality. It crushes difference in order to achieve harmony.[14] Instead the church's mission is to live its story faithfully, a story which celebrates difference within the harmony of God's peace.[15] This social, storied witness of Christian friendship is critical for the church's mission, since it embodies the story of God's salvation. Indeed the unique character of this social, peaceable friendship is seen in the way the church integrated the two distinct social orders of the ancient world, the *polis* or city and the *oikos* or home. Women, slaves and children who, in ancient societies, belonged to the home but were excluded from the city, were now welcomed into the city of God.[16] The task of theology is therefore to explore this Christian sociology, telling the story of God embodied in the church. Apologetics involves display rather than argument, a peaceable rhetoric of persuasive communal life.

Christians understand the secular to mean the time before the Parousia or end of all things rather than de-sacralised space.[17] Indeed 'England remains as a political body, a body within an ecclesiastical body'.[18] The mission of the church and its theologians is to expose false interpretations of the secular and remind English society of this heritage and its relevance to contemporary life. This means looking back to the medieval church and also to the Elizabethan Settlement advocated by Hooker, with its themes of common worship and a Christian commonwealth as we noted in Chapter 5. Hooker's church was not an idea so much as a reflection on the way Christianity manifested itself in a particular nation, through reiterative reading of the Scriptures, the tradition of Christian practice and the wisdom of God active in the wider world. God's word for English society today will likewise be found through attending to the interplay of these, aware that they all are infused with the grace of God. The contemporary mission of the church is to exhibit a richer interpretation of

---

[14] Milbank, *Theology and Social Theory*, p. 262.
[15] Milbank, *Theology and Social Theory*, pp. 262–8 and 327–9.
[16] Milbank, *Theology and Social Theory*, pp. 364–8 and 403–4.
[17] Milbank, *Theology and Social Theory*, p. 9.
[18] Milbank, *The Future of Love*, p. 273.

reality than 'secular' views, an interpretation which is rooted in the deep story of Scripture and the history of Christian practice. It involves supplying the tacit bonds of belonging which only religion can sustain.[19]

Vocal Friendship

The church is a social sign of the grace of God active in creation and shares in the story of God as a pilgrim community. Therefore language is of critical importance, language which does not represent reality but expresses it poetically.[20] The poetic involves God 'speaking to the creature through the creature'.[21] However since languages emerge from particular communities, Christians must learn their language as part of the church. This means restoring the notion of *paideia* or Christian education and training to discipleship.[22] *Paideia* involves learning to speak a language which expresses the Gospel embodied in the church. It is the language of holy living. Indeed Christianity is the recoding of Jesus' story which is a story of many stories since Christianity is not an ideology but the practice of the communities bearing Jesus' name.[23] Consequently theologians understand the significance of Christ (Christology) by studying the practices of the church as a tradition (ecclesiology). What matters is bodily solidarity rather than ideological coherence.[24] The church in the Spirit is a gothic bride which, like a gothic building, is built up incrementally and poetically in ways that reflect the Spirit's inspiration in different contexts and times.[25] Christians become charismatic as they are immersed in the practices of worship and learn to understand and speak the language of the Spirit. This may sound strange in modern contexts. However this will be part of its witness to and sharing of the friendship of God.

---

[19] Milbank, *The Future of Love*, p. xviii.
[20] John Milbank, *The Word Made Strange: Theology, Language, Culture* (Oxford: Blackwell,1997), p. 107.
[21] Milbank, *The Word Made Strange*, p. 3.
[22] Milbank, *The Word Made Strange*, pp. 25, 154.
[23] Milbank, *The Word Made Strange*, p.146.
[24] Milbank, *The Word Made Strange*, p.153.
[25] Milbank, *The Word Made Strange*, pp.185 and 277–8.

Hopeful Friendship

Gift is the key theological category for describing God's relationship with creation. Nevertheless creation is infected by evil and sin questioning whether creation can be a sign of hope or is simply tragic. Indeed after the Holocaust some radical approaches rooted evil in the fabric of reality making evil more fundamental than good and undermining hope for a peaceable future. Yet the church's story speaks of a fall from a primordial good. This assures Christians that evil is not the final word. Even in a world of terrible evil Christians can live with the hope that God will restore this original blessing. In the meantime they remain convinced of the goodness of finite creation. Evil is nothing in itself. At most it is a privation, which cannot destroy God's original blessing of harmonious peaceableness. Such peaceableness is fragile. However church practices, such as forgiveness and reconciliation, form peaceable Christian communities by transforming and reconciling a damaged past.[26] Likewise the chivalric code and the just war ideals of the medieval era show how Christians tried to tame violence and hold it to account in society.[27] The church may only be a glimpse rather than a full expression of God's future. However this glimpse is a hopeful sign and makes better sense of the world than the story of radical evil.[28] In this sense the church is the site of the true society.[29]

Conclusion

Milbank's theology is a 'theology [which] presupposes and reflects upon the practice of the church'.[30] He does not believe in a segregated secular since the mission of the church embraces everything that God has given. He argues that all human wisdom participates in the divine and revelation is 'lodged in all the complex networks of human practices ... [whose] ... boundaries are as messy as those of the church itself'.[31] Thus 'theological truth first of all abides in the body of the faithful' although this body is incomplete.[32] Hence, for Milbank, at

---

26 John Milbank, *Being Reconciled: Ontology and Pardon* (London: Routledge, 2003), p. 62.

27 Milbank, *Being Reconciled*, p. 41–3.

28 Milbank, *Being Reconciled*, pp. 105–6.

29 Milbank, 'The Church is the Site of the True Society', pp. 12, 14.

30 Milbank, *Being Reconciled*, pp. 106–8.

31 Milbank, *Being Reconciled*, p. 122.

32 Milbank, *Being Reconciled*, p. 122.

every Eucharist the church receives itself from the one who is outside it, that is from Christ, and is therefore transubstantiated or transformed into his likeness.[33] Thus God underwrites the sign of the church and ensures that Christian virtues are formed by grace rather than by the violent habits of Aristotelian happiness.[34] Virtues, such as charity and friendship, display the social character of Christian witness and life.[35] However Milbank's approach does raise a number of questions. Does he imply that Christians should disengage from the politics of modern, liberal societies?[36] Is this a retreat into a failed clerically controlled imperialistic Christendom which is unrealistic and excludes other truth-bearing communities beyond the church?[37] How far does Milbank uncritically accept the liberal view that equates religion with conflict? Is he over-confident about the social influence of intellectuals such as Scotus and Occam? Is he over-optimistic about recovering the pre-Scotian–Occamist tradition given all that has taken place since then? Surely we need to engage with the world as we find it rather than imagining we can return to something less problematic. Arguably the secular was not initially hostile to religious conviction but emerged as a way western societies tried to deal peaceably with conflicting religious convictions.[38] As mentioned above, the secular was initially a Christian attempt to respect differing Christian dialects and was therefore about acknowledging difference and listening to others in a way some feel Radical Orthodoxy rejects.[39] Yet in response it is important to note that Radical Orthodoxy is not closed to other forms of wisdom and politics beyond the church. It simply refuses to give them autonomy. Instead it situates them within a forgotten Christian narrative which needs to be recalled if a truthful account is to be had. In this sense mission is about recovering an understanding of a Christian secular as the true secular of the western tradition. This requires the church to pay more radical attention to its history, tradition and practices. It needs a robust church which is formed through the practices of common worship. It means becoming a church with a

---

[33]   Milbank, *Being Reconciled*, p. 123.

[34]   Milbank, *Being Reconciled*, p. 141.

[35]   Milbank, *Being Reconciled*, p. 153.

[36]   For these and other criticisms see Alister E.McGrath, *A Scientific Theology*, 3 vols (Edinburgh: T&T Clark, 2001–2003), vol. 1, p. 7 and vol. 2, pp.102–16.

[37]   Andrew Shanks, *God and Modernity: A New and Better Way to do Theology* (London: Routledge, 2000), pp. 101–2. See also similar comments by Daniel Izuzquiza in Martyn Percy, *The Ecclesial Canopy: Faith, Hope and Charity* (Farnham: Ashgate, 2010), pp. 167–8.

[38]   Jeffrey Stout, *Democracy and Tradition* (Princetown: Princetown University Press, 2004), pp. 103–15.

[39]   Steven Shakespeare, 'The New Romantics: a Critique of Radical Orthodoxy', *Theology* 103 (2000), pp. 163–77.

confident and distinctive voice. Christian mission is a form of love which loves its secularist neighbours by reminding them of English society's Christian roots as a Christian secular commonwealth.[40] It expresses this love even when that friendship is refused, either through apathy or in the form of evil, by continuing to embody a story which refuses to see these responses as more real than that love. This witness may involve absorbing the antagonism through peaceable cruciform suffering or challenging that evil more robustly as in the just war tradition. It is mission as the embodied speech of Christian friendship which out-narrates its rivals even as it itself remains an unfinished story itself.[41] The church is a pilgrim body rather than a holy city. It is not a utopian ideal but a glimpse of God's destiny for creation. It is a broken sign being transformed through worship into a more faithful sign of its peaceable character.[42]

Radical Orthodoxy suggests that Anglican mission should be characterised by a confident, if chastened awareness of the deep story of Christianity in English society and the contribution of the church to this history. Without this grounding, mission will appear reactionary or be taken captive by the unreflective present and will not represent a faithful truth-telling friendship. The mission of the English church therefore flows from the crucible of its worshipping life, embodied in peace-making communities which practise forgiveness and reconciliation. These practices form ecclesial signs which witness to the reign of God in life and whose members are able to describe the world in a language which clearly indicates the presence of God in all things. Mission, therefore, is first about becoming before it is about doing. It is about worship before it is about engagement. What emerges through testimony and activity flows from this formation. Such mission will express the character of God as hospitable and embracing of strangers, those excluded from contemporary society, and also as one who claims sovereignty over all of life. In this sense Anglican mission has to be radical.

---

[40]   Milbank, *Being Reconciled*, p.196.
[41]   Philippa Berry and Andrew Wernick (eds), *Shadow of Spirit: Postmodernism and Religion* (London and New York: Routledge, 1993), p. 48.
[42]   Milbank, *Being Reconciled*, p.179.

Chapter 7
Gospel Friendship

Oliver O'Donovan's work represents an Anglican re-telling of the story of Christianity in North Atlantic societies. Such a re-telling involves claims to truth and reflects an understanding of the way Anglicans share God's friendship with the world. Such storytelling must, however, be accountable to Scripture as the focus and core of that story. It is theology seeking to think out of Scripture.[1] Evangelical ethics must emerge out of the Gospel of Jesus Christ and this approach underlies O'Donovan's three major books on ethics, *Resurrection and the Moral Order: An Outline for Evangelical Ethics (1986)*, *The Desire of Nations: Rediscovering the Roots of Political Theology* (1996) and *The Ways of Judgment* (2005).[2] The first roots ethics in the created order rather than in the human will. The second explores the way such Christian ethics were expressed politically in European civilisation. The third explores these political concepts and the distortions to which they have been subject.[3] In so doing, O'Donovan 'turns to the Christ event and to the apostolic witness' as recorded in Scripture to underwrite his project.[4] However this does not mean that the church is marginal to his project even though he regards the practices of the church as less significant than the story of faith recorded in the Scriptures. On the contrary, O'Donovan wishes modern liberal western societies to recover their Christian identity by paying attention to their history and its sustaining theological themes. As Luke Bretherton comments, modern societies are forms of apostate Christianity which have lost their foundation, the Christ event.[5] The themes of this event

---

[1] Oliver O'Donovan, 'Response to Respondents: Behold the Lamb!', *Studies in Christian Ethics* 1/ 2 (1998), p. 96.

[2] Oliver O'Donovan, *Resurrection and the Moral Order: An Outline for Evangelical Ethics*, 2nd edn, (Leicester: Apollos, 1994), *The Desire of the Nations: Rediscovering the Roots of Political Theology* (Cambridge: Cambridge University Press, 1996), and *The Ways of Judgment* (Cambridge UK: Eerdmans, 2005).

[3] See John Habgood, 'Where we get our civic ideas from' Review of Oliver O'Donovan, *The Ways of Judgment* in *The Church Times*, (17 February 2006), p. 23.

[4] O'Donovan, *Resurrection and the Moral Order*, p. xv.

[5] Luke Bretherton, *Hospitality as Holiness: Christian Witness Amid Moral Diversity* (Farnham: Ashgate, 2006), pp. 61–3.

are performed by the church in its liturgy and narrated in the Scriptures. Yet this is not simply about recapitulation since the church is led by the Spirit into new insights and truths. The church is therefore tradition-situated rather than tradition-guided and the Spirit is more important than virtue to the church's vocation.[6] For O'Donovan the church does not represent a contradictory politics to that of its host society. Rather it represents Spirit-led Christian practice whose mission is to challenge those societies to recall their own Christian heritage and return to the country from which they have fled as prodigals. Like Milbank, this involves telling the story truthfully so that the friendship of God may be disclosed. The mission of the church is to be an evangelistic community, sharing the good news through sharing the Scriptural story and its out-workings in history, in order to enable others to locate themselves in this story.

Resurrection Friendship

For O'Donovan the focal expression of divine friendship is the resurrection, since it reveals the importance of creation to God and discloses its destiny. The resurrection ushers in the Kingdom of God which reaffirms and renews the integrity and ordering of creation.[7] Creation and Kingdom ethics are one and 'the way the universe is determines how man ought to behave in it'.[8] Consequently Christian ethics addresses every human being rather than simply those who have responded to Christ. Its freedom is freedom for Jesus Christ and is a Spirit-infused wisdom which displays a foretaste of the final reign of God to which the resurrection points. Thus to flourish humanity needs to attend to its destiny and its relationships.[9] This means paying attention to the chief end of humankind, namely to glorify God. Yet this end indicates that we inhabit a contingent creation, within which our freedom is relative to our creaturely status. It also shows that human history only has meaning because of God's ongoing ordering of the world. Without such ordering, history would dissolve into the perspectives of different and un-resolvable interests. It is the resurrection, therefore, which shows that the primal order of creation has been fulfilled and vindicated since it represents the recovery and transformation of lost humankind as part of that creation. Furthermore since the resurrection happens in time and creation, it preserves Christian ethics from being consumed

---

6   Bretherton, *Hospitality as Holiness*, pp. 72–5.
7   O'Donovan, *Resurrection and the Moral Order*, pp. xv–xvi.
8   O'Donovan, *Resurrection and the Moral Order*, p. 17.
9   O'Donovan, *Resurrection and the Moral Order*, p. 37.

by historicism. Historicism is the notion that our understanding of reality is determined and limited by human consciousness experienced within the limitation of time. Instead the resurrection confirms that ordered creation is the basic reality rather than human historical consciousness.[10] Creation as a whole is the basis of historical existence and is the origin of history. Thus, although our grasp of the world and indeed other eras is provisional, it is not divorced from them and can be mediated by language. This also prevents us from equating the created order with human sin and disorder since the resurrection confirms the goodness of creation. It stops Christian ethics from becoming human centred. Christian mission challenges all to respect the givenness of creation rather than believing that we are free from its constraints or unaccountable to it. This also ensures that social orders are never absolute, since as part of creation, they are contingent and provisional.

Ethics, therefore, depends upon our capacity to know the created order which requires that we understand everything in its relationship to the totality of things.[11] Such knowledge is inevitably about faith, since it involves knowing the whole from within rather than from outside creation. It is an inductive rather than a deductive approach. The church claims to learn such knowledge through reflective worship. Yet it does not claim to know everything about the end of history and consequently its ethics are provisional. The secret counsel of God cannot be discovered from within the dynamics of history. At best prophetic knowledge seen through the lens of the incarnation reveals that ethics are properly about love, which accepts and is conformed to the created order rather than rebelling against it.

Freedom and Friendship

According to O'Donovan our life as church, society and individual cannot be characterised as anarchic or self-interested freedom. Instead it must be about freedom for Jesus Christ or what Jesus Christ means as the one rooting the action of God within the created order. 'The [Enlightenment] project was misconceived from the beginning. Moral freedom can never be established on the basis of self-sufficiency and independence of the world. Freedom, if it is freedom to act within the world, must itself be of the world'.[12] Freedom, therefore, is

10 O'Donovan, *Resurrection and the Moral Order*, pp. 58–74.
11 O'Donovan, *Resurrection and the Moral Order*, p. 77.
12 O'Donovan, *Resurrection and the Moral Order*, p. 120.

about living in a way that respects our status as creatures. Equally authority (the reason for acting) is properly a gift from God to make such freedom possible. Yet this is not the arbitrary freedom of medieval philosophers Duns Scotus and William Occam. Rather God's authority is accountable to the covenants God makes and therefore is limited by respect for creation and salvation. It is however moral authority with a universal claim upon everyone since all inhabit a common creation.[13] Thus 'there is a common world about which questions of truth can be raised ... so that ... moral authority can challenge us and evoke our free response, even across the gulf of centuries'.[14] The freedom of the individual, so prized by both Protestantism and liberalism, is related to the freedom of the church or community as advocated by the Catholic tradition. In the church both individuals and communities find their freedom in each other as part of a common creation.[15] Since the ordering of creation is the moral field for ethics the form of the moral life involves a theological unpacking of the fruit of the Spirit. This is the particular, though not exclusive, calling of the church, since the moral life is lived within a common world shared by all within which the Spirit is active. The church's role is therefore to teach in ways that take account of the contextual and time-bound character of human life. Equally Christian character is shaped through this formative learning and is thereby equipped with the wisdom needed to live faithfully and repentantly in the world.[16]

Politics and Friendship

The moral life involves loving God and loving neighbour, though our neighbour is loved as the neighbour ordered to the love of God. This is why such love will always be political. Indeed we learn what it means to love our neighbour in the light of God as we pay attention to the ordering of creation. The goal of the moral life is to love in the light of the self-giving God revealed in Jesus Christ. This is the heart of the divine friendship for the world and O'Donovan's political theology aims to show us how we are to love our neighbour within the light of the self-giving God revealed in Jesus Christ. This is the ethics of power in society seen from the perspective of the Kingdom of God as the ultimate kingdom. Thus the political theology present in the liturgy of the church, such as the *Te Deum*, is not simply a series of scattered images but represents a distinctively Christian

---

13   O'Donovan, *Resurrection and the Moral Order*, p. 143.
14   O'Donovan, *Resurrection and the Moral Order*, p. 161.
15   O'Donovan, *Resurrection and the Moral Order*, p. 170.
16   O'Donovan, *Resurrection and the Moral Order*, pp. 204–25.

political vision. By telling the story of the works of God in the history of Israel and of Israel's Christ, a Christian political ethics emerges.[17] This reveals that religion and politics need each other since politics reminds religion that reality is seen through a glass darkly, whilst religion reminds politics of the importance of ethics and formation. Both though operate within the one history, which finds its goal in Christ, the 'desire of the nations'.[18] Similarly political theology and political ethics are not separate domains but are two moments in one train of theological thought which leads from the proclamation of the Gospel to political action. The first is a reflective exercise (what have we been shown of our political good?) whilst the second is a deliberative question (how then shall we pursue it?). Nevertheless Christian political ethics cannot be read from the pages of Scripture. Rather the 'concepts authorised from the narrative of Israel and Christ govern our deliberations about political ethics'.[19]

Christendom as Friendship

For O'Donovan contemporary political theology is rooted in Christendom's High Tradition (1100–1650AD) which emerges from earlier patristic and Carolingian thought. Even recent political theologies such as Liberation and Anabaptist-type theologies, like those of John Howard Yoder and Stanley Hauerwas, stand within the horizon of this earlier thought.[20] Consequently O'Donovan rejects both the German Enlightenment philosopher Kant's view that politics is corrupting and Augustine of Hippo's view that theology swamps politics. These have contributed to the cynicism with which modern people view politics as the agenda of interest groups. Neither is he persuaded by Liberation Theology's use of politics to illuminate God's truth. This trades on the idealism of Hegel and the materialism of Marx, who saw history as the key to understanding society. Great abuses have been performed when ethics and politics are united so that all existing authority is regarded as vested interests by those claiming to represent the poor. To ask 'whose good?' or 'who benefits?' simply reveals sectional interests rather than whether these are true.[21] Even an understanding of praxis (reflective action) depends upon whether we believe that we make our own worlds or whether we regard ourselves as creatures in God's creation.

17 'Response to Respondents', p. 92.
18 O'Donovan, *The Desire of the Nations*, p. 2.
19 'Response to Respondents', p. 93.
20 O'Donovan, *The Desire of the Nations*, p. 4.
21 O'Donovan, *The Desire of the Nations*, p. 11.

Furthermore Marxism is atheistic and has a headless view of society. In contrast the reign of God is crucial for a proper theological politics since it safeguards the goods of creation. It indicates the worthwhile character of politics which respects creation as a gift and the context of meaningful choice. The reign of God therefore locates authority not in institutions but in the political act of Christ performed on behalf of all. It speaks of a revealed history illustrated by Israel's story. Political theology emerges from a reading out of Scripture and shows that theology must include revelation rather than simply interpret history.[22]

The Reign of God as Friendship

The New Testament reveals a variety of ways in which the teaching and example of Jesus expose the politics of the reign of God. In Hebrews the new way of Christ supplants the old way of Israel. In the Gospels the new fulfils the old but still needs the old to be intelligible. For Paul the church isn't yet a formed political community but one that awaits its fuller clothing when God is fully known.[23] As a result there is a tension in Christian political theory between idealists, like the second-century African theologian Tertullian, who want the church to disengage from the politico-social order and pragmatists, such as Eusebius of Caesarea, ally of the fourth-century Emperor Constantine, who advocate engagement and affirmation. So for the fourteenth-century theologian, Wycliffe, a Tertullian idealist, human justice depends upon God sanctifying our relationship to our material possessions and political right emerges out of charity to God and neighbour since it must be rooted in the law of love. In contrast the sixteenth-century Thomists, Vitoria and the Salamanca school, held that political order is not rooted in redemption but in creation and the social character of human nature. Thus existing institutions should be supported in order to ensure the stability of the political order. In short they suggested a sort of Christian secularism and an autonomous political science without direct reference to God. On the other hand Papal politics contested this by seeing the church as a mediating order between these two approaches since it discloses the judging presence of God in society.[24] Yet what really matters for O'Donovan is the relationship of the church to Israel since this is a history of how God's kingly rule is mediated in corporate experience and how it is brought to fruition in the

---

[22] O'Donovan, *The Desire of the Nations*, pp. 21–2.

[23] O'Donovan, *The Desire of the Nations*, pp. 23–5.

[24] O'Donovan, *The Desire of the Nations*, pp. 25–7.

death and resurrection of Jesus Christ. Here is a history of redemption in which the truth is found within the unfolding patterns of history. Thus divine kingship is not rooted in force or power but in authority. This is not the command ethics of Duns Scotus or Karl Barth in which God determines an agenda from beyond. Nor does it represent our alienated wills in the way philosophers Hobbes and Marx believed. Rather it is rooted in the ancient Israelite understanding of providence which finds in the experience of political life an invitation to a deeper encounter with God through praise and worship, since worship recognises the presence of Yahweh in Israel.[25]

This providential presence is evident in the way constructive politics seeks for peaceable unity in society.[26] On the other hand attempts to control or fragment society by making absolute particular expressions of self-interest, such as despotic monarchy, imperialist agendas or powerful minority interests, show the corruption of politics. The prophetic tradition of Israel and the experience of exile are witness against such abuse. Politics, therefore, is the theatre of divine disclosure. Yet this disclosure has dual expression in church and state, rather than uniting church and political institutions. Jesus recognises that taxes must be paid to the political authorities during the interim era. Jesus exorcises demonic powers but not the Roman authorities. Thus 'the Beatitudes ... do not speak of "life in the Kingdom" as has often been said, but of the essential contradictions of that life which is seriously preparing for the Kingdom'.[27] By fulfilling the law and the teaching of the prophets Jesus fulfils Israel's tradition and its expectation and anticipation of a right way of living with God. In Jesus 'that promise is now to be made good, and the life of the community is to demonstrate it'.[28]

Church as Friendship

For O'Donovan Jesus proclaimed the coming of the Kingdom of God whereas the apostolic church told the story of what happened when the Kingdom came.[29] Nevertheless the counsel of God is hidden in the present and indeed the Scripture shows us that God is at work through Caiaphas and Pilate as well as Peter and Mary. This divine hidden counsel is evident within political orders when they are open to prophetic challenge and seek community. The former represents the

---

[25] O'Donovan, *The Desire of the Nations*, pp. 47–8
[26] O'Donovan, *The Desire of the Nations*, p. 72.
[27] O'Donovan, *The Desire of the Nations*, p. 108.
[28] O'Donovan, *The Desire of the Nations*, pp. 108–9.
[29] O'Donovan, *The Desire of the Nations*, p. 120.

surprise of God hidden in the political process whilst the latter reflects God's destiny for human society. Thus political theology is set in the four moments of the Advent, Passion, Restoration and Exaltation of Christ. The Ascension or Exaltation of Christ in particular reminds Christians that the mystery of glorification, though accomplished, still awaits disclosure. Hence all politics are provisional and will be judged in terms of this destiny.[30] For example, Christians respect the juridical order of the state and yet also remind the state that it has a duty to provide social space for the church to engage in its mission. Equally the state deals with intermediate judgments whereas the church's duty is to make public divine judgment. Thus the state is not a counter to the church. Rather the New Testament shows the mutual integration of three communities, Israel, empire and church and indicates that God has set his throne in the very context where Satan has set his. Consequently the church lives under the rule of God as the first fruits of the coming Holy City amidst ordinary society. This involves accepting a dual expression of authority as was the case during Israel's experience of empire, exile and post-exilic community. In both exilic and post-exilic forms 'dual authority corresponded to the fractured and enslaved condition of God's people'.[31] Now it corresponds to the progress of God's victory as God's people possess this victory and are able to push back the empire. The church is therefore a political society explicitly accountable to the hidden government of Christ. Yet this accountability also shows how secular government should rule because it is also accountable to God. Nevertheless since the visible authority of the church is ambiguous its leaders can never assume that their authority is identical to Christ's, as the Reformation argued against the Church of Rome.

For O'Donovan, therefore, the era of Christendom, lasting from 313 to 1791AD, was a faithful mission strategy whereby Christ's conquest drew subjects from under their rulers rather than engaging in open conflict with those rulers. The Constantinian Settlement set out in the Edict of Milan in 313 was a form of contextual theology since following 'the logical conclusion of their confidence in mission ... the kings of the earth had come to bow before the thrones of Christ'.[32] As such, Christendom was about the power of God to humble the haughty rather than about coercive power forcing conversion and involved alien powers becoming part of the church. Christendom properly involved a mutual service between two authorities, church and state. The church united truth and power since God's Kingdom is within the social order and its mission is to challenge

---

[30] O'Donovan, *The Desire of the Nations*, p. 133.
[31] O'Donovan, *The Desire of the Nations*, p. 158.
[32] O'Donovan, *The Desire of the Nations*, p. 194.

society to seek first the Kingdom of God. The state's task was to facilitate the church's mission but not to replace it. Church establishment acknowledged this and indeed the secular ruler was excluded from holding office in the church as a way of recognising the contingency of secular politics. Problems emerged with the conversion of the Germanic tribes, since a two-kingdoms Christendom became a two-governments Christendom with consequent competition about dominance. This led to the medieval Investiture Dispute with Papalists and Erastians in conflict, a conflict later evidenced, for example, between Geneva Calvinists and the English Church.[33]

Liberalism and Friendship

Contemporary liberal institutions which emerged from the Enlightenment remain dependent upon Christendom according to O'Donovan. Indeed they are forms of apostate Christianity. Thus Christians have a duty to challenge the blind spots of liberal politics and remind the latter of its roots. In addition the Christendom experiment recognised the provisional and contingent character of politics, thereby challenging utopian and dictatorial aspirations. The legacy of this is evident in the plural politics of today. Christendom enabled the church to foreshadow Christ's universal kingdom. It denied any political institution that role. In the meantime the church looks towards the goal of Christendom. This final hope counters the loss of hope amongst ideologies, such as Marxism or liberal capitalism, which conspire to lock people into a closed present. Yet the church's witness today takes place in the midst of a post-Christendom culture where the state no longer sees its duty as supporting the church's mission. This change in the relationship between church and state emerged historically from within evangelical Christianity as it sought to reduce government interference in its life.[34] It thereby ironically engendered 'a state freed from all responsibility to recognise God's self-disclosure in history'.[35] It implied that political authorities are incapable of evangelical obedience, leaving society driven by intrinsic and manipulative interests rather than divinely accountable moral purposes. Justice, for example, is now associated with a plurality of contending rights located in the subject rather than being derived from the ordering of creation and humankind's place within this. Authority is thereby undermined as subjectivism

---

[33] O'Donovan, *The Desire of the Nations*, p. 196–8.
[34] O'Donovan, *The Desire of the Nations*, p. 225.
[35] O'Donovan, *The Desire of the Nations*, p. 245.

inhibits common agreement. In addition this sort of state claims that it does not make religious judgments despite the fact that such judgments are evident in the boundaries it sets for religious participation.

O'Donovan's agenda is to show that the assumptions of modern society about law, social expectations, politics etc., have not emerged within a vacuum. They belong to an ongoing story whose roots lie within Christian political theory and which is remembered by the church. Advent, Passion, Restoration and Exaltation correspond in secular speech to freedom, justice/mercy, natural right and free speech. Even though modernity is here to stay and there is no way back to Christendom it remains true that 'modernity is the child of Christianity ... it has left its father's house and followed the way of the prodigal'.[36] This means that its notions of freedom and society, suffering, punishment, natural rights and so on represent corrupted expressions of Christian ethics. The church's challenge is live as a hidden polis witnessing to the Kingdom of God as a community inclusive of both the living and the dead. It has to re-inhabit its own political theology in order both to expose the pathology of modernity and to point in hope to the Kingdom wherein its civic destiny is rooted.[37]

Justice and Friendship

All this informs our understanding of secular government and its claims to authority expressed in the practice of judgment.[38] As mentioned above this authority emerges in western societies from a particular history which located human judgment under the sovereignty of Christ and the justice of the New Jerusalem. It is therefore a limited and provisional judgment pointing to the Final Judgment of Christ and discovered within our human experience of the world as the work of divine providence. This approach represents a tradition of communal wisdom which protects us against those who would seek to subvert or remove existing freedoms by using utopian ideals. It also challenges intuitive or conscience-determined judgments which subvert human freedoms even more than earlier spectator perspectives, since they represent unauthorised and unaccountable assertions in place of communally discerned justice.[39] Furthermore this raises questions about various theories of punishment. For example, punishment which aims at regeneration is tyrannical since it assumes

---

[36] O'Donovan, *The Desire of the Nations*, p. 275.

[37] O'Donovan, *The Desire of the Nations*, pp. 285–8.

[38] O'Donovan, *The Ways of Judgment*, p. 3.

[39] O'Donovan, *The Ways of Judgment*, pp. 75–77.

a divine perspective to which the church can only point with reserve. Similarly punishment which claims to be retributive is deceptive since it cannot achieve an equality of suffering relative to the crime. On the other hand punishment which is attributive can be a truthful, if contingent, response to the offence. All this is because only God can exercise equitable punishment. Human judgment can only echo rather than answer a crime.[40] Similarly Christian tradition indicates that the common good is not about the right of individuals to their own goods but is the right of the community to be social and that such social identity is rooted in the traditions and history of a society rather than in the self-consciousness of its members. This is what terms such as 'the people' properly seek to convey. Yet for O'Donovan political authority does not constitute a people. Instead it finds a people and recognises their common good rather than trying to integrate independent and subjective desires into a single coherent community. Furthermore the presence of foreigners in a community reminds that society of the greater world to which it belongs, a world which is signified in the international or catholic character of the church.

The church then is the post-political society and acts as the lens through which we look at the pre-political society of God's creation.[41] It shows up the latter's limitations and also its destiny. For example, in a market society it witnesses to the fact that community is prior to commerce and to competition. It reminds us that communication is the basis of our personhood rather than our personhood being rooted in an isolated individualistic identity. It indicates that 'what is "mine" is in some sense also "ours"', with consequent political and ethical implications.[42] In addition the church as a catholic society questions the consumerist family and reminds society that the household was originally a community ordered to productive work.[43] As such it critiques self-preoccupation, the legacy of Protestantism's concern for individual conscience which, when combined with post-Enlightenment subjectivism, undermines social accountability and self-giving and destroys the credibility of social institutions and equates them with oppressive structures. In contrast for the Christian 'the self-judging believer ... is not an isolated individual but a social one'.[44] The subject is situated and determined by relations within the community.

---

[40] O'Donovan, *The Ways of Judgment*, p. 114.
[41] O'Donovan, *The Ways of Judgment*, pp. 238–41.
[42] *The Church Times* (17 February 2006), p. 23.
[43] O'Donovan, *The Ways of Judgment*, pp. 268–75.
[44] O'Donovan, *The Ways of Judgment*, p. 312.

Conclusion

O'Donovan reminds western societies that they are rooted in Christian politics and cannot make sense of themselves without paying attention to this history and its ongoing influence on contemporary life. This exposition of the way the Gospel has shaped these societies represents his understanding of Christian friendship for these societies. Of course O'Donovan's approach is not uncontested. Can resurrection and the moral order be distinguished? Should not the church embody a contrast pilgrim politics rather than a supportive residential politics in which Christians think they should rule? Was the loss of Christendom God's discipline to show the church how it should survive freely and un-complacently in Babylon, living by its wits, rather than developing political theologies which seek to rule or underwrite these societies?[45] Does O'Donovan represent an authoritarian conservatism seeking to restore a past order rather than seeing the church as a community taking part in a wider discourse within civil society, particularly with those who are shaken by life's traumas? Indeed is there a given order within which humans live or rather an unfolding disclosure of Christ's resurrection life in all life, which Christians should follow rather than react against?[46] Where does the Spirit's leading the church into truth fit with this? Do large scale interpretative concepts such as resurrection try to embrace too much of the Bible and fail to pay attention to particular genres and stories in the Bible?[47] Such questions indeed open up a robust conversation. Yet as we explore the character of Anglican mission it is the way O'Donovan expounds the long and integrated story of Israel, the church and European societies and its relationship to creation which is of most interest. He shows us that it is impossible to understand or sustain contemporary European societies within which Anglicanism emerged, without paying attention to the formative role of Scripture and the church in those societies. He has an Anglican view of mission in which the resurrection integrates creation and redemption and in which Christian ethics and politics are not divorced from common ethics and politics. This is why he criticises more sectarian evangelical traditions. Christendom was a Christian political experiment in which a whole commonwealth sought to live within the Christian story. Although this Christendom experiment is no longer

---

[45]   Stanley Hauerwas, *Wilderness Wanderings: Probing Twentieth Century Theology and Philosophy* (Colorado: Westview Press, 1997), p. 200.

[46]   Andrew Shanks, *God and Modernity: A New and Better Way to do Theology* (London: Routledge, 2000), pp. 92, 103–7.

[47]   Richard A. Burridge, *Imitating Jesus: An Inclusive Approach to New Testament Ethics* (Grand Rapids, Michigan: Eerdmans, 2007), p. 384 and footnote 117.

possible in the way it was in the past, O'Donovan argues that societies such as England depend upon a truthful conversation with and re-appropriation of this legacy. He shows how the self-giving friendship of Christ in the church became a catalyst for the politics of western societies and how the church's vocation today is to remind these societies of this as they try to forget their heritage. His challenge to the church is to recognise that worship is the way by which we remember and are constituted as witnesses and heralds of this reality. Mission is more than simply inviting people to personal faith. It is about participating in God's cosmic and political drama whose expression in English society is inexplicable without attention to the stories of Israel, Jesus and the church.

Chapter 8

Graceful Friendship

Rowan Williams's theology is grounded in an Anglican politics of friendship. Williams believes that we discover truth in conversation rather than by unilaterally asserting our points of view. Truth and unity belong together. We discover that we are God's friends as we learn what it means to be friends of one another. Grace is therefore discovered through the Body of Christ and cannot be experienced in its fullness if that body is dismembered. Hence re-membering the body through graceful conversations is at the heart of Williams's project. In addition such graceful holiness, formed in the church as it worships God, offers material resources for understanding God and salvation. Faith in flesh, therefore, is critical to Christian theology if that theology is faithfully to grasp the character of God. Theology is the difficult task of patiently exploring the graceful sign of the church, graceful not in the sense that the church is always gracious, but in the sense that God is present in the sign of baptised Christian communities participating in God's mission in the world.[1]

Friendship in the Gaze of Love

Williams regards reality as held within the divine gaze.[2] This inclusive gaze, embodied in the incarnation, involves both exposure and judgement. However this is the exposure of disarming acceptance and is the judgement of love. Precisely because it is a loving gaze, the character of the judgement involved is all the more challenging since it is not a general love or judgement but a particular one, which engages with the messy details of our particular lives. This is why worship and prayer are central to the character of theology and to the vocation of the church. Indeed praying and knowing belong together.[3] Thus a considerable amount of his theology explores Christian spirituality in works such as *The Wound of*

---

[1]   Mike Higton, *Difficult Gospel: The Theology of Rowan Williams* (London: SCM, 2004), p. 3.

[2]   Higton, *Difficult Gospel*, pp. 16–18.

[3]   Benjamin Myers, *Christ the Stranger: The Theology of Rowan Williams* (London: T&T Clark International, 2012), p. 99.

Knowledge: Christian Spirituality from the New Testament to St John of the Cross and *Silence and Honey Cakes: The Wisdom of the Desert.*[4] For example in his study of a number of Christian spiritual writers in *The Wound of Knowledge* Williams seeks to show how the mystery of God constantly challenges all human attempts to control religion and reminds human beings that it is their sinfulness which renders God mysterious.[5] God's freedom and love, expressed in Christ, are not at the behest of sinful human agendas. Thus engaging with God in worship and discipleship radically challenges human-centred living. In *Silence and Honey Cakes*, he uses the four themes of otherness, personhood, fleeing and staying to explore how discipleship is a pilgrimage of living with others in reverence, attention and healing embraced by the challenge of the love of God. Each Christian has a distinctive vocation within the community of the church and Christian formation involves fleeing from false self-projections and conformity to the world. Discipleship is about staying faithfully with others and the self in the church, which is a community pledged through baptism to one another in God. It is about being together as a display and exploration of what it means to live in the gaze of God. Other contemplative books, such as *Ponder these Things: Praying with Icons of the Virgin*, *The Dwelling of the Light: Praying with Icons of Christ* and *Open to Judgement* further explore the relationship between spirituality, embodiment and witness. As someone influenced by the Eastern Church, Williams sees this approach to spirituality and witness as a reminder to western Christians of the importance of contemplation and divinisation, or being formed into a visible holy people.[6] Spirituality is a transforming journey into God, which forms Christians into icons of Christ. Sermons are moments of reflection upon the practice of reading Scripture together as church, a practice which reminds Christians that their lives are explicitly open to the scrutiny of God. Hence Christian formation makes us tangible witnesses to the world and the church is itself continually becoming an icon of divine grace.

---

[4]   Rowan Williams, *The Wound of Knowledge: Christian Spirituality from the New Testament to John of the Cross* (London: Darton, Longman and Todd, 1979) and *Silence and Honey Cakes: The Wisdom of the Desert* (Oxford: Lion, 2003).

[5]   Myers, *Christ the Stranger*, p. 114.

[6]   Rowan Williams, *Ponder these Things: Praying with Icons of the Virgin* (Norwich: Canterbury Press, 2003); *The Dwelling of the Light: Praying with Icons of Christ* (Norwich: Canterbury Press, 2003) and *Open to Judgement* (London: Darton, Longman and Todd, 1994).

Friendship, Scripture and the Church

Rowan Williams's work on the third-century Arian controversy reflects his view of the church as an icon or window into the mystery of God. The Arian controversy was a debate between Arius and Athanasius about the divine status of Christ. It reveals how the practices of the Christian community form us to see the activity of God in the world. Williams argues that Athanasius did not defeat Arius because his biblical and theological case was watertight. What trumped Arius was the witness of the fourth-century world church. Here was a provisional sign of the universal community of God, a witness that God was in Christ redeeming the world. According to Athanasius only God could bring about universal salvation. Human agency of itself is too finite. Thus the Arian dispute was fundamentally about the significance or sign of the church. For Athanasius the sign of the church gathered at the Council of Nicaea offered material support for the doctrines of Christ's divinity and of the Trinity. Hence the church illuminates the meaning of the Gospel. In *Arius: Heresy and Tradition* Williams describes the conflict as one between Arius, the conservative, Scriptural literalist and Athanasius, the more theologically minded, explorer of the salvation embodied in the new imperial church.[7] Arius felt theology must be constrained by the wording of Scripture and a simple doctrine of God. The character of the community should not influence interpretation. Abstract text and abstract theology were sufficient. For Athanasius, the character of the community represented meaningful flesh, flesh whose meaning is in its body. This meaningful flesh contributes to a faithful interpretation of Scripture. In short Athanasius flags up the role of the church in interpreting the Scriptures. Scripture remains the source of the core revelation of God. However the story of Scripture and the ongoing embodiment of that story in the church are not divorced but wedded to each other. They illuminate one another since what the church becomes is interrogated by the Scriptures and yet also illuminates them. On occasion this interpretive relationship will involve fresh ways of understanding the 'meaning' of the stories present in those texts. The faithfulness of such fresh insights is tested by their congruence with the Scriptures and by the witness of the church. This is 'a debate about the kinds of continuity possible and necessary in the Church's language',[8] and of the role of theology in resolving complex disputes, which are not easily grasped by a simple appeal to Scripture.[9]

---

[7]   Rowan Williams, *Arius: Heresy and Tradition* (London: Darton, Longman and Todd, 1987). See also Higton, *Difficult Gospel*, pp. 42–3.

[8]   Williams, *Arius*, p. 234.

[9]   Williams, *Arius,* pp. 236–8.

It reveals that, 'access to the incarnate Word is in Scripture and the corporate life of the Church'. Hence he seeks an 'ecclesiastical' reading of Scripture'.[10]

Such an 'ecclesiastical' interpretation of Scripture sheds light on a number of critical themes for Christian believing. The first theme concerns the intimacy rather than the isolation of God. Arius, in an attempt to protect the otherness of God, divorces God from creation and redemption. He thereby undermines the security of salvation as Jesus becomes a mere human agent rather than God-with-us. Arius's God, according to Athanasius, is not directly involved in either creation or redemption.[11] The second theme concerns the character of our knowledge of God. Athanasius's theology gives a different interpretation to apophatic theology or theology reflecting upon the unknowability of God. Arius argues that unknowability means the inaccessibility of God. He stresses the utter difference and distance of God from creation. For Athanasius, apophatic theology is about the accessibility of God in Christ. This does not imply an exhaustive knowledge of God but rather means that Christ indicates who and what God is.[12] From this Williams is able to show that the love of God present in Christ informs the way God's will is expressed. There is no arbitrariness in God. God acts as God is. Thus God may be mysterious but God is not unknowable, since what God is is how Christ was and is. The third theme emerging from the witness of the Constantinian church is the relationship of Scripture to theology. For Arius, a literal or surface reading of Scripture raises questions about Trinitarian language and hence of the salvific claims of Athanasius. 'Son of God', for Arius, implies subordinationism, that is the subordination of the Son to God the Father. For Athanasius faithfulness to Scripture is about being faithful to the deeper vision of God and creation which worship and Scripture engender. The incarnation is underscored by the existence of a church of universal character evident in the church of his day. Hence there is a symbiotic relationship between worship, theology and Scripture as each illuminates the other. Ironically a conservative commitment to Scripture can actually mask the intentions of Scripture. In contrast fresh ways of articulating the faith are needed as new challenges confront the church. Such fresh expressions of faith aim to renew the tradition as they engage in conversation with these new challenges. Hence words that are not found in Scripture, such as *homousios* or 'Trinity', become servants of this cause.[13]

---

10   Williams, *Arius*, p. 239.
11   Williams, *Arius*, p. 240.
12   Williams, *Arius*, pp. 241–2.
13   Williams, *Arius*, pp. 234–35.

A fourth theme relates to the theological significance of the church following the conversion of the Emperor Constantine. The Arian controversy reflected contemporary ambivalence about the implications of the Constantinian Settlement since the church was no longer a self-conscious sect but now the imperial faith. Some, such as Eusebius of Caesarea, saw this as a sign of the universal truthfulness of Christianity. Others, such as the desert fathers, felt that the soul of Christianity had been compromised.[14] For Williams, 'what the Church discovered in the painful years after Nicaea was that its own inner tensions could not after all be solved by a *deus ex machina* on the imperial throne, and that its relationship with the empire intensified rather than solved the question of its own distinctive identity and mission'.[15] What emerged from this controversy was the importance of the church as a distinctive community which reads Scripture together in critical distance from society. The intimacy of God with his people, embodied in the church, gave that community an authority to interpret life, which was more truthful than that offered by imperial propaganda. A contemporary example of the loss of this critical distance occurred in Nazi Germany and the German Christians. Only the Confessing Church and the Barmen Declaration kept alive the critical distance necessary for truthful interpretation. The fifth theme relates to the meaning of the Christ. After Athanasius the church was clear that the incarnation exposes the integration of the will, nature and character of God. There is no created mediator between God and creation; no history in God, only a history of God. Hence God is known because he acts in uttering his Word through whom creation and redemption are realised. Theology is therefore about following the activity of this Word in life. It is responsive reflection, which enables Christians to say that God's faithfulness to God's character, expressed in Christ, is the ground of our faith that God is actively for us. God's life in Christ represents active self-differentiation and gift reflecting that God is relational as the Trinity indicates.[16] Hence theology begins with the practices and language of the Christian community, past and present. The church performs its faith and although the true meaning of Scripture and the church's story awaits the disclosure of the Parousia or the End, the provisional, contextual and contingent manifestations of this story are signs of the divine story at work in the world.

---

[14] Evidence for Eusebius' interpretation of the Constantinian Settlement can be found in Eusebius of Caesarea, *The History of the Church*, trans. G.A. Williamson (London: Penguin, 1965), pp. 380–413.

[15] Williams, *Arius*, pp. 236–7.

[16] Williams, *Arius*, pp. 238–9.

Friendship and Theology

Thus the theological importance of the Arian controversy informs the way Williams grapples with the complexity of reality which includes the contemporary Anglican Communion.[17] Reality needs working at if we are to understand it. God is not easy to grasp and often surprises us.[18] The temptation is to seek easy answers and swift closures to challenging questions and thereby fail to do justice to the character of what is being explored. This is a particular temptation for the western mind, which segregates God and life, effectively divorcing God from the materiality of creation. Instead it is the graced, tangible character of creation as gift that illuminates our understanding of God. Indeed this enables Christians to be patient in the brokenness of life and to maintain a conversation when issues refuse swift resolution.[19] For Christians God is the generative source of this gift and God enables creation to flourish, develop and grow with its own integrity. In consequence discipleship is about learning how to recognise the presence of God in all of life and live accordingly, a demanding education which takes considerable time and training.[20] His own approach to this is in the collection of essays, *On Christian Theology*, the nearest book we have to a 'Theology of Rowan Williams'.[21] Yet this is not a systematic theology but one which begins with the practices and language of the Christian community.[22] For Williams, academic Christian theology is dependent upon the informal theology of worship. This informal theology is Christian speech, the contemporary voicing of Christian language, which describes and converses about God's activities in a contingent world. Its character is threefold. First it is celebratory since it explores the implications of the worship of Christian people. Secondly it is communicative since it illuminates Christian speech for those estranged from it. Thirdly it is critical since it challenges complacent and lazy Christian thinking.[23] Theology in this mode is therefore conversational and invites response. As speech it engages other ways of understanding in a quest to grasp more deeply and clearly God's ways with the world. Hence Christian theology is hospitable to all forms of truth-seeking and as speech it is neither fixed nor finished. As speech it also binds speakers to each other and avoids

---

17 Higton, *Difficult Gospel*, p. 3.
18 Myers, *Christ the Stranger*, pp. 2, 17.
19 Myers, *Christ the Stranger*, pp. 52–4.
20 Higton, *Difficult Gospel*, pp. 61–87.
21 Rowan Williams, *On Christian Theology* (Oxford: Blackwell, 2000).
22 Williams, *On Christian Theology*, p. xii.
23 Williams, *On Christian Theology*, p. xv.

the sort of linguistic sectarian enclave implied by George Lindbeck's cultural linguistic thesis.[24] Christian conversation with the world therefore is generative rather than simply proclamation.[25]

Consequently as the church performs its faith in a conversational manner it is formed to understand more clearly how God is at work in the world and what is the meaning of Scripture. Yet it always acknowledges the mystery of God's action, refusing to see its theology as problem solving but instead as paying attention to the strangeness of God.[26] Thus the literal interpretation of Scripture can only be known by God, since the church's interpretation of God's agenda and of the Scriptures is always contingent, informed by the limitations of its context and sinful condition. Indeed Williams advocates eschatological literalism, by which he means that the true interpretation of the Scriptures will only be known fully at the End or *Eschaton*. In the meantime there will be competing interpretations of Scripture and the ways of God. This plurality can provoke fundamentalism as interpreters react by seeking a single solution too swiftly and naively.[27] Yet just as the Arian controversy showed that interpreting Scripture was more complex than simply quoting Scripture, so engaging with religious plurality is not straightforward. Exclusivism, inclusivism and pluralism are often presented as responses to religious plurality. Yet Williams believes that each of these approaches diminishes the distinctiveness and respect due to difference since they assume that one community can police and arbitrate between the various different groups. Exclusivism argues that one faith is the exclusive pathway to God. Inclusivism argues that one faith can include others within itself as lesser but valid pathways to God. Pluralism argues that each path to God is equally valid. In contrast Williams again argues that the fullness of revelation awaits the End.[28] Only then will the true interpretation of religious and other expressions of plurality be understood. In the meantime inter-faith encounters should negotiate differences in a piecemeal manner as they try to find areas of common agreement. This will involve different faiths sharing their stories openly with each other rather than remaining in deferential silence. Hence conversation is the best course since in conversation mutual understanding, enrichment and challenge take place.

---

[24]   George A. Lindbeck, *The Nature of Doctrine, Religion in a Post Liberal Age* (Philadelphia: Westminster Press, 1984).

[25]   Williams, *On Christian Theology*, pp. 31–5.

[26]   Myers, *Christ the Stranger*, p. 102.

[27]   Williams, *On Christian Theology*, pp. 44–59.

[28]   Williams, *On Christian Theology*, pp. 167–80.

Theology therefore is not to be confused with God's perspective. Instead it is about showing how the complexity of reality comes to judgement before God as the Christian community learns how to discern God's activity in contemporary life. Such theology needs three key dispositions: surrender through repentance, praise as an indication of the non-utilitarian approach of theology and prayer as openness and attention to the divine. Theology, therefore, is not about great universal theories. It is hostile to blasphemies, such as nuclear war or technological self-confidence. Instead theology is the prayerful following of God's ways in the world rooted in a common hope for the world. It seeks to heal us by freeing us from deceptive fantasies about ourselves and reality.[29] This following is embodied publicly in the church. Truth and reality therefore emerge as Christian speech converses with life. It is therefore responsive, a learning how to speak the faith in changing circumstances and with changing knowledge. Tragedy reminds Christians that the world has an integrity which is not simply at the mercy of human imagination and manipulation. It thereby challenges a human-centred and constructivist approach to understanding the world, since constructivist confidence in human power would imply that the tragic should not happen.[30] The incarnation therefore is not a concept but the implication of the particular story of Jesus and its universal appeal. As mentioned above, the doctrine of the incarnation arose because there was now a universal, representative community called the church. Only God could unite such diversity in a common salvation. Hence insights about the incarnation emerged through reflection upon the character of the body in the light of the Gospel stories. As Lord, Jesus challenges and repositions all other powers, since Jesus represents God's judgement about the relationship of these powers to God. Nevertheless this judgement is the judgement of love. It offers justifying grace rather than condemnation.[31] Such revelation is not a package of ideas but the effect of God's generative life in history. God is revealed as diverse people experience and embody God's universal salvation in their lives. In addition, since we live in history, revelation is ongoing as the church discovers God in new, though related ways, to those held in the past. Again the empty tomb reminds the church that Christ has gone ahead rather than away and that Christ is not contained in the church. Hence the church is that community whose life speaks of God's universal hospitality and grace. It is the community which knows the story of God by living it. If, like the Church of England, it has an intimate relationship with the state, then its

---

[29] Myers, *Christ the Stranger*, pp. 35, 107–11.
[30] Williams, *On Christian Theology*, pp. 3–14.
[31] Williams, *On Christian Theology*, p. 249.

task is to remind the latter that it is relativised by the more catholic community of God's church. The relationship is certainly not about power or privilege.[32]

Friendship as the Church

Given that theology is rooted in the particular stories of Jesus, the Word uttered by the Father, the church's calling involves a journey into the Father with the Son in the Spirit. This is often a journey into apparent darkness even though it is this is the sort of blindness which comes by trying to look into the sun.[33] As a result Williams's study of the church involves paying attention to the way the story of God in Christ shows how the church is to be a sign of that cosmic story.[34] First, the Gospel is the life of a people, not an abstract ideology about God. The tangibility of the incarnation is underwritten by the tangibility of church's witness which is not the imitation of Christ but the expression in human lives of the effect of the Gospel. The church is the effect of this Gospel and as the Body of Christ it is meaningful flesh. Secondly, the empty tomb reminds the church that it is not in control of Christ. Christians follow where Christ has gone before rather than taking Christ with them into the world. The witness of the church is about living in this light rather than in any other light. Third, the incarnation indicates that the church is properly sacramental. Christ participates in the church as it expresses its vocation through worship. Hence as the church worships, something of Christ is inevitably 'seen' and the church is a visual theology. This 'sight' may not be clear, given the presence of sin in the body, but Christ is a guaranteed presence and hence an effective presence. Fourth, the church is a learning community as it is formed to follow Christ through time and in different contexts.[35] This learning is about taking note of new contexts but also seeing continuities with the tradition. These enable the community to recognise the lessons of God in ever new circumstances. Fifth, baptism gives Christians their primary identity. This 'church identity' is a gift of God which is neither negotiable nor malleable. As a bestowed identity it therefore escapes the problems attached to the unstable, fluid and isolated self of modern life. In addition this identity is relational and social. Baptism is about belonging to a community.

---

[32] Williams, *On Christian Theology*, pp. 233–4.
[33] Myers, *Christ the Stranger*, p. 32.
[34] Williams, *On Christian Theology*, pp. 61–87 and Myers, *Christ the Stranger*, p. 14.
[35] Richard A. Burridge, *Imitating Jesus: An Inclusive Approach to New Testament Ethics* (Grand Rapids, Michigan: Eerdmans, 2007), p. 391.

Friendship and the Christian Story

The church's story is rooted in the core narratives of the Scriptures and therefore Scripture is the core resource for theology. Contrary to the claims of some of his critics, Williams has a very high regard for Scripture. However such a high view exposes some of the short circuiting that takes place among many who regard themselves as biblically focused and committed to a literal interpretation of Scripture. As indicated above, a properly literal interpretation pays close attention to the character and style of the Scriptures themselves, rather than simply approaching the words in a wooden manner. In addition, the baptismal identity of Christians means that interpreting the Scriptures is a communal affair, listening not simply to contemporary voices, but to those of the tradition. Thus a simple return to an abstract New Testament is not sufficient to understand the vocation of the church in contemporary society. Instead, the way the church in history attended to God indicates an analogous approach for the contemporary church. Anglicans are bound together because they are Reformed Christians who accept the threefold order of ministry, the classical creeds and regard their governing authority as the vernacular Bible. They reject a centralist executive hierarchy and see faith as grace dependent. In addition, Anglicans refuse to limit God's work simply to human life. God is found in the flux of reality and it requires spiritually sustained patience to discern God in all of this. Thus the Church of England emerged by rejecting the idea of the church as one political entity among others. It is not an interest group but a community whose interest is catholic or for all.

In *Anglican Identities* Williams offers commentaries on seminal English Anglican theologians as a way of enabling a conversation about an Anglican way to proceed.[36] William Tyndale's characterisation of Christians as debtors to love reveals that time and patience are critical factors in learning the sort of practical love which can work creatively at resolving disputes.[37] Richard Hooker's contemplative pragmatism and sapiential theology provide distinctive resources for Anglicans seeking to listen to the voice of God today. Contemplative pragmatism involves ordinary congregations prayerfully discerning God's call on their lives in their own contexts rather than the imposition of an idealistic blueprint for the whole church. Sapiential theology reflects a way of life which is rooted in serious communal reflection upon Scripture, tradition and reason.

---

[36]   Rowan Williams, *Anglican Identities* (London: Darton, Longman and Todd, 2004).

[37]   Williams, *Anglican Identities*, pp. 9–23.

Such wisdom reflects the contingent and provisional character of faith.[38] It also recognises that God's transformation of the church takes time. Bishop Wescott represents respectful openness, or liberality, which takes the Scriptures and the past seriously but recognises the need to turn over the soil of tradition as new questions are asked.[39] Archbishop Michael Ramsay provides an epiphanic or revelatory vocation for church and clergy. The church is fundamentally called to witness to what God is doing rather than seeking to replicate the agendas of late modern commerce and consumerism. The principal task of the clergy is to gather people together to contemplate the cross rather than to provide a sleek, organised collective of Christian activists.[40] Consequently the church is the message as it gathers for Eucharist and is transformed into meaningful flesh. Thus the Christian community does not need to do anything in order to make itself a better message. It simply needs to be open and attentive to God's nourishing presence and let God generate an appropriate witness through it. Finally Dom Gregory Dix's anthropology represents a distinctively Christian grasp of human identity lived in the gaze of God. For Dix the Christian is *homo eucharistus*, a thanksgiving human being rather than *homo economicus*, a wealth-creating human being. The Christian's identity is rooted in the story of grace rather than in the story of late capitalist consumerism. Justification by grace through faith is therefore a gift, grace which liberates us from the need to justify ourselves or to determine the church's success.[41]

This understanding of Anglican identity explains why history matters. If the church is God's new human race in embryo, an icon of God's intention for humankind, then apologetics involves showing how the church's story embodies the divine.[42] Equally if Christian identity is embodied in time the contemporary church needs to listen to its faith ancestors if it is to understand how to live faithfully today. Thus in *Why Study the Past? The Quest for the Historical Church*, Williams aims first to show that we understand our identity through telling a story about our past, second to show how Church history helps to expose the divine in our human story and third to show how today's church is knit together with its spiritual ancestors and nourished by them as it confronts new challenges. In the process he is at pains to demonstrate that the past is strange

---

[38] Williams, *Anglican Identities*, pp. 24–55.
[39] Williams, *Anglican Identities*, pp. 72–86
[40] Williams, *Anglican Identities*, pp. 87–101.
[41] Williams, *Anglican Identities*, p. 108.
[42] Rowan Williams, *Why Study the Past? The Quest for the Historical Church* (London: Darton, Longman and Todd, 2005).

to us rather than the present in different clothing.[43] Hence understanding the past is challenging and stretching. Yet this is true of all forms of understanding since everyone and everything, including God, is a stranger. Thus as we explore the way our Christian ancestors grappled with faith in their own day, we learn how to do the same today. For example, the meaning of martyrdom for the early church, the issues at stake in asserting the freedom and grace of God in the Reformation and the significance of singing and praying using words from other generations or contexts help us to understand what Christian identity and unity mean when new challenges confront the church in our day.

Friendship and Modern Societies

Williams' understanding of God and the church means that he has considerable concerns about modern societies shaped by human-centred ideals of the eighteenth-century Enlightenment. In *Lost Icons: Reflections on Cultural Bereavement*, he argues that modernity has diminished childhood and allowed it to be colonised by consumerism. Consumerism has also rendered adults infantile and undermined charity by promoting aggressive competitive acquisitiveness. The self-centred individualism of modernity has undermined older Christian understandings of the relational self and left no place for the other. Furthermore modernity no longer has any sense of formation and education.[44] It has stripped the medieval vision of rich, love infused reality and replaced it with a thin self-preoccupied consumerist vision which rewards destructive and corrosive behaviours.[45] Certainly Christians must engage with the world as it is, tragedy and all, rather than trying to escape or construct the world to suit particular tastes and needs. However Christian identity does not glorify the isolated self but recognises its relational character expressed in giving and receiving. Such a social and embodied view of identity indicates how Christians are to become icons of God or meaningful flesh.[46] To become such an icon involves exercising the contemplative pragmatism of Hooker; that is, living as those who pay attention to what we discover in the world, accepting that creation is about limitation and allowing God to speak in and through all of this.

---

[43] Williams, *Why Study the Past?* p. 24.

[44] Rowan Williams, *Lost Icons: Reflections on Cultural Bereavement* (Edinburgh: T & T Clark, 2000).

[45] Rowan Williams and Larry Elliott (eds), *Crisis and Recovery: Ethics, Economics and Justice* (Basingstoke, Palgrave MacMillan, 2010), p. xi.

[46] Higton, *Difficult Gospel*, pp. 89–100.

This has particular implications for how Christians understand education, politics, economics, art and ecology. Firstly, education is less about measurable information outcomes and more about who we become as we are educated. It is primarily about character and virtues rather than about functions and skills. Secondly, politics is properly an inclusive conversation, a form of common worship, rather than the policing of social plurality by an élite or unaccountable power.[47] Conversation entails response to and respect for difference and otherness and in political terms is tested by how far those with power pay attention to the poor who are excluded from such power. Truthful politics is therefore characterised by a refusal to crush or colonise the other in the name of ideals or power. It recognises that what is common and communal is more fundamental that what is competed over and contested. This understanding of politics implies a limited state since no state has the right to guarantee its own survival by completely destroying its opponents.[48] It advocates a procedural rather than a programmatic state, one that fosters a conversational plurality or 'argumentative democracy' of mutual recognition rather than a singular secularism which ignores the complex identity of its citizens by reducing them to abstract individuals within a market state.[49] Equally it challenges the church to exemplify truthful social living if the world is to experience justice in its politics.[50] 'The church needs to be a place in which the formation of character, the enabling of recognition, is of first importance', since its vocation is in part to build the character of citizens who can foster societies of justice and peace.[51] Indeed the critical question every society has to answer is what sort of society we need to become if people are to flourish. Thirdly, economics or 'housekeeping' is about life shared in common whose aim is to grow and flourish in beneficial ways. It is about how society builds a home together and therefore is about shared well-being. This suggests that mutuality is at the heart of a Christian vision of economics analogous with the Body of Christ and expressed in forms of giving. This is about crafting a common life which therefore includes attention to appropriate character and virtues.[52] Fourthly, art involves paying attention to the integrity of reality in order to explore the complexity of reality. This approach resists the sort of swift

---

[47] Higton, *Difficult Gospel*, p. 119.

[48] Higton, *Difficult Gospel*, p. 130–31.

[49] Rowan Williams, *Faith in the Public Square* (London: Bloomsbury, 2012), pp. 20, 147, 166.

[50] Stanley M. Hauerwas, *Performing the Faith: Bonhoeffer and the Practice of Nonviolence* (London: SPCK, 2004), p. 28–9.

[51] Williams, *Faith in the Public Square*, p. 270.

[52] Williams and Elliot (eds) *Crisis and Recovery*, pp. 19–33.

theological closure feared by many artists and protects art from the temptation to see itself purely in functional or emotionally subjective terms. If the church proclaims that God's love respects the integrity of that creation, then loving creation through art involves representations which respond to, draw out and are infused by the integrity of what is being created. Thereby art itself is generative and enriches creation.[53] Such an approach indicates a respect for the otherness of creation which relates to its creator independent of us.[54] This means that Christians resist ecocidal approaches to life whose patterns of consumption destroy the possibilities of life. Such approaches may not manifest themselves as immediately ecologically destructive but the hubris of financial institutions and the destruction of moral ecology in unregulated capitalism feed through into a careless consumerism without regard for the future of the earth or future generations.[55] Such a way of life is life without landmarks, in which we are always 'nowhere in particular' and therefore have no sense that where or when we are has meaning. In the face of this, religious communities with their ritualised memory and sense of place contain resources to resist the destructive character of this approach to society and creation.[56] In kneeling, believers make themselves signs which witness that 'I am answerable for all I do'.[57]

Friendship and Peace

Williams therefore advocates peaceable living that respects the integrity of the other and resists violence which destroys the other. Religion is not just another attempt by an interest group to grab power and privilege through conquest. It is about witnessing to what is beyond which does not need our violence to be realised.[58] His is therefore an organic Catholicism.[59] In *The Truce of God* he notes the way violence has colonised North Atlantic cultures through the mass media and entertainment media.[60] This has brought about a sense of uncontrollability and unpredictability in life leading to escapism and victim culture as people

53   Rowan Williams, *Grace and Necessity: Reflections on Art and Love* (Harrisburg PA, Morehouse, 2005), pp. 167–70.
54   Williams, *Faith in the Public Square*, p. 185.
55   Williams, *Faith in the Public Square*, pp. 185, 200, 242, 219.
56   Williams, *Faith in the Public Square*, pp.235–7.
57   Williams, *Faith in the Public Square*, p. 325.
58   Williams, *Faith in the Public Square*, pp. 304–5.
59   Myers, *Christ the Stranger*, p. 38.
60   Rowan Williams, *The Truce of God* (Glasgow: Collins, 1983).

feel powerless to affect life.[61] Violence is consequently normalised and people become desensitised to the overwhelming violence of nuclear war. Yet Mutually Assured Destruction (MAD) is effectively mass suicide which the church must resist since it is a community that refuses to assent to its own survival at the cost of the whole scale destruction of another society. Indeed the visible catholicity of the church is a sign of universal hope for all people and is consequently more fundamental than sectarian state interests.[62] Furthermore since Christians believe that the world is God's gift that world is not ours to destroy. Thus the peace he advocates is Eucharistic peace or the space Jesus opens up for faithful living. This is not a selfish peace nor a retreat from the complexities of life. It is certainly not a peace based upon the 'balance of power' as favoured by the arms industry and liberal politics. Instead it is a call to privilege life and simplicity, to live as 'poor in spirit', to engage creatively with those whom we are in conflict with and to deal internally with our own demons.[63] In short it is to live in a way that speaks of the peace of Christ liturgically expressed in the Eucharist.

Peacemaking of this sort has implications for how the church deals with sexuality issues. In the article 'The Body's Grace', Williams invites Christians to revisit traditional understandings of sexuality and sexual behaviour in the light of contemporary questions and understandings of the human sexuality.[64] He argues that desire, or eros, reflects the relational character of human beings. Thus it is positive where it enlarges life and destructive where it exploits and manipulates.[65] This is at the heart of the Christian tradition's commitment to lifelong monogamous fidelity and celibacy and to the narrative self. The creation-redemption drama of the Scriptures illustrates how creation is desired, formed and loved by God through time. For Williams the sexual question, as with all ethical issues, is about how a community orders its life to reflect holy living appropriate to the Body of Christ.[66] His is a form of ecclesial ethics rather than rule-based or consequentialist ethics. Recognising that many marriages are exploitative, that some gay and lesbian relationships display the characteristics of fidelity and longevity and noting that biblical material, contraceptive practice and female genital structures raise questions about a simplistic equation of sexual activity and reproduction, he wonders whether joy rather than producing children is the primary good of faithful relationships. If so could there be space

---

[61] Williams, *The Truce of God*, pp. 11–21.
[62] Williams, *The Truce of God*, pp. 29–33, 68–74.
[63] Williams, *The Truce of God*, pp. 80–102.
[64] Rowan Williams, 'The Body's Grace' (Lesbian and Gay Christian Movement, 1989).
[65] Williams, 'The Body's Grace', p. 6.
[66] Higton, *Difficult Gospel*, pp. 135–6.

for gay and lesbian relationships, which, though not marriage, are nevertheless analogous to marriage's commitment to lifelong monogamy?[67]

Conclusion

In this chapter I have tried to show how Williams helps us grasp the rich character of Anglican character, vocation, witness and mission through his reflections on theology, history, contemporary society and the arts. His is a gracious theology premised on the friendship of God, a way of life which refuses to live violently by attempting to control everything. It is about living in step with an unfolding and open story confident in God's peaceable destiny for all.[68] Christian discipleship requires 'repentant attention' in worship and a timeful patience akin to the challenge that listening to or performing music requires.[69] Thus the truthfulness of Christian doctrine cannot be separated from the witness of holy lives.[70] Indeed for Williams, doctrine is not about explanation or about defining ideological positions. Rather doctrine is to make possible a truthful and transforming encounter with Christ.[71] It is meant 'to hold us still before Jesus'.[72] Theology is therefore contextual speech or speech that is testing out its capacities to describe the divine presence in particular contexts. It is therefore never abstract but is about faith in flesh that explores friendship with God at this particular time.[73] Worship is therefore at the heart of Anglican discipleship, a contemplative standing naked in the gaze of the loving God embodied in Christ. It involves relinquishing control and false self-images and discovering a secure baptismal identity out of which a confident testimony and form of life can be lived. Anglican witness is therefore expressed in the reality of an argumentative, outward facing, pilgrim community discerning together a way of faithful Christian living which remembers those who have gone before us on this journey. It is a slow and patient way of travelling and Williams has been criticised for being too open to the more intransigent perspectives within the Anglican Communion and preferring a tragic dissonance to a joyful resolution.

---

[67] Williams, 'The Body's Grace', p. 7.
[68] Hauerwas, *Performing the Faith*, p. 17. See footnote 7 as well.
[69] Hauerwas, *Performing the Faith*, pp. 100, 104–5. See also p. 107 footnote 98.
[70] Hauerwas, *Performing the Faith*, p. 23. See footnote 20.
[71] Hauerwas, *Performing the Faith*, p. 67.
[72] Rowan Williams, *Christ on Trial: How the Gospel Unsettles our Judgement* (London: Fount, 2000), p. 37 quoted in Hauerwas, *Performing the Faith*, p. 23, footnote 20.
[73] Hauerwas, *Performing the Faith*, pp. 83–4.

He seems at times to be so committed to self-emptying that some express concern about his deepest convictions.[74] Perhaps this reflects his Welsh roots and Russian Orthodox interests?[75] Certainly his theology and his practice resist closure.[76] Yet such criticism misses the character of the graced relationships he believes should characterise Christian friendship which take time to achieve in a complex world. Indeed Williams' picture of this timeful performing and improvising faith through the image and story of dance captures something of the meaning of mission in God's slow time. It indicates what 'a pedagogy of peaceful Christian performance' might amount to.[77] It reflects graceful Anglican friendship.

[74] Rupert Shortt, *Rowan's Rule: The Biography of the Archbishop* (London: Hodder & Stoughton, 2009), p.9.

[75] Myers, *Christ the Stranger*, pp. 115–16.

[76] Shortt, *Rowan's Rule*, p.2.

[77] Shortt, *Rowan's Rule*, pp. 107–9.

Chapter 9
Listening Friendship

Hermeneutics literally means the interpretation of messages, the art and practice of understanding. It is about understanding other people as people rather than as objects. It is about receiving something unexpected from the encounter which often surprises us. Understanding is a form of practical friendship or love in action which follows the dynamic of common worship as a conversation with God involving those different from ourselves.[1] The discussion below shows how such listening is central to the character of Anglicanism.

Friendship and Difference

Anthony Thiselton is an Anglican theologian rooted in both church and university whose work on philosophical and biblical hermeneutics explores how the church can listen to the sound of God in the human life world.[2] In an early article on 'Truth' he argues that the meaning of language only emerges as we are trained to understand how the language works and what it enables us to see.[3] Training and the habits which sustain this training depend upon belonging to a community within which we learn to speak and understand the language so that we can grasp the truth it engages with. This does not mean that truth is a community's construction since a theological understanding of truth asserts that truth depends upon God and can only be fully known when God reveals it at the *Eschaton*, or end of all things. However truth is encountered in history and is discerned through the wisdom of communal rather than individualistic judgements. This also means

---

[1]   Anthony C. Thiselton, *The Hermeneutics of Doctrine* (Cambridge UK: Eerdmans, 2007), p. xvii.

[2]   The following material forms part of my paper '"Let us cook you your tea, vicar!" Church, hermeneutics and postmodernity in the work of Anthony Thiselton and Stanley Hauerwas' in Stanley E. Porter and Matthew Malcolm (eds), *Horizons in Hermeneutics: A Festschrift in Honor of Professor Anthony C. Thiselton* (Grand Rapids Michigan/Cambridge UK: Eerdmans, 2013), pp. 268–85.

[3]   Anthony C. Thiselton, "Truth" in Colin Brown (ed.), *The New International Dictionary of New Testament Theology*, vol 3 (Exeter: Paternoster, 1978), pp. 894–5.

that the Bible's truth does not exist as a timeless abstraction but has to be proved again and again in each generation.[4] In *The Two Horizons*, Thiselton follows the philosopher Gadamer by arguing that we cannot understand the things of God or the human life world by using a method because a method is an approach which ignores the realities of time, the situatedness of human existence and the fact that we relate to one another as subjects rather than observe each other as objects. Method assumes that the empirical approach of the natural sciences is the only way of understanding. It equates understanding with explanation. Yet this fails to see that understanding human beings involves encounter, disclosure and surprise. Revelation and mystery are involved since hermeneutics is not about explanation through the observation of an object, but about listening to a disclosure in the language of the speaker. This *phronesis* or practical wisdom, the *sensus communis*, (a community's wisdom embedded in its tradition), enables human understanding to take place. For example when we encounter manifestations of human minds, such as a work of art or a game, we are drawn into the world of the work of art or game and interpret it contingently from within this dynamic relationship. Practical wisdom is therefore an art rather than a technique. It recognises that interpretation is not an abstract activity but rather an embedded one reflecting our location within interpreting communities which have their own prejudices or pre-judgements. Neither the community nor its prejudices, or traditions, determine understanding since in the event of interpretation the two horizons of 'interpreter' and 'text' engage with each other as the 'text' is listened to and new insight emerges.[5] However the social character of both language and identity mean that interpretation is a communal activity and, for Christians, one which necessarily includes the church. Nevertheless since we belong to many communities in a variety of ways, each community's understanding is inevitably experienced relative to other communities' understandings. Hence, although as an ordained Christian Thiselton's primary community is the church, as a scholar he is also part of the university community. Both university and church represent different, though related, 'life games', each with their own rules. However they do need 'the transmission and testing of the knowledge that is mediated through *the community and the tradition of which the individual scholar is a part*'. Hence as a member of the church Thiselton brings insights which contribute to his work as a

---

⁴   Thiselton, "Truth" in Brown (1978), pp. 899–900.

⁵   Anthony C. Thiselton, *The Two Horizons: New Testament Hermeneutics and Philosophical Description with special reference to Heidegger, Bultmann, Gadamer and Wittgenstein* (Exeter: Paternoster, 1980) pp. 294–314.

scholar.[6] For Thiselton, theology, therefore, is not simply for the church but rather represents a discourse available to and testable by those beyond the church since theology is a claim to universal truth. Yet theology self-consciously recognises that it is rooted in a tradition and community with a complex story about God and the world. Consequently for a Christian scholar hermeneutics is about acknowledging the generative though not determinative involvement of Christian identity in understanding life.[7]

Friendship and the Stranger

This subtle relationship forms the backcloth to Thiselton's exploration of the interpretation of texts which involves a commitment to listening to the other.[8] This echoes our earlier discussion in Chapter 2 about Christian friendship as distinctively orientated to the other or stranger. He is particularly concerned to challenge theological approaches which 'in transforming theology into questions about the community (i.e. into ecclesiology), or knowledge into contextual practice (i.e. into social history) ... leave no room for the creation as the work of grace in Christian theology, and no room for new horizons in hermeneutics.'[9] This false approach is called socio-pragmatic hermeneutics and holds that communities read texts in ways which simply reflect their communal self-interests and values. However in reacting to the false objectivity of modernity this approach is itself conservative and closed. There is no possibility of surprise or disclosure. There is no listening to or dialoguing with another directly or through a text. Instead the encounter is a pretext for reinforcing existing community traditions. Yet community traditions develop as they engage with new questions in new contexts. Certainly there is recognisable continuity with the past but there is also a porous, open and dialogical character to understanding. Communal traditions are not hermetically sealed but are soft systems which act as settings within which understanding takes place and which inform the starting point of further interpretation.[10] They condition but do not construct our understanding. Public worship represents such a setting but it

---

6   Anthony C. Thiselton, 'Academic Freedom, Religious Tradition and the Morality of Christian Scholarship' in Mark Santer (ed.), *Approaches to Authority, Community and the Unity of the Church* (London: SPCK, 1982), p. 30. Thiselton's italics.

7   Thiselton, 'Academic Freedom', p. 36.

8   Anthony C. Thiselton, *New Horizons in Hermeneutics: The Theory and Practice of Transforming Biblical Reading* (London: Harper Collins, 1992).

9   Thiselton, *New Horizons*, p. 7.

10   Thiselton, *New Horizons*, p. 9.

does not pre-determine the way the Bible will be listened to and understood on every occasion. Similarly the theology of the cross subverts any self-interested way of interpreting the human life world and God which might seduce the church, since it de-centres individual and corporate self-interest particularly within the church.[11] Nevertheless communal or common understanding is at the heart of an incarnational faith, such as Christianity, since revelation operates through the inter-wovenness of word and deed and the action and witness of the community. The latter gives credibility and facilitates understanding of the word which is both spoken and read since 'the text is more than a "docetic" or "disembodied" system of signifiers'.[12] Likewise the language of this community as it is spoken or practised in contemporary life draws its credibility from the public tradition of the community. Indeed since stories create communities this is the way in which the claims of particular communities are voiced.[13] Nevertheless narrative can itself become a bid for power or simply a game of texts if there is no accountability beyond the narrator or narrating community.[14] Thus for the church, narratives 'activate the eschatological call of Christian pilgrimage, in the sense of beckoning onwards towards new future action'.[15] The end acts as a check on temptations to convenient interpretation whilst the promises present within them speak of extra-linguistic possibilities and de-centre the present as fixed point of reference.[16]

Friendship as Paying Attention

Hermeneutics is therefore fundamentally the practice of listening to a person or persons rather than the act of viewing objects. It is about paying attention to the particular questions that human living raises rather than generating abstract theories about humanity. Even when interpreting texts, we are listening to a voice.[17] As such it involves understanding, love and respect for the 'other'. It is also a communal activity, since listening is dependent upon a shared language,

---

[11]   Thiselton, *New Horizons*, p. 28.
[12]   Thiselton, *New Horizons*, p. 75.
[13]   Thiselton, *New Horizons*, pp. 354–5, 481.
[14]   Thiselton, *New Horizons*, pp. 485–506.
[15]   Thiselton, *New Horizons*, pp. 569. See also Anthony C. Thiselton, 'Human Being, Relationality and Time in Hebrews, 1 Corinthians and Western Traditions', *Ex Audito* 13 (1997), pp. 76–95.
[16]   Thiselton, *New Horizons*, pp. 606–7.
[17]   Maggie Dawn, 'I am the Truth: Text, Hermeneutics and the Person of Christ' in Duncan Dormor, Jack McDonald and Jeremy Caddick, *Anglicanism: The Answer to Modernity* (London: Continuum, 2003), *Anglicanism*, p. 74.

and generates *phronesis* or practical wisdom, the wisdom which grows through a timeful engagement with the particulars of human life. Questions about truth are therefore ones which test the coherence of this wisdom, rather than trying to make it correspond with an abstract ideal.[18] Hermeneutics is particularly important to the church since its doctrine does not emerge from abstract thinking but from the contingent, communal practices and performance of worship.[19] Doctrine reflects a form of reflective listening to questions which arise from ecclesially situated existence.[20] Christology, for example, is not an abstract study in ideas about the identity of Jesus of Nazareth, but a way of forming disciples into the sort of life which his story displays. Christology is therefore a practical activity rather than a theoretical one and is about transformation of life rather than simply intellectual interest.[21] It is a drama of self-involving speech-acts rather than the detached thinking of a spectator.[22] Consequently believing is always embodied in habits, commitments and action within the context of a communal life which is located and contingent. These generate a distinctively Christian character as disciples are trained in the shared language, practices and traditions of the community.[23] Belief is consequently about habits more than clear thinking. It is a way of life rather than a package of ideas.[24] Doctrine therefore is the communal endorsement and transmission of these habits as expressed and embedded in the life, worship and action of the Christian community.[25] To understand doctrine therefore requires participation in the life of this community since doctrine is a language or conversation that emerges from within a form of life rather than representing an abstract form of human thought.[26] It is the fruit of paying attention to Christian discipleship.

Friendship as Openness

Consequently the church's teaching is always provisional since new questions will arise which require a review of existing tradition as these questions are

---

[18] Thiselton, *The Hermeneutics of Doctrine*, pp. xvi–xix.
[19] Thiselton, *The Hermeneutics of Doctrine*, p. 5.
[20] Thiselton, *The Hermeneutics of Doctrine*, p. 3.
[21] Thiselton, *The Hermeneutics of Doctrine*, p. 7.
[22] Thiselton, *The Hermeneutics of Doctrine*, p. 9. See also Thiselton, *New Horizons*, pp. 324–5.
[23] Thiselton, *The Hermeneutics of Doctrine*, pp. 19–23.
[24] Thiselton, *The Hermeneutics of Doctrine*, p. 28.
[25] Thiselton, *The Hermeneutics of Doctrine*, p. 34.
[26] Thiselton, *The Hermeneutics of Doctrine*, pp. 55–9.

attended to. The church's doctrinal language is therefore constructive rather than simply conservative, allowing for new insights to be gained which cohere with the existing narrative of God's dealings with the world.[27] This entails ecclesial formation, education and training whose primary context is worship and whose practical wisdom is open to discovering more of the truth. Furthermore this formation and training develop a distinctive character which displays patience, tolerance, respect for the other and a disposition to listening, a 'hermeneutics of altereity'.[28] Tradition and performance are therefore mutually enriching, enabling the church to improvise in new situations in ways faithful to its identity and generative classical texts.[29] This dialectic expands understanding and enables a faithful transcending of past perspectives. It displays theology as a reflective practice rather than an ideology. As a result there will be some tension between the contingencies of context and readership relative to claims for truth. To some extent, the multiplicity of little discipleship narratives contribute to the ongoing grand narrative of God in the world just as the canon of Scripture functions as a coherent plurality which generates Christian tradition and doctrine.[30] As mentioned above, Thiselton resists the reduction of the truth claims of theology to ecclesiology or ethnocentric consensus. Truth remains the goal beyond the limits of contingent communal reasoning and understanding and is rooted in the object of inquiry that exists in its own right.[31] Yet Christian doctrine is substantial if not finished and its classic texts reflect a choir of many voices which together have a formative effect on new generations of Christians living in different and varied situations.[32] Doctrine therefore represents truth on the way rather than an abstract certitude outside of time and place.

Friendship and the Ordinary

Listening to the other and refusing to be self-referential are therefore fundamental markers of the church, particularly in its Anglican expression. As Jeff Astley argues, this means that the church should listen to the faith of ordinary disciples with the same respect as it accords to trained theologians and ministers. These ordinary disciples are the majority of Christians who have received no formal

---

27   Thiselton, *The Hermeneutics of Doctrine*, p. 74.
28   Thiselton, *The Hermeneutics of Doctrine*, pp. 86–8, 101.
29   Thiselton, *The Hermeneutics of Doctrine*, pp. 88–90.
30   Thiselton, *The Hermeneutics of Doctrine*, pp. 127–36.
31   Thiselton, *The Hermeneutics of Doctrine*, pp. 128–9.
32   Thiselton, *The Hermeneutics of Doctrine*, p. 144.

theological training and yet interpret their faith in language and concepts which contribute to the fullness of common worship.[33] This practical contextual form of theology emerges through reflection upon action.[34] It is a wisdom theology of response formed through participating in the practices of discipleship.[35] In short practice comes before conscious faith revealing that theology is a way of life, a habitus, rather than simply an intellectual activity or emotive feeling. As such, ordinary theology underwrites the patristic conviction that theology is primarily contemplation rather than speculation.[36] Indeed Anglicans learn their theology through their prayers which are the offering of ordinary life to God within the context of public common worship. Such theology is about performance, is lay and is relatively tentative. It is kneeling theology which theologises about conventional, customary and common religion.[37] It is therefore different from clerical theology and challenges clergy to teach the faith in ways that enable ordinary disciples to voice their own theological insights. What is clear is that this is significant and meaningful theology since it represents churchgoers' views of their salvation and the way they understand their lives before God.[38] Inevitably the subterranean character of this ordinary theology makes it a challenge to get hold of and therefore to understand.[39] However, as Gadamer has shown, the way to understand the human life world is to look and listen to how the language works.[40] Practices indicate convictions. Often these will appear incoherent or too biographical yet, as we have noted, Anglicans recognise the fruitfulness of narrative as a way of understanding their stories. If ordinary theology is less critical than academic theology is comfortable with, then this challenges its critics to greater patience and a careful listening to the embedded wisdom present in these testimonies. Understanding is the responsibility of the whole community, which needs to listen to those who speak in unconventional ways. Yet this surely reflects the pastoral character of Anglican mission, which listens before beginning a conversation about the things of God. Anglican

---

[33] Jeff Astley, *Ordinary Theology: Looking, Listening and Learning in Theology* (Aldershot: Ashgate, 2002). See also Jeff Astley and Leslie J. Francis, *Exploring Ordinary Theology: Everyday Christian Believing and the Church* (Farnham: Ashgate, 2013).

[34] Astley, *Ordinary Theology*, p. 2.

[35] Astley, *Ordinary Theology*, p. 34.

[36] Astley, *Ordinary Theology*, p. 54.

[37] Astley, *Ordinary Theology*, p. 72, 93.

[38] Astley, *Ordinary Theology*, p. 66.

[39] Astley, *Ordinary Theology*, p. 70.

[40] Astley, *Ordinary Theology*, p. 112–3.

theology is predominantly ordinary theology, the 'sensus fidelium', a theology of a community open to the world.[41]

Friendship and Congregational Listening

Although Anglican churches are normally parochially structured, congregations are important signs of the grace of God in ordinary life. Indeed, as we have already noted, Bernice Martin asserts, 'sociologically a distinctive aspect of Anglican congregational life is the way that it manifests itself in the mundane local networks of social relationships and associational sympathies, and their subsequent realisation are to be found in the networks of face-to-face relations as exemplified in the local life of a parish'.[42] Consequently Anglican ministry is not ideological but interpretative, helping people make sense of their life in relation to God.[43] Thus ways of working with congregations need to be appropriate rather than standard, since the latter de-contextualises them, is theoretical and instrumental rather than hermeneutical and relational.[44] One fruitful way of achieving this involves a narrative approach since this enables us to see how the Bible becomes storied in the life of a given congregation and how its memory is embedded in its habits and rituals.[45] It pays attention with a loving rather than an arrogant eye.[46] It recognises that congregations are ecclesial cultures or texts which need to be sensitively read if they are to be understood.[47] Thus in her work on contemporary congregations, Helen Cameron discerns five ecclesial cultural forms: first, the parish as a public utility; second, the gathered congregation as a voluntary organisation; third, the small group church akin to book groups or party plan; fourth, the 'third place church' inhabiting secular spaces such as a café church; and fifth, the magnet church, which creates safe spaces in which children, young people and families can follow the Christian way.[48] Through such attention to the character and stories of congregations we learn how faith

---

[41]　　Astley, *Ordinary Theology*, p.161.

[42]　　Matthew Guest, Karin Tusting and Linda Woodhead, *Congregational Studies in the UK: Christianity in a Post-Christian Context* (Aldershot: Ashgate, 2005), p. 60.

[43]　　Guest, *Congregational Studies*, p. 68.

[44]　　Guest, *Congregational Studies*, pp. 139–49.

[45]　　Helen Cameron et al. (eds), *Studying Local Churches: A Handbook* (London: SCM, 2005), pp. 47–9.

[46]　　Cameron, *Studying Local Churches*, p. 221.

[47]　　Helen Cameron, *Resourcing Mission: Practical Theology for Changing Churches* (London: SCM, 2010), pp. 20–22.

[48]　　Cameron, *Resourcing Mission*, pp. 23, 148–51.

is interpreted across a wide range of contexts and a wide canvas of human experience. They reveal the distributed nature of Anglican witness. Furthermore, as Malcolm Grundy and Richard Impey have argued, listening to the wisdom of the congregation enables each congregation to discern its mission and identify appropriate leadership. This prevents clergy imposing abstract agendas upon congregations and ensures that future plans are owned by the congregation as a whole.[49] Congregations are healthy if all involved appreciate the particular dynamics which size, history, disposition and diversity generate.[50] This requires external facilitation, listening and mutual respect in order to enable all to own the outcomes of this process and become agents of mission rather than simply pawns of clerical ambition. In the process of mutual listening congregations clarify which of four different purposes they are most drawn to: worship and service, worship and fellowship, worship and campaigning or simply worship.[51] Each purpose will impact on the organisation of the congregation, the way people feel they belong and the sort of leadership they need. Where there are clashes within a community about its purposes, careful consultancy can expose and develop strategies to respond to them. However some divisions may be unresolvable within one congregation, since these purposes reflect deeply held outlooks about faith and life.[52] Listening, however, can be particularly fruitful when appointing new clergy, since it can disclose whether there is enough common agreement for fruitful working. All of this is rooted in the notion of wisdom as a communal, contingent, contextual grasp of how to live before God.[53] Understanding how to engage in the mission of God is something we discern together through careful listening to the Spirit within the situatedness of a congregation's life and circumstance. It is a dimension of common worship and community living. There is no spectator or singular view and so the process is inevitably conflictual and contestable. To be part of the church is to be part of such a community and is why baptism determines belonging rather than private choice or interest group decisions. This situatedness also reminds us that Anglican mission is about territory and faithful conversation.[54] Hence

---

[49] See Malcolm Grundy, *Understanding Congregations: A New Shape for the Local Church* (London: Mowbray, 1998) and Richard Impey, *How to Develop Your Local Church: Working with the Wisdom of the Congregation* (London: SPCK, 2010).

[50] Grundy, *Understanding Congregations*, pp. 23–4; and Impey, *How to Develop Your Local Church*, pp. xii, xiv–xv, 16–30.

[51] Impey, *How to Develop Your Local Church*, pp. 34–6, 39–40.

[52] Impey, *How to Develop Your Local Church*, pp. 56–67.

[53] Impey, *How to Develop Your Local Church*, pp. 117–33.

[54] Timothy Jenkins, *An Experiment in Providence: How Faith Engages with the World* (London: SPCK, 2006), p. 23.

buildings and saints matter as resources for communal memory and to indicate the significance of place.[55] 'Holiness is built into the story of a place so that the Christian community can be built up in faith by association with it'.[56] Church buildings are therefore signs and symbolic places for parishes, not simply utilities for congregations.[57] They help to combine the Christian story with the local community's story and remind Christians that their discipleship is necessarily rooted in a place as well as a community. [58]

Friendship and Attentive Living

As mentioned above, hermeneutics, or the way we interpret, is a form of attentive listening rather than a theory or method. It is the way we understand others in the contingencies of life. This informs the ethos of life and, for Anglican Christians, this ethos witnesses to the distinctive character of the attentive friendship of God. Thus Samuel Wells argues that Christian ethics integrates ways of listening, grasping local stories, being present to people and the practices of Anglican worship. This has particular impact when trying to understand the distinctive ethos or witness of an Anglican congregation in an inner urban parish.[59] Such witness is the embodiment of God's friendship expressed in the practical living of Christian congregations in ways which are responsive to differing contexts. This is how an ancient faith can continue to represent itself in changing situations.[60] In so doing the Christian story and the practices of the church shape and empower Christians to become improvisers of their faith and thereby keep the story going. [61] Hence the Bible is not so much a script as a set of training resources to shape the habits and practices of a community. Christian ethics is therefore about forming habits rather than giving us rules or calculating outcomes.[62] Such habits inform the imaginative resources of Christians,

---

[55]   Jenkins, *An Experiment in Providence*, p. 33.

[56]   John Inge, *A Christian Theology of Place* (Aldershot: Ashgate, 2003), p. 84.

[57]   Inge, *A Christian Theology of Place*, p. 114.

[58]   Inge, *A Christian Theology of Place*, pp. 118, 131

[59]   Mark Thiessen Nation and Samuel Wells., *Faithfulness and Fortitude: In Conversation with Stanley Hauerwas* (Edinburgh: T&T Clark, 2000), pp. 117–36.

[60]   Samuel Wells, *God's Companions: Reimagining Christian Ethics* (Blackwells: Oxford, 2006), p.1. and Hauerwas and Wells (eds), *The Blackwell Companion to Christian Ethics*, pp. 14, 44.

[61]   Samuel Wells, *Improvisation: The Drama of Christian Ethics* (London: SPCK, 2004), p. 11.

[62]   Wells, *Improvisation*, p. 12.

enabling them to discern a different future. Thus 'Christian ethics and theatrical improvisation are both about years of steeping in a tradition so that the body is so soaked in practices and perceptions that it trusts itself in community to do the obvious thing'.[63] The outworking of this can involve befriending difficult and dangerous people whose lives are caught up in complex and challenging realities. In such situations being with people signifies God's friendship in Christ more effectively than working for people, working with people or even being for people. Such friendship is characterised by presence, silence, touch, words as signs of the reign of God.[64] It enables Christians to face fear with faith.[65]

This way of keeping the story going coheres with Anglican notions of formation and discipleship. It recognises the importance of regular liturgically shaped gatherings of the Christian community which form congregations to recognise the work and call of the Spirit in contemporary life and its place in the drama of God. It stresses the importance of church-based training if we are to understand our vocation since 'the church's creative energies are largely concerned with preparing its members to respond by habit to unforeseen circumstances'.[66] Since Christian ethics is the outworking of baptism, this involves embedding the memory of the Christian story given at baptism deep within the community's common life through the repetitive practices of worship.[67] Such practices are 'good ways to relate to one another, are honed in community, developed by tradition, learned by apprenticeship and embodied in habit'.[68] The heart of Christian ethics is therefore the local congregation and its ordinary disciples.[69] It is summarised in a conviction that 'God gives his people everything they need to worship him, to be his friends and to eat with him'.[70] It is a liturgically informed ethic in which the liturgy trains Christians in the language of God and enables them to understand how they should live faithful to the story this language narrates.

---

[63] Wells, *Improvisation*, p. 17.

[64] Samuel Wells and Marcia A. Owen, *Living Without Enemies: Being Present in the Midst of Violence* (Downers Grove, Illinois: IVP Books, 2011), pp. 24–6, 58, 65–7.

[65] Samuel Wells, *Be Not Afraid: Facing Fear with Faith* (Grand Rapids, Michigan: Brazos, 2011).

[66] Wells, *Improvisation*, p. 78.

[67] Wells, *Improvisation*, pp. 149, 197.

[68] Wells, *God's Companions*, p. 2.

[69] Wells, *God's Companions*, p. 5.

[70] Wells, *God's Companions*, p. 1.

Conclusion

The church is a community committed to understanding truthfully. This is essential if its mission is to cohere with the agenda of the Spirit. Through careful listening to God and others it learns to hear their voice and begin to understand them. This is in contrast to approaches which assume that it is possible to discern the truth without being part of such communities. It involves listening to ordinary disciples in order to grasp the fuller narrative of God's working in human lives and ensures that this story is publicly told. Listening in this way is about respect for otherness, a respect Anglicans believe to be at the heart of mission and evident in the incarnation. It reflects the self-giving and attentive friendship of God for creation. Such a commitment to listening and respecting the stranger is learned through paying attention to the witness, the stories, practices and performance of very diverse Christian communities. Anglicans do not believe that we can understand God's ways on our own or indeed, as individual congregations, important though these are. We understand as we are in conversation with both the local and catholic community. Yet these conversations are grounded in the tangible practices of gathered communities, who know Christ as friend and are trained in the disciplines of worship to improvise upon Scripture in contemporary life. Understanding, therefore, is something which emerges rather than something we possess. It is embedded in the habits which shape our ethics. It reveals that Anglicans are liturgical charismatics, formed through the disciplines of public worship to be able to improvise within God's mission wherever they find themselves.

Consequently congregational stories illuminate the ongoing story of God in contemporary life. These congregations of the church are part of that catholic community, contemporary and past, performing contemporary improvisations of the divine story as embodied apologetics of the Gospel. Their micro-practices contribute to the mission of God since their embodiment, witness, story, habits, character, hospitality, friendship, memory and improvised performances on the Scriptural script are substantial contributors to the plausibility of the Gospel. Anglican mission involves interpreting the story of God as it is embodied in the Scriptures and in the ambiguous performances of the church, past and present. Congregations are not simply reservoirs for Christian activists, but instantiations of graced life, webbed into a greater story which gives theological significance to their ecclesial practices. As Martyn Percy comments, 'the belief that God is Father, Son and Holy Spirit is not an arid set of directives, but rather a faith that is embedded in a community of praxis that makes beliefs work'.[71] In consequence 'the theological programme ... invites theologians to take more notice of local contextual ecclesial and operant, pastoral practice as primary theological material, rather than such praxis merely being seen as the outcome of discerning and interpreting formal theological or denominational propositions'.[72] Taking notice and listening are ways of respecting the integrity of others that reflects the self-giving love of God in Jesus Christ. They represent a refusal to subsume particulars within an abstract scheme and a commitment to the uniqueness of each human being and their community.

---

[71] Martyn Percy, *Shaping the Church: The Promise of Implicit Theology* (Farnham: Ashgate, 2010), p. 4.

[72] Percy, *Shaping the Church*, p. 14.

Chapter 10

Wise Friendship

Wisdom involves living truthfully and fruitfully within the contingencies of life and is a vital dimension of theology as the Wisdom traditions of both Old and New Testaments disclose. It is also a way of life to which Anglicans feel particularly drawn as we saw in Chapter 5. Wisdom is sceptical about blueprints, abstract theories or utopian dreams, preferring instead to find ways forward which learn from the past but are aware that we always travel into a new country. According to Daniel Hardy, Christian wisdom emerges through a conversation between theology and contemporary knowledge. We learn God's wisdom through the formative rhythms of worship as those on a pilgrimage within a church and world embraced by God's light. This approach binds things together in an age of fragmentation, deeply aware of the interconnectedness and complexity of reality and its relationship with God.[1] It seeks depth in an era seduced by the superficial. It relishes the dynamic character of reality when others seek stability. Using the image of the burning bush, Hardy believes that 'the divine can indwell the world without damaging it or taking it over'.[2] Theology therefore aims to expose the relational activity of the Trinitarian God in scientifically, historically or socially mediated reality, a God who seeks friendship with all that is created.[3] Hardy is therefore committed to the intelligible, integrated and yet demanding character of reality. This is neither confessional theology in the tradition of Karl Barth nor positivist theology in the fashion of religious studies. Rather it is a third way which accepts the positive concerns of confessional theology but is more open and critical, seeking God's liberality in all things. It accepts the openness of religious studies but is concerned with relating truth and practice to God. It embraces the liberal quest for God within the complexities of modern life

---

[1]   David Ford and Dennis Stamps (eds), *Essentials of Christian Community* (Edinburgh: T&T Clark, 1996), p. 3.

[2]   Daniel W. Hardy with Deborah Hardy Ford, Peter Ochs and David Ford, *Wording a Radiance: Parting Conversations on God and the Church* (London: SCM, 2010), pp. 12–36.

[3]   See Patterson's construal of Hardy's 'realism' as perichoretic; God known in relation to human contextuality. This implies the under-determinedness of both creation and the church. Susan Patterson, *Realist Christian Theology in a Postmodern Age* (Cambridge: Cambridge University Press, 1999), pp. 101–6, 141.

but dissents from its turn to the subject and has reservations about contextual theology which dissects where God knits things together.[4] 'Theology is the architecture of life with God' and worship re-locates us in the fundamental activity of God towards humankind in the world so that we can discern blessing in the ordinary stuff of life.[5]

Friendship with Magnificent Complexity

'A Magnificent Complexity: Letting God be God in Church, Society and Creation', captures Hardy's vision of wisdom theology.[6] His fundamental desire is to rescue theology from captivity to the limitations of the human mind or ancient texts. Instead the resources for theology are in church, society and creation.[7] Theology is 'a responsible activity claiming for its comprehension a universal validity – an outward-directed movement toward what is to be known, and an appraisal of it which meets a commitment to universal standards – not an activity of self development'. It is a personal but not subjective or constructivist way of knowing since it uses 'skilled intuition which is open to, and under the control of reality'.[8] Nevertheless knowing involves imagination and participation akin to listening to a complex story. We remain open to what the story is telling us when faced by its ambiguity and diversity, seeking to deepen and enrich our understanding of reality through an ever richer grasp of it. There is therefore an intrinsic relationship with that which is beyond our consciousness, a relationship conditioned by that 'other' rather than being the project of human aspiration. For Hardy the dynamic and dialectical nature of this approach points towards the mystery of Christianity's Trinitarian view of God.[9]

Theology is therefore self-involving, historical and mediated as it emerges through wrestling with the complexities of life.[10] Since God, faith and existence are woven into history and in the specific life of Jesus Christ, theology pays

---

4   Ford and Stamps, *Essentials*, pp. 6–9.
5   Ford and Stamps, *Essentials*, pp. 18–19.
6   Ford and Stamps, *Essentials*, pp. 307–55.
7   For the reparative character of his project see *Wording a Radiance*, p. 23.
8   Daniel W. Hardy, 'Christian Affirmation of the Structure of Personal Life', in Thomas F. Torrance (ed.), *Belief in Science and in Christian Life: The Relevance of Michael Polanyi's Thought for Christian Faith and Life* (Edinburgh: Handsel Press, 1980), p. 72.
9   Torrance, *Belief in Science and in Christian Life*, p. 88.
10   Daniel W. Hardy, 'Today's Word for Today: Gerhard Ebeling', *Expository Times* 93 (Dec 1981), p. 68.

attention to history as well as to the cosmos since history relates us to Christ.[11] 'We must allow the divine realities to declare themselves to us' through correlating the Christian story with the story of science or history.[12] Each assumes the givenness of their object and approaches it 'a posteriori', recognising that God is discerned in and through the process of investigation.[13] This way of discerning God's activity is evident in the common Christian practice of England, or 'the things that are established'.[14] Such common practice is not detached from traditional authorities, such as Scripture and Tradition. Rather it mediates them and thereby allows them to be scrutinised. This ensures that theology is public, since common experience is the experience of the whole rather than of an ecclesial sect. It includes all that modernity has fragmented and segregated through specialisation, such as science, history, the arts, etc. Hardy therefore challenges forms of English theology which have become detached from this common practice in their preference for abstraction, a church focus or academic specialisation in place of engagement across the whole field of human endeavour. Instead the presence of God can be seen in the way ordinary people live, think and pray together and the future for theological research involves 'sensitivity to the vitalities of current thought and life' since commerce with the world inevitably is commerce with the transcendent, the mystery of 'God with us'.[15]

Friendship and Praise

Religion, therefore, cannot be reduced to a subset of human thought or culture.[16] Instead religious and non-religious traditions are an ongoing response to transcendent truth.[17] This response is most explicitly and profoundly active in Christian worship, which is a symphony of 'praise as ... an attempt to cope with

---

[11]   Hardy, 'Today's Word for Today', p. 70.

[12]   Hardy quoting Torrance in 'Thomas F. Torrance' in David F. Ford (ed.), *The Modern Theologians: An Introduction to Christian Theology in the Twentieth Century* (2 vols, Oxford: Blackwell, 1989), vol. 1, p.71.

[13]   Ford, *The Modern Theologians*, vol. 1, p. 73.

[14]   Ford, *The Modern Theologians*, vol. 2, pp. 30–71 and Daniel W. Hardy, *God's Ways with the World* (Edinburgh: T & T Clark, 1996), pp. 279–91.

[15]   Hardy, *God's Ways*, pp. 42–6.

[16]   John Hull (ed.), *New Directions in Religious Education* (Lewes: The Falmer Press, 1982), p. 111.

[17]   Hull, *New Directions*, p. 115.

the abundance of God's love'.[18] Praise is the creative logic of overflow, freedom and generosity which perfects perfection.[19] Worship acknowledges God as most fundamental to the community and involves 'taking up the whole of reality into praise of God'.[20] Praise is the way the Christian community understands God as adequately as possible since it affirms the interaction of God with the world. Indeed 'the core of astonishment around which it all spirals is that God is free to be involved with His creation from the 'inside' as well as from the "outside"'.[21] Christian wisdom, therefore, explores the transcendentally sustained character of reality, its theological pregnancy and how worship and the presence of redeemed sociality illuminate this. Worship is defined by God's movement towards us and positions us in the presence of truth.[22] The divine always reaches beyond itself in order to establish a relationship between creation, society and the church. Consequently relationship is at the heart of the divine agenda.[23] The call of the church in worship is to sing into existence the multi-braided reality in which we live.[24] The political role of the church is to 'provide a more concrete manifestation of what ... [social life] might mean for human affairs in general'.[25] This redeemed sociality, or the transformation of people into fullness of life, is the aspiration of all social life. It therefore implies a co-ordination of purpose between church and general society, since both share this common goal of contributing to a true society and both must guard against the reductionist simplifications of modernity represented in collectives, individualism or a belief that God is disengaged from the world.[26] Sociality, though it has varied expressions, still integrates broader societal hopes with ecclesial ones. It is not located in the apostolicity of the church but in how God is active and present in creation, a presence which expresses itself in ever richer unfoldings of society.[27] Redeemed sociality therefore is a qualitatively richer expression of the inherent sociality present in creation, a drawing out of the truth present in creation.[28] The

---

[18]   Daniel W. Hardy and David F. Ford, *Jubilate: Theology in Praise* (London: Darton, Longman and Todd, 1984), p. 1.
[19]   Hardy and Ford, *Jubilate*, pp. 6–8.
[20]   Hardy and Ford, *Jubilate*, p. 48.
[21]   Hardy and Ford, *Jubilate*, p. 81.
[22]   Hardy, *God's Ways*, p. 12.
[23]   Hardy, *God's Ways*, p. 16.
[24]   Hardy, *God's Ways*, p. 37.
[25]   Hardy, *God's Ways*, p. 174.
[26]   Hardy, *God's Ways*, p. 176.
[27]   Hardy, *God's Ways*, pp. 193–4.
[28]   Hardy, *God's Ways*, p. 206.

challenge to the churches is to promote what is good in social life rooted in the deepest awareness of the truth of God's work in all human life.[29]

Friendship and the English Church

The church in England has a special vocation in this regard since it is historically embedded in English society. It should therefore continue to be 'immersed in the devices and means by which the public sustains itself' rather than being tempted to follow the American tradition of withdrawal or of European idealism.[30] In so doing the church in England will sustain the unique character of English society in which the institutions of government, law and church foster the common good.[31] This is goodness realised through tested practice within the complexities of society rather than through abstract rationality. The gathered church, therefore, points society at large to its proper identity, destiny and source in God. Its mission is to show communities, nations and international life their own true life, since 'the social life of people is actually a direct manifestation of God's work amongst them and their response to it'.[32] The Church of England in particular has a unique vocation since it is not a confessional church nor simply a witness or sacrament. Rather, as an 'ecumenical' church with a variety of ideas of church within itself, it embodies faith as wisdom. It displays social life as life lived by participating as a united, resourced and engaged community in God.[33] Worship, ministry and common life incorporate ordinary life into God's continuing work. Thus 'Anglicanism ideally follows a distinctive pattern in which the gift of God in Jesus Christ is embodied in worship, wisdom and service in an historical continuity of contextually sensitive mission'.[34] It is a movement directed by and to the holiness of God forming communities of holy trust, whose mission seeks the incorporation of all into comprehensive fulfilment in God.[35] For Anglicans this is a fallible, historical journey very different from the ontological approach of Roman Catholicism, the mystical approach of Orthodoxy and the actualist approach of Reformed Christianity. Anglicans are more pragmatic. They take things as they find them and work in relation to them. They value moderation

---

[29] Hardy, *God's Ways*, p. 207.
[30] Hardy, *God's Ways*, p. 209.
[31] Daniel W. Hardy, *Finding the Church* (London: SCM, 2001), pp. 62–75.
[32] Hardy, *God's Ways*, p. 217.
[33] Hardy, *God's Ways*, pp. 218–9 and Hardy, *Finding the Church*, pp. 81–93.
[34] Hardy, *Finding the Church*, p. 2.
[35] Hardy, *Finding the Church*, pp. 19–25.

and participation, gathering and working with others on the ground. They live within their historical context, walk with Jesus and wait for change to come. In short, Anglicans take the long view of history as a context of God's activity. They seek witness, openness and embrace rather than conquest and triumph.[36] For Anglicans the church is a history of God's activity which is open and self-extending.[37] It does not exist for its own benefit but to show a godly form of social life to the world as a way of healing the social life of that world.[38] As Hardy comments, 'I wish to give greater prominence to the interweaving of national, political and legal issues with those of religious conviction and identity'.[39] Such a mission is sympathetic to ecumenical engagement as a way of embodying and respecting distinctiveness as well as reflecting the ecumenical and provisional character of the Church of England itself.[40]

The church therefore has an important educational role in society because its life dramatically exemplifies a rich social vocation for the world.[41] It is a church of collegial friendship, characterised by abduction, attraction and fullness.[42] The church itself is educated as its desires and affections are abducted (drawn to) and re-orientated by the light of God.[43] In this abduction the church becomes a pilgrim society which expresses and opens up the way of God. Through this Christians slowly discover their vocation and identity in the work of God.[44] Hardy uses the word 'granulate' to describe this 'inside-out' healing.[45] The church, therefore, represents a hermeneutic of wisdom, distilled through reflection on history, which unpacks the dense content of reality whose truth is found in the praise of God.[46] This was the agenda of Paul as he discovered the presence of Christ and his transformative wisdom in the materiality of the world itself.[47] The world and the church have the signs of God's life within them.[48] As living wisdom the church

---

[36]   Hardy et al., *Wording a Radiance,* pp. 76–8.
[37]   Hardy et al., *Wording a Radiance*, pp. 31–3.
[38]   Hardy, *God's Ways*, p. 225.
[39]   Ford and Stamps, *Essentials*, p. 335.
[40]   Hardy, *Finding the Church*, pp. 135, 159.
[41]   Hardy, *Finding the Church*, p. 244.
[42]   Hardy et al., *Wording a Radiance*, p. 111.
[43]   Hardy et al., *Wording a Radiance*, pp. 42–7.
[44]   Hardy et al., *Wording a Radiance*, pp. 58–61.
[45]   Hardy et al., *Wording a Radiance*, p. 64.
[46]   Hardy, *God's Ways*, pp. 244–6.
[47]   Hardy, *God's Ways*, p. 251.
[48]   Hardy, *Finding the Church*, p. 213.

displays the inter-wovenness of the world, humanity and God.[49] In the pursuit of wisdom it uncovers how things are ordered in relation to each other and to God. It therefore locates everything within the larger whole of God's creation and regards human knowledge as infused with the goodness of this creation and properly subjected to the Good. Truth combined with the Good equates to wisdom which is the life of God immersed in the goodness of the created world.[50] To be wise is to find the 'balance' of things, the right point in the relationships of the self, others, world and God. Given the disruption of reality which we call sin, the challenge of uncovering the self-sustaining character of wisdom is a struggle and requires finding God's ways in the midst of this disruption.[51] This is what the incarnation represents. Through it we are brought into a relationship with the one responsible for the order of creation. Wisdom therefore brings everything into the light of God. It seeks the common good in a way which the academy has abdicated from pursuing. Indeed 'religion is the binding of all into wisdom'.[52] It sees coherence between the dynamism of the world and the dynamism of God.[53] Hence ecclesiology is 'the activity of assembling all that needs to be assembled to promote the fullness of human society'.[54] Spirituality is also a form of wisdom, since our spiritual exercises are always undertaken living in particular situations and within particular fellowships so that we can live as whole people where we are.[55]

Thus theology recognises and searches for the dynamic presence of God in the world and its history.[56] God is to be found in the ordinary world of human relations and the truth of history is found within the particularity of the past, the 'knots of history' rather than in the mind of the historian.[57] The Bible is not an exhaustive account of God's engagement in history but indicates the way God deals with the world particularly seen in the incarnation.[58] Religion is not simply human experience but reflects the dynamic structures of reality beyond the human mind. Theology must therefore rediscover the pivotal place of

---

[49] For what follows see Daniel W. Hardy, 'The Grace of God and Earthly Wisdom', in Stephen C. Barton (ed.), *Where Shall Wisdom be Found? Wisdom in the Bible, the Church and the Contemporary World* (Edinburgh: T&T Clarke, 1999), pp. 231–47.

[50] Hardy, *Finding the Church,* p. 219.

[51] Hardy, *Finding the Church*, p. 52.

[52] Hardy, *Finding the Church*, p. 46.

[53] Hardy, *Finding the Church*, p. 59.

[54] Hardy et al., *Wording a Radiance*, p. 70.

[55] Hardy et al., *Wording a Radiance*, pp. 110–13.

[56] Hardy, *God's Ways*, pp. 311–17.

[57] Hardy, *God's Ways*, pp. 275–7.

[58] Ford and Stamps, *Essentials*, pp. 328–35.

worship in order that the 'transcendental notes of being', unity, truth, goodness and beauty, may be raised to their zenith in the vitality of God.[59] The movement of the transcendent yet immanent reality of God is the primary determinant of everything since 'the proper content of worship, of community and of ethics is established by the One who is worshipped, who is remembered through the tradition and anticipated in our midst'.[60] These traditions are only a defence against a-historical accounts of truth and morality in so far as they are rooted in and nourished by the worship of God.[61] Yet such tradition is the wisdom which represents the outcome of the Christian community's digestive process of sifting and gradating the multiple ways God relates to creation.[62]

Friendship and the Face

Since wisdom involves respecting the richness of the particular, it pays careful attention to the uniqueness of each person and resists conflating distinctions within generalisations. For David Ford worship and wisdom belong together since worship is an ongoing attention to God within the contingencies of created living which orientates the believer and enables them to make Christian judgements. 'Praise, worship and blessing are the key relationship within which to know God and … the most helpful dynamic through which to appreciate the "ecology" of God, people and the rest of creation in interaction'.[63] Worship generates the Eucharistic self, the self 'orientated towards Jesus Christ and other people'.[64] It forms 'communities of the face' who are open to the stranger whose face is a reminder of the particularity, uniqueness and irreducibility of each human being.[65] Living in the shadow of the Enlightenment and the Shoah or Holocaust, Christians in Europe need to resist the faceless and totalising self which dehumanises people and allows them to be exploited and even exterminated.[66] Instead they should embody a hospitable self, which sees others not as threats but as those we trust and pay attention to.[67] The other person is not

---

[59]   Hardy, *God's Ways*, p. 308.
[60]   Ford and Stamps, *Essentials*, p. 313.
[61]   Ford and Stamps, *Essentials* (1996), p. 312.
[62]   Ford and Stamps, *Essentials* (1996), p. 319.
[63]   Ford and Stamps, *Essentials* (1996), p. 5.
[64]   David F. Ford, *Self and Salvation: Being Transformed* (Cambridge: CUP, 1999), p. 10.
[65]   Ford, *Self and Salvation*, p. 23.
[66]   Ford, *Self and Salvation*, pp. 21, 47.
[67]   Ford, *Self and Salvation*, p. 89.

lost sight of or squeezed into our own self-image. Their otherness is respected and befriended. What enables us to be in communion is worship since here we discover our liturgical self which is a communal singing self and a Eucharistic self shaped in the image of Christ, since to worship the face of Jesus is to be faced by Jesus.[68]

Friendship and Learning

This vision of a worshipping, wise church has implications for the church as a learning community since the way the church learns informs what it learns.[69] Rooted in the wisdom traditions of the Old Testament, Christians learning involves an intense communal conversation between Scripture and society. This interweaving of sacred and secular, of Jerusalem and Athens, displays the character of Christian wisdom. It reflects a high view of the church and of communication. For Anglicans, following Hooker, it shows that learning is an ongoing journey since it takes place within the contingencies of history. There is no absolute vantage point but only settlement after settlement. Wisdom, therefore, acts as a counterweight to the instrumental and calculative forms of knowledge which dominate contemporary society.[70] These lack the capacity to form communities and discern overall meaning for living. In contrast, wisdom enables Christians to engage in an ongoing interpretation of life with God, or a continual reading of Scripture.[71] This approach is rooted in a theology of desire and discernment, the love of wisdom and wise loving, which seeks to learn in the Spirit. Churches therefore become schools of desire and wisdom in which Christians learn to love God for God's sake displaying 'a wisdom of worship, prayer and discerning desire that is committed to God and the kingdom of God'.[72] Indeed 'the theological wisdom of faith is grounded in being affirmed, being commanded, being questioned and searched, being surprised and opened by new possibilities, and being desired and loved'.[73] For Christians living in

---

[68]   Ford, *Self and Salvation*, pp. 120–30, 192–211.

[69]   The following paragraph is from my notes taken at the Bishop of Sheffield's Shrove Tuesday Lectures, David Ford, 'Learning the Faith' (unpublished) on 7 March 2000.

[70]   David Ford, *Christian Wisdom: Desiring God and Learning Love* (Cambridge: Cambridge University Press, 2007), p. 1.

[71]   Ford, *Christian Wisdom*, p. 2.

[72]   Ford, *Christian Wisdom*, p. 3.

[73]   Ford, *Christian Wisdom*, p. 5.

the west this is an approach which refuses to divide sacred and secular.[74] It is about learning through the secular and yet challenges the latter to recall its religious roots.[75] Education is therefore about transformation rather than simply systematic information.[76]

This invitation to continual reading of Scripture is evident in the way Ford engages with the wisdom cries in Luke-Acts, John, Job and Paul under the impact of the Shoah on western Christian thought. It is also what drives Scriptural reasoning with other Abrahamic faiths. Both approaches evoke a desire for wisdom. In Luke wisdom is seen in the way the story of Jesus and the early church is told.[77] This story shows wisdom cries to be pleas for discernment of God's action in life. They indicate that Christians discover wisdom in and through the contingencies of life rather than through abstract speculation.[78] Discipleship is therefore a historic journey of developing insight and learning in which tradition functions as a guide to help us see Scripture as a resource infused by the Spirit. This dynamic approach to interpretation points to new ways forward exemplified, for example, in the midrashic reading of Genesis 1 in the Prologue to John's Gospel.[79] Here is an example of how to interpret Scripture 'centred on the intensities of local living and face to face relationships while having a global vision of God's purposes and the responsibilities these inspire'.[80] Hence wise interpretation involves the practice of re-reading older texts as can be seen elsewhere in the Old and New Testaments. This re-reading is not arbitrary because it is done before God in the company of other Christians and is tested by its transformative outcomes. In this way Scripture actually grows its readers through the interaction of community (past and present) and texts.[81] Like Job this involves searching for wisdom in the most trying of circumstances in which loving God for nothing emerges through the testing and sifting of discipleship. Reading Job in the light of the Shoah follows the restorative tradition of remembering and repair exemplified by Ezra the scribe.[82] The story of Jesus also has affinities with Job since it involves the transformation of desire into a God-

---

[74]   Ford, *Christian Wisdom*, p. 9.

[75]   David F. Ford, *The Future of Theology* (Chichester: Wiley-Blackwell, 2011), pp. 43–7.

[76]   Ford, *Christian Wisdom*, p. 12.

[77]   Ford, *Christian Wisdom*, p. 43.

[78]   Ford, *Christian Wisdom*, p. 50.

[79]   Ford, *Christian Wisdom*, pp. 53–8.

[80]   Ford, *Christian Wisdom*, p. 62.

[81]   Ford, *Christian Wisdom*, p. 69.

[82]   Ford, *Christian Wisdom*, pp. 139, 147.

centred wisdom since both live and die for God's sake.[83] Similarly in Corinthians Paul speaks of the maturing of faith through living wisdom Christology.[84] All of this helps the church to discover wisdom in worship, a hallowing of the name of God whatever the cost. Furthermore Luke-Acts shows that improvisation is possible beyond any precedents in the life of Jesus as the church reads the whole council of Scripture in dialogue with others.[85] Meaning, or the quest of wisdom, emerges through discussion as Christians re-read the tradition in the light of contemporary challenges.[86] Singing is a particular expression of this since as it sings a culture remembers, takes to heart, indwells and communicates its most passionate cries.

The church, therefore, is to be a school of desire and wisdom exhibiting the four marks of the church. It is a school of desire for unity grounded in Walter Kasper's idea of responsible receptivity. It seeks to be a school of desire for holiness in its worship, prayer and penitence. It is a school for catholicity which includes all sections of humankind. It is a school of desire for apostolicity as it continues to articulate the authentic and authoritative teachings of the apostles. As such, Christian theology rejects the modern university's divorce of knowledge and love.[87] It is also open to the insights of those beyond its core community since Scriptural reasoning with Jews and Muslims is about friendship rather than consensus. Equally it ensures that theology remains in the public square, contesting an imperialist secularism in favour of greater plurality and reminding secularism that it is but one tradition among many and not the most influential nor resourceful for making sense of contemporary life. Such friendship is most evident when learning with disabled people, such as those in the L'Arche communities. Here friendship enables strangers to discover each other's wisdom and thereby educate one another.[88]

Conclusion

Hardy and Ford are Anglicans whose theology is situated within this English tradition. They seek God's wisdom in the interaction of Scripture, theology and human knowledge. They remind us that all human knowing is limited and

---

83 Ford, *Christian Wisdom*, p. 159.
84 Ford, *Christian Wisdom*, pp. 186–7.
85 Ford, *Christian Wisdom*, pp. 202–7.
86 Ford, *Christian Wisdom*, p. 227.
87 Ford, *Christian Wisdom*, p. 269.
88 Ford, *Christian Wisdom*, pp. 350–71.

fallible. They show why it is necessary to belong to conversational communities with a robust tradition of practice and reflection if we are to approach the bright mystery of God's truth in the world and share this mystery with others. They also show us why this quest emerges through the practice of Christian worship. For Ford, the church is a 'piece of humanity where Christ really has taken form'.[89] In this way he and Hardy reflect their Anglicanism, a way of faith which recognises that we learn how to follow Christ as church within the limitations of created life and its history. It is a form of life which seeks to weave together rather than divide, which is dynamic and open to new insights and which is capacious and porous. At its best this has been and remains the character of the Church of England. It is an embedded mission befriending the complexity of society and reality. It is a church which seeks to discern how Christ may take form in English society today with a wisdom which refuses simplistic idealism or pragmatism. Instead it seeks for God's Spirit within all that we are part of, confident that this is God's good creation and that God wills our good. Some might argue that this sort of Anglican wisdom is too easily accommodated to the agenda of the world; that this wisdom is conciliatory rather than critical. Yet wisdom is about love, about the benevolence of God towards creation. The patient work of wisdom refuses simplistic approaches to reality. It is a theology for the long haul which respects the gift and complexity of creation and the mystery of God. In a culture saturated with the excesses of commercial competition and the seductions of military power, both of which have brought western societies to the brink of disaster, a wise and patient form of life has many attractions.

---

[89]   Ford, *The Future of Theology*, p. 114.

PART III
Challenge

Chapter 11

Social Friendship

November is now one of the more religious months in the English calendar. Remembrance Day and Remembrance Sunday seem to be the nearest thing our society has to a corporate lament. The three days of All Hallows tide (Halloween, All Hallows (All Saints) and All Souls) preceding this also focus on reflective memory and the fragility of human existence even in the midst of American 'trick or treat'. It is a sort of Advent season before Advent. Yet it also shows the latent presence of religion in popular culture as themes of death, suffering, fragility, darkness, evil and contingency look for *religio*, some sort of connecting together or re-membering, which gives these themes meaning. Churches try to do this through symbolic ritual and this is appropriate since, as Chief Rabbi Jonathan Sacks has argued, a key task of religion is to make meaning. 'Science takes things apart to see how they work. Religion puts things together to see what they mean'.[1] This is an ambiguous vocation as popular piety and organised religion meet in a space which neither controls completely. Yet the very orientation of the season towards the church or even the churchyard, reflects a deeper connection to religion and Christianity than is recognised by secularist sceptics and some Christians. As Timothy Jenkins argues, it is vital to learn the language of popular culture if the character of its religiosity is to be understood.[2] In contemporary society it is easy to assume that the secular, popularly understood as the autonomy of politics and its freedom from religious control, implies the absence of the divine from public life. Ironically noisy secularists and even some Christians collude with this secularisation thesis to convince society that much of England is godless.[3] Yet as will be apparent below, the picture is not so clear cut as this suggests. Certainly for Christians the resurrection reveals that Jesus is Lord of the whole of creation. Everywhere is God's territory and this notion of divinely inhabited space is at the heart of Anglican mission vision captured in

---

[1]   Jonathan Sacks, *The Great Partnership: God, Science and the Search for Meaning* (London: Hodder & Stoughton Ltd, 2011), p. 2.

[2]   Timothy Jenkins, *Religion in English Everyday Life: An Ethnographic Approach* (Oxford: Berghahn Books, 1999).

[3]   Alan Billings, *Lost Church: Why We Must Find it Again* (London: SPCK, 2012), p. 38.

the meaning of parish. As John Inge and Philip Sheldrake have pointed out, such parish space is in fact about place, a named space with meaning and history.[4] Parishes are places with a mission history as well as a mission challenge. They represent a story about God's work with this particular group of people. They symbolise the claim of Christ to the whole of England. Furthermore, as Mark's Gospel indicates, Jesus' mission involved the crowds as well as the disciples. Many of the crowds did not become disciples but Jesus still shared blessing with them. This too is the essence of parish mission. Congregations have a mission to all the crowds of the parish, praying that some may consciously discover the love and grace of Christ for themselves and be drawn into the discipleship community of the church. Hence it is important to be present among all communities in our society in order to witness to this and to contest the secularist myth.[5]

The Secular and Society

So what has led to the popular view that secularism is the default view of North Atlantic societies? The thinker who has done most to explore this question is Charles Taylor in his magisterial work, *A Secular Age*.[6] According to Taylor, institutional life within North Atlantic societies, such as England, is no longer publicly accountable to God and the Christian story in anything more than formal terms. Religious practice has declined significantly and belief in God is contested rather than assumed. The religious square is now a plural space with different faith traditions competing for attention and popular culture increasingly focuses on the here and now rather than the hereafter. So for the first time in human history these societies function on the basis of a purely self-sufficient and exclusive humanism without reference to any reality beyond this. Human flourishing no longer acts as a rationale for religion. This new world has emerged through a story of disenchantment following the rise of the natural sciences and the formation of what Taylor calls the isolated 'buffered self'

---

[4]   See John Inge, *A Christian Theology of Place* (Aldershot: Ashgate, 2003) and Philip Sheldrake, *Spaces for the Sacred: Place, Memory and Identity* (Baltimore, Maryland: The John Hopkins University Press, 2001).

[5]   For a summary of the secular debate see David Martin, *On Secularisation: towards a Revised General Theory* (Aldershot: Ashgate, 2005) and David Herbert, *Religion and Civil Society: Re-thinking Public Religion in the Contemporary World* (Aldershot, Ashgate, 2000) pp. 29–59.

[6]   Charles Taylor, *A Secular Age* (London: Belknap Harvard, 2007).

which locates meaning and self-control in the mind rather than in the beyond.[7] In this it contrasts with pre-modern identity which was communal, porous and anxious about being colonised by alien powers.[8] Ironically Christianity contributed to the development of the buffered self as monastic perfectionism together with the Reformation's 'rage for order' and focus on individual piety overwhelmed a more relaxed communal practice of faith, contributed to the rise of totalitarianism and gradually led to the disconnection between popular piety and formal religion. As science spoke more about universe than cosmos, nature rather than creation, popular understanding of the world changed from seeing it as a divinely infused place to an empty space.[9] The deconstruction of medieval sacramentalism by the Reformers also acted as an engine for disenchantment, as did the stress upon faith in ordinary life. Together they contributed both to a more disciplined society enforced by the increasing power of the nation state and to a sense that human agency, articulated in the protestant work ethic, was responsible for shaping life.[10] Cartesian rationalism was the logical outworking of this as the lonely self reasoned and willed its way through life as a disembedded identity seeking its own freedom. It is what the philosopher Roger Scruton calls a 'culture of desecration'.[11]

Yet ironically this very freedom had to be controlled by a state comprised of equally independent individuals. Thus with individualism emerged the collectivism of the powerful state which used concepts, such as 'the people' or 'society' to bind society together in ways which replaced fractious religious communities following the Wars of Religion. God was now put on trial and required to give account of divine activity in the universe or remain a distant deist deity. Humankind was judge and jury. Flourishing was the goal of these new collectivist states, which despite the horrors of the French Revolution and the wars of the twentieth century, seemed able to offer their citizens a more reliable quality of life than the churches as science and industrial production combined to deliver the good life, at least to the affluent classes. Truth no longer required participation in the practices of a religious tradition. Instead it could be found through abstract thought or experiment leading to an excarnational spectator approach to knowledge.[12] Meaning and purpose were no longer seen as inherent

---

[7] Taylor, *A Secular Age*, p. 25–7.

[8] Taylor, *A Secular Age*, p. 35.

[9] Taylor, *A Secular Age*, p. 58.

[10] Taylor, *A Secular Age*, pp. 102, 118, 124.

[11] Roger Scruton, *A Political Philosophy: Arguments for Conservatism* (London: Continuum, 2006), p. 133.

[12] Taylor, *A Secular Age*, p. 335.

within creation but were imposed by human thought, agency and will upon an otherwise meaningless universe. This view of reality was disseminated by secular education whose advocates were not necessarily sympathetic to religious conviction.[13] Consequently this story became the standard view bolstered by an expressive individualism and collectivism which acted as a channel for human emotion. Both contested the demands of religious formation and questioned the moral value of suffering. Thus spirituality has now taken the place of religion as the language of transcendence, a very subjectivist approach reflecting a consumerist 'pic n mix' and therapeutic approach to truth.[14] In addition the British synthesis of 'British means decent means Christian' has broken down and more authoritarian religious approaches appear to do well in this new world because they offer insecure individuals clear guidance about all dimensions of life. In contrast more liberal traditions tend to fare worse, since their approaches are less prescriptive and consequently less disciplined. What this means is that committed religious practice represents an increasingly alien form of life in these parts of the world. The USA may remain something of an exception, since its settlement and political traditions fostered a very different, more voluntarist approach to religion which until recently has managed to generate much more robust congregational participation than in Europe.[15] For Taylor, religion, particularly Christianity, therefore will only survive if it can recover confidence in its great story and its capacity to engage creatively and contingently with the possibility of transformation and peace expressed through other focused *agape* love. This is not about a nostalgic return to Christendom but about improvised performances of life which demonstrate the possibility of participating in the love of the deep reality of God.

To Anglicans in England the arrival of this secular age represents a profound ambiguity. The present shape of the Church of England is inextricably bound up with the Reformation. Yet, as we have seen in Chapter 5, the Reformation in England sought to hold together what was fragmented in Europe. Hence the more catholic sense of common worship within the horizon of a long tradition and memory were retained alongside insights about the primacy of Scripture, the importance of personal piety and the value of sound learning. The English church as a whole was less ideologically driven than its Reformation counterparts in Europe, despite attempts by some sections of it to clarify convictions more explicitly. Common worship rather than a common confession held the English

---

[13]   Taylor, *A Secular Age*, p. 423–4.
[14]   Taylor, *A Secular Age*, p. 618.
[15]   Taylor, *A Secular Age*, p. 523–32.

church together. Yet this very latitudinarian approach has found it difficult to withstand the assaults of the sort of secularism which Taylor outlines. Particularly since World War II the public indicators of Christian practice have all been declining and with this, the perceived impact of the Church of England in society.[16] For many, like Bob Jackson, this reflects the end of Christendom.[17] For Michael Moynagh, this reflects three turns: the ecclesial turn as people, particularly younger women, stop attending church; the ethical turn as the expressivist self overwhelms notions of duty and accountability; and the economic and social turn in which information technology, customising and networks corrode traditional notions of value and belonging upon which the church depended.[18] Yet these changes may not actually imply that England is a secular society in the popular sense, even if it has elements of Charles Taylor's description.[19] David Martin argues that secularisation is a complex and multiple reality across the globe and that the particular way it has emerged in the North Atlantic societies represents an expression of western, Latin, Reformation Christianity.[20] Indeed he argues that some secularisation is intrinsic to Christianity itself as it distinguishes between the world and the Kingdom of God.[21] Consequently he does not accept a Whig interpretation of secularisation which sees it as part of a progressive modernisation narrative. Many societies modernise but do not embrace western secularism, and newer forms of faith, such as Pentecostalism, work with the grain of the secular without being swallowed up by it. Indeed in some ways Pentecostalism represents a very late-modern and capitalist form of faith which has been more successful in attracting the poor than Liberation Theology.[22] Furthermore much sociological thinking is circular since it imposes a pre-existing idea of the secular upon the complexity of reality. In addition the

---

[16] The 2011 census shows 60 per cent of the population claiming Christian allegiance compared with 70 per cent in 2001.

[17] Bob Jackson, *Hope for the Church: Contemporary Strategies for Growth* (London: Church House Publishing, 2002), pp. 61–6.

[18] Michael Moynagh with Philip Harrold, *Church for Every Context: An Introduction to Theology and Practice* (London: SCM, 2012), pp. 73–93.

[19] For example Linda Woodhead, in 'The Quiet Revolution in UK Faith', *Church Times* (10 Feb 2012), p.12, argues that Christianity has mutated into a privatised form of faith with the spirit of re-enchantment evident in pilgrimages, the re-sacralisation of wells, prayer cairns on mountain tops and quests for bodily healing.

[20] Martin, *On Secularisation*, pp. x, 8, and David Martin, *The Future of Christianity: Reflections of Violence and Democracy, Religion and Secularisation* (Farnham: Ashgate, 2011), pp. 105–7.

[21] Martin, *On Secularisation*, p. 3.

[22] Martin, *On Secularisation*, pp. 34–42 and 73.

ideological interests of the rising nineteenth-century professional classes which contested the legitimacy of religious discourse in the public square, the rise of alternative pursuits which rivalled church, such as Sunday sport and Sunday shopping, state control of education and female lifestyle changes have all led to the popular belief in secularisation.[23] Yet the increasing popularity within Europe of more ancient forms of religion such as pilgrimages and festivals which attract more participants than services in church buildings, raise questions about the depth of secularisation. There is no simplistic secularising story.[24] The future of world Christianity is likely to be Pentecostal and in the Global South.[25] However in contexts such as England churches will need to help people recover their lost language through what Martin calls the 'sacramental iconology' of worship and by sharing the story of faith.[26] This means restoring more dramatic and participatory expressions of faith, practices which engage people rather than simply tell them. Faith as a performance of life rather than information about life will be more fruitful.

Vicarious Friendship and Society

Furthermore public manifestations of practice may not be an adequate indicator of the religious views of most English people, particularly given the history of the nation and indeed of Europe as a whole.[27] For example, there is the difference between the rhetoric and practice of faith, the irony of churches which are perceived to have low social significance yet having a high social profile and the way major national events still look to the churches for forms of ritual and meaning.[28] For Grace Davie this is about 'believing without belonging' and challenges the notion of secularisation as the decline of belief. For Alan Billings it is belonging but neither attending nor believing. Such a disposition can also be seen in events such as the *Seeing Salvation Exhibition* in 2000 which saw large attendance rates and written responses, suggesting a latent interest in the Christian story, though not one expressed in traditional

---

[23]   Martin, *The Future of Christianity*, pp. 106–24.
[24]   Martin, *On Secularisation*, p. 53.
[25]   Martin, *The Future of Christianity*, pp. 23, 62–82.
[26]   Martin, *On Secularisation*, p. 176.
[27]   Grace Davie, *Religion in Modern Europe: A Memory Mutates* (Oxford: Oxford University Press, 2000), p. 2.
[28]   Grace Davie, *Religion in Britain Since 1945: Believing without Belonging* (Oxford: Oxford University Press, 1994), p. 1.

ways.[29] Belief does not disappear but changes as diminishing regular practice combined with exposure to a more plural religious landscape generates an informal syncretism even though this is still seen as broadly 'Christian'. People are un-churched rather than secularist.[30] Consumption rather than production dominates their life and consequently religious practice has become a matter of choice rather than of duty.[31] Without a vibrant religious market place like that in the United States, the attraction of Pentecostalism for the poor where welfare states don't exist or the attraction of gatherings among communities such as the African Diaspora, Christianity among the indigenous Europeans, including the English, is seen as a public utility vicariously representing a consenting but not participating majority.[32] Changes in the social landscape, particularly in the case of women, have contributed to this state of affairs making tradition bearing more precarious.[33] Yet although regular Anglican attendance levels dropped by 50 per cent between 1960 and 1985 the parochial system still survives, contact with the broader community continues through the occasional offices and major festivals, and establishment remains a reality.[34] Indeed in terms of social welfare provision, the period between 1980 and the Millennium encouraged an effective re-establishment of the churches since governments saw them as effective deliverers of care particularly in areas of major deprivation.[35] Furthermore support from other faiths for the established church rose during this period since they prefer a benign Anglican establishment to a more robust secular settlement which would be less sympathetic to them because it would marginalise all faiths.[36] Anglican congregations may be smaller and older, with some notable exceptions in suburban and new urban university contexts, yet

[29]   Paul Avis (ed.), *Public Faith? The State of Religious Belief and Practice in Britain* (London: SPCK, 2003), pp. 29–37.

[30]   Davie, *Religion in Britain Since 1945*, p. 48. See also Davie, *Religion in Modern Europe*, p. 8. and Grace Davie, *Europe: The Exceptional Case: Parameters of Faith in the Modern World* (London: Darton, Longman and Todd, 2002), p. 5.

[31]   Davie, *Religion in Britain Since 1945*, pp. 18–21, 194 and Grace Davie, *The Sociology of Religion* (London: Sage, 2007), pp. 36–8.

[32]   Davie, *Europe: The Exceptional Case*, pp. 28–79, 137–47 and Davie, *The Sociology of Religion*, p. 86.

[33]   See also Callum Brown, *Religion and Society in Twentieth Century Britain* (London: Pearson Longman, 2006).

[34]   Davie, *Religion in Britain Since 1945*, p. 52. For statistical detail see Jackson, *Hope for the Church*, pp. 2–12 and Lynda Barley, *Churchgoing Today* (London: Church House Publishing, 2006).

[35]   Grace Davie, Paul Heelas and Linda Woodhead (eds), *Predicting Religion: Christian, Secular and Alternative Futures* (Aldershot: Ashgate, 2003), pp. 6–7.

[36]   Davie, *Religion in Britain since 1945*, p. 147.

this is not unique since all forms of voluntary belonging are being squeezed by the impact of economic consumerism and media dominance.[37] However a smaller, though often more active body of committed Christians continue to act vicariously for the large number of nominal Anglicans.[38] This smaller gathered church must avoid becoming a self-preoccupied consumerist church. Instead, for Davie, it should maintain a lively and engaged parochial witness which invites parishioners into a deeper way of life. The Church of England may indeed be a weak 'state' church which represents rather than dominates. However its key impact is through local transmission of the communal religious and often social memory on behalf of the rest. Sometimes it will be in conflict with other memory managers such as the media.[39] Yet its presence and embeddedness in English society indicates that secularism is in fact the ideological agenda of an élite within English society rather than the default position of the majority. As Martyn Percy suggests, there is still an ecclesial canopy over English society.[40] Most people look to the churches for rites of passage and meaning making, even if there is evidence of an exchange of religion for spirituality among elements of the post-materialist, mainly female, middle classes.[41] As Robin Gill argued 20 years ago, the perception of decline in churchgoing participation was encouraged by over-building of churches in the nineteenth century following the 1851 religious practice census and latterly by suburbanisation, the impact of social mobility and the changes in female roles in society.[42] Yet one of the dangers with statistics is that Free Church ideas of membership are used to determine Anglican and Roman Catholic size when these are not membership churches.[43] Furthermore during the nineteenth and early twentieth centuries most regular religious participation was in childhood through the Sunday School Movement rather than in adulthood. This has now declined in the face of massive rival

---

[37]   Davie, *Religion in Britain since 1945*, p. 189. See also Davie et al., *Predicting Religion*, p. 6.

[38]   Davie, *Religion in Modern Europe*, p. 38.

[39]   Davie, *Religion in Modern Europe*, pp. 53–80 and Davie, *Europe: The Exceptional Case*, pp. 16–21.

[40]   Martyn Percy, *The Ecclesial Canopy: Faith, Hope and Charity* (Farnham: Ashgate, 2012).

[41]   Paul Hellas and Linda Woodhead et al., *The Spiritual Revolution: Why Religion is Giving Way to Spirituality*, (Oxford: Blackwell, 2005), pp. 5, 70, 78–127.

[42]   Robin Gill, *The Myth of the Empty Church* (London: SPCK, 1993), p. 189. See also Brown, *Religion and Society*.

[43]   Paul Avis (ed.), *Public Faith? The State of Religious Belief and Practice in Britain* (London: SPCK, 2003).

recreational competition as mentioned above.[44] Yet there is significant evidence that churchgoing impacts positively and vicariously in society. Surveys show that churchgoers are more altruistic, volunteer more and are more ecologically aware than those who don't attend.[45] In this sense believing and belonging must include behaving. Ironically the fact that the religious convictions of these churchgoers are not publicised contributes to the myth of secularisation.

Clerical Friendship and Society

One of the major changes over the past 250 years in the relationship of church to society has been that of clerical identity.[46] The role has become more focused as a religious professional. Consequently it is more specialised. Historically the cleric was a generalist occupying a role somewhere between a hobby and a profession. It was primarily a symbolic role resourced by the living or by personal income. Congregational size was often small. In 1800 there were only six communicants at St Paul's Cathedral and in 1807 two thirds of clergy were non resident.[47] Yet with the rise of the professions in the nineteenth century, the clergy appeared more amateur and marginal and so there was pressure to compete. This was intensified by the evangelical and Anglo-Catholic renewal movements, both of which emphasised a more distinctive, serious role for the clergy and their attire.[48] Professionalisation and more robust theological education also raised expectations. Yet the capacity of the church to resource this increasingly came under pressure and now forms a major challenge to dioceses. Such financial pressure also encouraged congregationalism as congregations became income generators which need tending if the mission of the church was to continue. This also changes the relationship between congregations and dioceses. For some better resourced congregations the diocese remains marginal to their survival whereas for more fragile congregations it is increasingly vital. Equally as the diocese becomes a broker of financial viability it becomes more powerful and tempted to centralise decisions, unify practice and pursue a closet market

[44] Gill, *The Myth of the Empty Church*, pp. 110–12.

[45] Robin Gill, *Churchgoing and Christian Ethics* (Cambridge: Cambridge University Press, 1999), p. 51.

[46] Martyn Percy, *Clergy: Origin of Species* (London; Continuum, 2006), p. 7.

[47] Percy, *Clergy: Origin of Species*, p. 67.

[48] Percy, *Clergy: Origin of Species*, pp. 26–30, 88. See also Percy, *Shaping the Church: The Promise of Implicit Theology* (Farnham: Ashgate, 2010), p. 56.

model of church.[49] Yet one of Anglicanism's great strengths is its elasticity and unwillingness to be definitive.[50] It is a drama rather than an idea, a performance rather than information and therefore has a localist feel to its expression. The context informs how the drama is enacted. Martyn Percy suggests that the Church of England is now an agent of 'occasional conformity'.[51] Conversion is often about re-turning. This outward-facing role ensures that the church does not turn inwards and contribute to a double secularisation: that of the state and that of a sectarian intense congregationalism. As Percy comments, 'England has never been an outwardly religious country, if church attendance is anything to go by'. Instead the relationship is about 'relating and mutating', a sort of 'haphazard, semi-secular, quiet English Christianity'.[52] This is a relationship in which few people choose *not* to relate to the church and indeed most visit a church at life-changing events. It is also why Percy believes that an organic, incarnational and institutional church rooted in the *terroir*, the distinctive cultural soil, of English society is likely to impact more in the longer term, than more intensive and marginal congregations.[53] Here are the anchors of meaning and memory which provide engagement with wider society. Here patience and charity predominate, a 'passionate coolness' which connects the practices of faith to ordinary life and sustains the tradition of faith against corrosive globalising capitalism.[54] Here wise clergy who embody the Benedictine virtues of hospitality, service and attention enable a ministry of presence and engagement to bear fruit.[55] In short, ministry is about character and availability more than it is about task, caste or even skills. It is about parsons embodying and sharing with others in Coleridge's vision of a wise clerisy which guides society.[56] It is less about specialists who control marginal spaces in that society.[57] In consequence, as Wesley Carr suggests, mission is often about re-focusing rather than supplanting people's spiritual interests and desires through listening to their stories.[58]

Such an organic and engaged role for the church with clergy would suggest that the chaplaincy role of the parson remains central to Anglican mission. This is particularly so if, as Alan Billings asserts, the English actually belong, albeit

---

49 Percy, *The Ecclesial Canopy*, pp. 19–23.
50 Percy, *The Ecclesial Canopy*, p. 86.
51 David Martin quoted in Percy, *Shaping the Church*, p. 39.
52 Percy, *Shaping the Church*, p. 55.
53 Percy, *Shaping the Church*, p. 102.
54 Percy, *The Ecclesial Canopy*, pp. 179, 194.
55 Percy, *Shaping the Church*, pp. 133–41, 164.
56 Percy, *The Ecclesial Canopy*, p. 10.
57 Percy, *Shaping the Church*, p. 164.
58 Avis, *Public Faith?*, p. 86.

occasionally and often vicariously, but don't really believe.[59] Their real creed is optimistic secular humanism which has become even more ambivalent about all formal religion since the atrocities of 11 September 2001 in New York. This chaplaincy mission is expressed through the occasional offices, the symbolising of major annual events such as Remembrance and Christmas and in the Church of England's capacity to contain the fall-out from major catastrophes. It is a very different approach from that of the Free Churches and from the churches of the USA and raises questions about models of ordained ministry which render the clergy congregational minsters, Anglo-Catholic priests, social activists and personal therapists, none of which are rooted in the deeper story of Anglican mission in England. The character of Anglican mission is more nuanced, offering places of occasional attendance and spaces where spiritual questions can be engaged with.

Friendship and English Culture

English Anglican mission, therefore, needs to pay careful attention to English culture and history and the importance of Englishness if it is to engage with the spiritual heart of England fruitfully and appropriately.[60] According to Nigel Rooms there are nine characteristics of the English. These are social dis-ease, satirical humour, moderation, hypocrisy, empiricism, eeyorishness, class-consciousness, fair play and courtesy, which are often captured in phrases such as 'typical' or 'I know my place' or 'sorry'.[61] Archetypal stories, such as Robin Hood, also illustrate this core narrative. This English character reveals not so much a secularist society as society reserved about imposing forms of religion. As a nation the English prefer peace to truth and prefer to live with disagreement than enforced conviction.[62] The Church of England in many ways reflects this diffidence and reserve about ideological approaches to faith, preferring a more nuanced quiet friendship which provides a better bridge for sharing the Gospel than more strident approaches. Even the culture of celebrity does not really threaten this implicit religion. As Pete Ward argues celebrity is a proto-religion rather than a real religion. It is too frivolous to be a formal religion and cannot

---

[59]   Billings, *Lost Church*, p. ix.
[60]   Nigel Rooms, *The Faith of the English: Integrating Christ and Culture* (London: SPCK, 2011), pp.1–22.
[61]   Rooms, *The Faith of the English* (2011), pp. 44–53, 68–72.
[62]   Percy, *The Ecclesial Canopy*, p. 63.

sustain the community, creed and commitment of the latter.[63] Yet this proto-religion explores many important religious themes such as the sacred self albeit in a narcissistic way. It therefore raises questions about sacralisation, polytheism and questions about the good life.[64] The public manifestation of this is a celetoid society in which celebrities, commerce and media collude to construct celebrity in ways which are self-interested, seductive and consumerist.[65] They parody spirituality, myth and ritual through a form of expressive individualism which invites its participants to see themselves as empty vessels needing to be filled with the narratives and commodities of celebrity. This is often irreverent spirituality with celebrities like Madonna co-opting religious symbols into their acts and offering brief and intriguing insights into their lives through confessional chat shows. Celebrities act as ironic saints of an idolatrous, consumer culture yet within this discourse are themes of judgement, heaven, faithfulness, holy families, fame, revelation, incarnation, sin and redemption which offer conversation points with authentic Christian conviction.[66] Mission, therefore, involves recognising potential conversations and finding ways of facilitating them.

Graham Ward therefore argues that Anglicans must be culture readers, seeking to understand their neighbours in ways which enable them to share the story of faith appropriately.[67] For most people life in contemporary England is urban, lived in the post-modern consumer-shaped city. The city represents a utopian dream in which 'libidinal monads' can have all their desires satisfied.[68] Yet the Christian community should not condemn such societies or withdraw from them. Instead they should live among them as signs of a deeper transformation symbolised in the Eucharist. Such communities display a different eros or desire which is orientated to God. Graham Ward sees the church as that community which re-enchants the world through the micro-practices of its witness since Christian activity is part of the Spirit's divine action in a world which is increasingly a global city.[69] This is particularly important in North Atlantic societies where, Ward believes, three trends are corrupting this utopian urban dream. The first is a political crisis of democracy. The second is economic

---

[63] Pete Ward, *Gods Behaving Badly: Media, Religion and Celebrity Culture* (London: SCM, 2011), pp. 3, 57.

[64] P. Ward, *Gods Behaving Badly*, p. 7.

[65] P. Ward, *Gods Behaving Badly*, p. 45.

[66] P. Ward, *Gods Behaving Badly*, pp. 110–127.

[67] Graham Ward, *The Politics of Discipleship: Becoming Postmaterial Citizens* (London: SCM, 2009), pp. 9, 24.

[68] Graham Ward, *Cities of God* (London: Routledge, 2000), p. 56.

[69] G. Ward, *The Politics of Discipleship*, pp. 13, 29.

globalisation. The third is the cultural impact following the new visibility of religion since 1989 and especially September 2001.[70] The crisis of democracy has arisen as representative politics and the rise of the bureaucratic state have led to cynicism about macro-politics. As a result identity politics and a consumerist, spectator approach to life have contributed to soulless capitalism which has overwhelmed a more rooted, responsible capitalism. Globalisation has led to powerlessness and fear which encourages more authoritarianism as lobbying and a manipulative media subverts truthful political discourse. Globalisation adds to this unstable environment with its surfeit of experiences and inflated consumerism. Yet this is only possible because of cheap, exploitative labour. By hiding this reality globalisation encourages forgetfulness and promotes secularism though a complete focus upon the immediate. It makes money divine in a deceptive utopianism as all becomes increasingly virtual and insubstantial. This also fosters a sort of de-traditioned religion with its vision of infinite freedom, unlimited consumption, a dematerialised and unlimited world, 'a utopian vision of an international community stable and beyond conflict'.[71] Life is effectively marketised and countries increasingly become corporations. Yet ironically globalisation and the rise of new media confront secular westerners with other religions and with resurgent Christianity particularly of the global south. This re-positions western secularists as a world minority rather than the future to which the world is travelling and is subtly affecting culture. On the one hand a noisy new atheism reacts against intolerant religious fundamentalism. Yet at the same time religiosity has re-emerged in western societies through books such as the Da Vinci Code and the Harry Potter series which are forms of religion premised around entertainment. Adverts increasingly use religious language and symbols to sell products in this post-secular world. If religious communities are to challenge the corrosive character of this late-modern, post-secular society they will need to speak out on an interfaith basis to get a hearing. Christians in particular must embody practices of hope, love and faith if impact is to be had. This form of service is proper *liturgia*, a service rendered to the city which integrates politics, ethics and aesthetics to show that the good life is also the beautiful life which is the true life.[72] For Christians this is a communal performance since discipleship is not simply following Christ but being formed together to be Christ-like communities. It is also a situated social performance, an offering which contributes to the transfiguration of society. The church,

---

[70] G.Ward, *The Politics of Discipleship*, pp. 34–8.
[71] G.Ward, *The Politics of Discipleship*, p. 107.
[72] G.Ward, *The Politics of Discipleship*, p. 183.

therefore, is not simply another stakeholder of the city but is called to affirm the good, celebrate transcendent aspiration and yet challenge the godless, dehumanising character of new cities. This calling to be a 'cathedral in the midst of the city' challenges the immediacy of 'lifestyles without a conscience' present in the city.[73] This is the church as meaningful flesh and sacramental body, re-performing rather than imitating the way of Christ. It is politics which reflects a democracy rooted in the command to love one another and involves listening, watching and prayer.[74]

Conclusion

Christendom may no longer be what it was, but in England we cannot escape its legacy nor pretend that it was all a mistake. Christendom was a contingent mission strategy appropriate to its era. It has not disappeared even if some elements in public life speak as if this is the case. Indeed in some ways Christendom has returned at local level as churches become service providers and the most recent census reaffirms a majority still identifying with Christianity in England. Yet England is not the USA and we should not expect its religious practice to be modelled on that very different social and historic context. That said, mission in a secular age represents a major challenge to contemporary Anglicans in England. The secular is a deeply embedded ethos within North Atlantic societies and is likely to be the norm for the foreseeable future. There are vested interests within western societies, such as England, which seek to defend this secular status quo. Yet the impact of hard secularism on the ground seems more modest. Indeed there is evidence that the value of faith is becoming more apparent in public life, despite attempts by so-called new atheism to demonise it.[75] There still remains affection for and semi-ownership of parish churches by most people for major events of life and census statistics stubbornly indicate that the majority of the population wish to be regarded as Christian, particularly outside the metropolitan areas. The English church anticipated the English nation and state. It is part of the fabric of English society which means that its mission is not about entering virgin territory. Instead it is about re-engaging with a population which believes tentatively and belongs occasionally. This requires a nuanced, embedded approach to mission which works with the grain of the

---

[73] G.Ward, *The Politics of Discipleship*, pp. 207–20.
[74] G.Ward, *The Politics of Discipleship*, pp. 278–82.
[75] See Jonathan Birdwell and Martin Littler, *Faithful Citizens* (London: Demos, 2012).

English character. The vicarious and representational role of the church remains important. Yet the major challenge to this approach is finance. Today's Church of England is congregationally resourced yet trying to maintain a parish model of mission in a way unknown to its ancestors. At the same time, as we shall see in the next chapter, it is trying to explore fresh expressions of church. This puts enormous pressure upon the existing system, particularly upon its professional ministry. Furthermore whilst celebrity may not be taken as seriously as its advocates would want, it does represent a major distraction to serious faith. This is a further challenge to parishes as their capacity to cope with its impact is limited. Anglican mission therefore needs Christian communities of depth and commitment who bear witness in all the communities of England to the difference Christ makes yet who avoid the trap of earlier reforming zealots whose approach alienated the population and thereby contributed to secularisation.[76]

---

[76] For an exploration of this see John B. Thomson, *Church on Edge? Practising Christian Ministry Today* (London: Darton, Longman and Todd, 2004), pp. 85–95.

Chapter 12

Fresh Friendship

Fresh Church?

There is a lively debate within the Church of England about the sort of church it should be in contemporary England.[1] Martyn Percy argues that there is still a need in English society for public religion. Yet whilst the future of its mission may need to be seen in more ecumenical and engaging ways, there is no sign that society wants to leave religion alone.[2] Nevertheless notions of locality, central to the Anglican parish, are changing, and there is a need to find ways of responding to this just as happened in response to the era of urbanisation in the nineteenth century.[3] Thus whilst Sara Savage sees many positives about the parish as a generous space woven into the fabric of English society, she also detects a dark side which needs addressing, evident in the 'norm of niceness', poor conflict management, the disproportionate number of dysfunctional people drawn towards congregations and the ambiguities of the clerical role. Grace Davie, as we have seen, is also concerned about an increasing tension between a utilitarian view of church held by the majority of the population and the more passionate view of the committed minority, which may actually make it more difficult to keep in touch with that majority.[4] Likewise Ann Morisy worries that there is now too high a threshold for belonging and argues instead that the church needs to create contexts for people to sense God's presence in their lives.[5] In a similar vein Robin Gamble remains confident that traditional parish mission configured around notions of presence, proclamation and persuasion can bear fruit if it is well planned and passionately engaged with, whilst Rowan Williams sees in the parish church a sign of the availability of God and of the loyalty of

---

[1]   See Angela Shier-Jones, *Pioneer Ministry and Fresh Expressions of Church* (London: SPCK, 2009) and Michael Moynagh, *Church for Every Context: An Introduction to Theology and Practice* (London: SCM, 2012).

[2]   Steven Croft (ed.), *The Future of the Parish System: Shaping the Church of England for the 21st Century* (London: CHP, 2006), pp. 13–14.

[3]   Croft, *The Future of the Parish System*, p. 7.

[4]   Croft, *The Future of the Parish System*, pp. 40–41.

[5]   Croft, *The Future of the Parish System*, p. 130.

the church to its society.[6] This sign maintains Anglican credibility, speaks of the hospitality of God and encourages ordinary people to attend to the world of the spirit.[7] On the other hand Graham Cray argues that the values of a missionary church must test existing models of the church to see if they remain faithful to the Gospel and Steven Croft wants to develop fresh expressions of church for those 60 per cent of the population who don't relate to present parish mission. He argues for a more missional understanding of the diaconate and for fresh expressions initiatives to be rooted in good theology and cultural exegesis. They also need to demonstrate maturity by aligning themselves with the four marks of the church and enabling people to travel towards baptism and Eucharist.[8] Such improvisations of church, however, cannot ignore the long memory which many parishes still represent expressed both in their architecture and stable demography.[9] Social mobility today is not as widespread as many think and indeed fewer people moved house in 2002 than in 1952 and, between 1984 and 1994, households relocating fell by 50 per cent. The principal change is that couples with two jobs tend to drive more rather than move house with consequent impacts on the road network.[10] As Moynagh comments, 'local churches have a long-term future because for most people everyday life remains local'.[11] What has changed is the coherence of communities as time pressures and the effects of choice undermine a shared understanding of communal life and values. Consequently churches need to be where people are and to find ways of sharing faith appropriately. Hence all expressions of church need to find fresh ways of engaging contemporary English culture and the idea of a divide between traditional expressions and fresh expressions of church is nonsense.

Fresh Evangelism

Steve Hollinghurst therefore argues that the Gospel in contemporary society must generate indigenous expressions of faith which relate to realities on the ground rather than holding fast to past practice if it is to engage fruitfully with the changing world.[12] He believes that many Christian communities in Britain

---

6   Croft, *The Future of the Parish System*, pp. 95–102.
7   Croft, *The Future of the Parish System*, pp. 54–9.
8   Croft, *The Future of the Parish System*, pp. 75, 81, 145.
9   Croft, *The Future of the Parish System*, p. 156.
10   Michael Moynagh, *Emergingchurch.intro* (Oxford: Monarch Books, 2004), p. 77.
11   Moynagh, *Church for Every Context*, p. 91.
12   Steve Hollinghurst, *Mission Shaped Evangelism* (Norwich: Canterbury Press, 2010).

have lost touch with the cultures around them and need to engage in an act of 'double listening' to emerging cultures and to the church's own story in order to hear God speaking through both.[13] In the first instance this means paying close attention to the story of Christendom's decline in Britain over the last century, for example by taking seriously Callum Brown's assertion that the changing role of women since the 1960s and the rise of a consumer society, rather than rationalist secularisation, have had the greatest impact on declining religious practice.[14] It means realising that Christian and other religious groups which have made some headway in Britain or the USA often represent forms of client-based religion which either collude with the consumerist quest for happiness or are conservative, refugee churches reacting against the changing cultural landscape. Neither response is adequate. Nor is the hope that immigrants from sub-Saharan African Christianity will bring about the revival of Christianity in Europe. Instead the church in the West must find ways in which elements of the Christian story can be good news for its emerging cultures.[15] This involves attracting rather than arguing people to faith. It means entering into new cultures and letting others experience the grace of God through the mutual sharing of life and testimony. It is about allowing faith and worship to emerge over time rather than trying to bring worship to people. It is about engaging with the sort of questions that contemporary people are asking about destiny, meaning, creation, worship and suffering in a language they understand and in the contexts where they gather such as car-boot sales, supermarkets, mind, body and spirit fairs, music festivals and internet social networks. This is about building relationships on others' territory, creating exploratory space for faith which responds to the questions posed and which listens and lets God transform people in God's own time. It is not spiritual consumerism. The church must therefore become a more improvising and risk-taking community, going to where people are rather than requiring them to come to where the church is.[16]

Hollinghurst's challenge is forceful and apposite. Yet what will fire existing congregations to be part of this evangelistic calling and how will the Gospel be embodied in persuasive and sustainable ways which represent depth and durability? Improvisation requires confidence, imagination and capacity which are not always present in fragile Christian communities. There needs to be a rootedness in the deeper Christian story if fresh expressions of church are to be sustainable or they may simply fizzle out within one generation or subgroup's

---

[13] Hollinghurst, *Mission Shaped Evangelism*, p. 1.
[14] Hollinghurst, *Mission Shaped Evangelism*, pp. 9–51.
[15] Hollinghurst, *Mission Shaped Evangelism*, p. 167.
[16] Hollinghurst, *Mission Shaped Evangelism*, p. 225.

life cycle.[17] In the past Anglicans maintained this relationship through liturgy. Liturgy is worship which is both upward and outward looking since its root meaning is the idea of service to wider society. At its best worship connects and forms Christians to serve the mission of God. Worship nourishes and trains Christians to perform their faith in ways that cohere with the activity of God. Worship is therefore crucial for confidence, imagination and capacity, the making of space for God (*capax dei*). In addition worship is evangelism since God refuses to be absent when his people gather. Mission-shaped evangelism flows from and is present in faithful worship through which ordinary Christians learn the story of grace and are equipped with the skills to improvise upon this story in whatever context they find themselves in. Mission-shaped evangelism therefore emerges from a worship-shaped church.

Fresh Sacraments?

Consequently the performance of worship is a critical issue for the mission of the contemporary church. A common complaint about the Fresh Expressions Movement is that it is an initiative of evangelicals and charismatics with little appreciation of the formative character of sacramental practice. Yet sacramental practice can enrich and resource fresh expressions of church particularly in a culture which is suspicious of simple, clear answers to the challenges of life.[18] Mystery, symbol, story, silence, community and worship offer a landscape of Christian practice which can engage and refresh those exploring faith beyond the traditional church. Good liturgy does not impede engagement with contemporary culture but rather is a Spirit-infused medium which can make connections in something as tangible as the sensory worship of the Mass. A focus on story prevents discipleship becoming over abstract and idealist. The challenge is to mine and improvise upon Christian tradition rather than seek novelty as a way of becoming relevant to unstable cultures. Examples of this approach range from stories about *Visions* in York and the new monasticism of *MayBe* in Oxford, to reflections on the particular flexibility of Anglicanism and its liturgical richness within a postmodern context as in the history and

---

[17] Martyn Percy, *Anglicanism: Confidence, Commitment and Communion* (Farnham: Ashgate, 2013), p. 127.

[18] Steven Croft and Ian Mobsby (eds), *Fresh Expressions in the Sacramental Tradition* (Norwich: Canterbury Press, 2009).

practice of *Contemplative Fire*.[19] Fresh ways forward do not have to reject the past. Rather they can improvise upon the tradition in ways that express how God is with us today.

Stale Friendship?[20]

The Fresh Expressions Movement has broadly been positively received across the Church of England. However there are voices which ask whether this is the correct way forward. Most notable amongst these are Andrew Davison, Alison Milbank, John Hull and Alan Billings. Davison and Milbank argue that *Mission Shaped Church* and the Fresh Expressions Movement represents an uncritical collusion with contemporary consumerism and is based on shoddy theological and sociological thinking.[21] In short these initiatives are so friendly with contemporary cultures that they lose their moorings and cease to represent Anglican mission at all. They point to the mere 19 pages of explicit theological reflection in *Mission Shaped Church*, note the divorce of form and content in much talk about church and culture throughout the book and see in this a Gnostic tendency which separates faith from embodiment.[22] In particular they argue that much discourse from the Fresh Expressions Movement subverts Anglican mission by detaching Christian community from its accountability to place, the particular and the material, in favour of a free-floating, abstract and portable faith.[23] Indeed some critics of *Mission Shaped Church*, such as John Hull, actually reinforce this by suggesting that an abstract notion of the Kingdom of God should control the way the embodied church engages in mission.[24] The Fresh Expressions Movement therefore presents faith not as a form or way of

---

[19]   Croft and Mobsby, *Fresh Expressions in the Sacramental Tradition*, pp. 9–15, 52–65, 87–99, 100–113.

[20]   The title comes from 'Stale Expressions: The Management-Shaped Church' in Milbank, *The Future of Love: Essays in Political Theology* (London: SCM, 2009). John Milbank sees the Fresh Expressions Movement as a collusion of evangelicals and liberals, who both are ambivalent about the church as a community of harmonious difference. Instead of embracing the Anglican ethos he holds that they prefer ecclesiastical management. The problem he does not deal with is the financial driver underlying the push towards a more mission-orientated church.

[21]   Andrew Davison and Alison Milbank, *For the Parish: A Critique of Fresh Expressions* (London: SCM, 2010).

[22]   Davison and Milbank, *For the Parish*, p. vii.

[23]   Davison and Milbank, *For the Parish*, pp. 29, 45.

[24]   Davison and Milbank, *For the Parish*, p. 50.

life but as a package of portable ideas whose clothing can mutate according to contemporary cultural demands. It is basically a conformist religious collusion with capitalist consumerism. This contrasts with recent philosophy and long-term Christian practice which indicate that meaning is present in the form rather than independent of it.[25] The form of the inherited church is not redundant clothing which can be discarded. Instead it is infused with grace. Thus the way that the church has emerged is as a spiritual reality which orientates and controls the way the church develops. Salvation is not private or abstract. Rather Christians await a church-shaped salvation.[26] Faith is about a practical imitation of Christ which follows our incorporation into Christ through baptism. It is shaped by the disciplines and practices of the Church, which are the first fruits of the Kingdom of God.

In the light of this, parishes appear much more inclusive, flexible and conversational with the cultures around them than fresh expressions of church which segregate and fix a moment of culture and have no prophetic response to that culture. Indeed many in the Fresh Expressions Movement seem to have little sense of effective history and represent an un-Anglican flight from tradition.[27] They advocate innovation over improvisation, prefer novelty over stability and offer pastiche over authenticity as the virtual or ideal trumps the actual or real. They have little sense of belonging to the church as a trans-cultural, trans-historical body and promote a private, detached faith, a sort of utopia which literally does not exist. In contrast mission is about unveiling the eschatological church, the company of God's people. It is not about implanting the church in a foreign space. In this sense the historic parish represents a strong sacrament of hospitality, particularly for the poor who, unlike the middle classes, cannot move to the locations of their choice. The parish as a place of long-term prayer represents a sacred place of memory, which the de-traditioned mobile middle classes often under-appreciate. It also challenges the incipient competitive congregationalism which surrounds a good deal of talk in the Fresh Expressions Movement.[28] Instead of subverting the parish and thereby playing into the hands of secularist critics, the church should recover confidence in its historic mission strategy, promote liturgical seasons, colourfully re-engage the culture with its festivals and music and tell its story imaginatively through the performance of its life together. In short the church's life should be lived through its liturgy.[29]

---

[25] Davison and Milbank, *For the Parish*, pp. 5–7.

[26] Davison and Milbank, *For the Parish*, p. 48.

[27] Davison and Milbank, *For the Parish*, pp 64–73, 93–117.

[28] Davison and Milbank, *For the Parish*, pp. 144–63.

[29] Davison and Milbank, *For the Parish*, p. 209.

At the heart of this criticism, ironically, is a concern that such approaches actually subvert the church's vocation to be an inclusive, outward facing, embedded presence in English society and thereby undermine its historical mission.[30] In *Lost Church*, Alan Billings registers his concern that today's church is losing an ear for the large number of ordinary parishioners who belong but do not attend much and have faith rather than beliefs.[31] With declining attendance rates church leaders are tempted to give attention to the committed, the believers, at the expense of the former or seek to develop ways of engaging with those who don't attend in a way that subverts the Anglican project of providing open, hospitable space for those with faith but hesitant beliefs. He is concerned that such initiatives conflate faith and beliefs, see discipleship as about correct ideas rather than trust and understand mission in a way which subverts a tried and tested Anglican polity (parishes) with something which he is not convinced can be called church.[32] He sees this agenda as captive to and reacting to secularisation and strident public atheists who also want faith to be about beliefs since the latter can be attacked more easily. Neither represents the Church of England's understanding of faith or mission which he wants to recover and both open up a gulf between the sympathetic mass of the population and a more strident, insecure church determined to establish a clear brand. Yet this is happening, ironically, at a time when voices are emerging in public life criticising the certitude agenda of new atheism and re-appreciating the value of 'religion' in society.[33]

So is this critique fair? Certainly the theological and philosophical criticisms of Davison, Milbank and Billings are pertinent and challenge the Fresh Expressions Movement to think more rigorously about its ecclesiology and apologetics.[34] For Moynagh, however, the expectations that these 'new contextual churches' should be modelled on inherited and often introverted parochial models is neither biblically nor theologically sound. Mission is an attribute of God so 'it follows that just as mission is not a second step for God it must not be a second step for the church'.[35] New contextual churches therefore are not simply reacting to a perceived decline and disconnection between inherited church and contemporary western society, nor are they seeking to be

---

[30]   Alan Billings, *Lost Church: Why We Must Find it Again* (London: SPCK, 2012), pp. x, 104–7.

[31]   Billings, *Lost Church*, pp. 1, 58, 63.

[32]   Billings, *Lost Church*, pp. 103–7.

[33]   Billings, *Lost Church*, p. 14ff.

[34]   Moynagh, *Church for Every Context*, takes up this challenge.

[35]   Moynagh, *Church for Every Context*, p. 124.

relevant to is as a sort of interest group church. Rather they represent culturally appropriate missional engagements with their host society in ways that cohere with the self-giving mission of God and they seek to become contextually rooted ecclesial communities.[36] Certainly fresh expressions of church which uncritically embrace sub-cultures of society and dismiss the potential of parochial mission should be challenged and discarding liturgy and even sacraments may for some collude with elements of contemporary culture in a corrosive manner. Thus it is vital that such initiatives remain connected to the wider catholic church whose worship practices, such as confession, reading Scripture, interceding, the sacraments etc. train Christians to recognise the working of the Spirit in life and are themselves infused by Christ (Matthew 28:20).[37] As Moynagh says, 'relationships cannot be separated from the practices that embody them' and indeed it is in the conversations of faith that practices are refined and tested rather than simply conserved.[38] Furthermore such ecclesial relationships are prevented from becoming emotive when they are tested by inherited practices. Liturgical formation therefore ensures that the church maintains a critical distance from contemporary culture in order to discern where the Spirit is present in a given culture. Since Anglicans in particular have understood their identity to be constituted by common worship, faithfulness necessarily takes priority over relevance to contemporary culture. Indeed this is how the church is relevant to contemporary culture since it is 'fresh' precisely because it emerges from the Gospel which transforms Christians into witnesses like Christ critically engaging with the cultures of their day. This should be the norm for the whole church since to be an expression of the church is to be a church which grows in its *terroir*, or cultural soil, but in a manner faithful to its calling.[39] Only thus can it be a fresh expression of church rather than a form of spiritual narcissism colluding with an ambiguous culture.[40] Improvisation, therefore, requires that Christians are proficient practitioners of faith rather than those who side step the costly challenge of discipleship formation in order to appeal to whatever contemporary culture regards as significant. As mentioned above, becoming a Christian involves learning a new language in order to understand all things

---

[36] Moynagh, *Church for Every Context*, pp. 126–31..

[37] Stanley Hauerwas, 'The Liturgical Shape of the Christian Life: Teaching Christian Ethics as Worship' in David Ford and Dennis Stamps (eds), *Essentials of Christian Community* (Edinburgh: T&T Clark, 1996), pp. 35–48.

[38] Moynagh, *Church for Every Context*, p. 113.

[39] Percy, *Anglicanism*, p. 47.

[40] Percy, *Anglicanism*, p. 132.

within the story of Christ.[41] Christian communities are fresh and relevant to the wider church and society if they form recognisably Christian disciples who can be faithful witnesses within the contexts they inhabit.[42]

Such a challenge applies to all expressions of church. Given the statistical reality of attendance figures facing the Church in England, too optimistic and romantic a view of the parish also needs questioning.[43] In addition other factors which drive the Fresh Expressions Movement, such as finance and the age profile of both congregations and clergy need to be faced by traditionalists. Greater use of self-supporting ministry may sustain the existing model for another 20 or 30 years, but this is not enough.[44] Many parishes are evidently not engaged fruitfully with their host communities. Often parish congregations are themselves segregated sub-cultural groups which now reflect the segregated character of contemporary English society and uncritically collude with surrounding cultural norms. Indeed church traditions can never be wholly isolated from their cultures nor is there any single and agreed pure church culture against which all can measure themselves.[45] What is clear is that public worship may not be as accessible to the majority population as in the past as links with wider culture become more tenuous.[46] In addition, economic segregation means that few parish congregations, particularly in urban areas, now fully represent the diversities and varieties which signify the catholicity of the church. This is why, for Anglicans the diocese rather than the parish is the local church since a diocese represents a more catholic and focused sign of the church. Within a diocese inherited and fresh expressions of church can exist fruitfully and accountably as joint examples of improvising, theologically reflective, Anglican mission, some of which may be non-territorial 'parishes' akin to religious orders or chaplaincies, whilst others

---

[41] See George Lindbeck, *The Nature of Doctrine, Religion in a Post Liberal Age* (Philadelphia: Westminster Press, 1984) and 'The Church as God's New Language' in Hauerwas, Christian Existence Today: Essays on Church, World and Living in Between (North Carolina: The Labyrinth Press, 1988), pp. 47–65.

[42] I am indebted for many of the insights above to Sam Pollard, 'Spirit-Dependent Discipleship and Contextual Mission: Establishing Stanley Hauerwas as a Resource for Contemporary Missiological Debate' unpublished MSS, Bristol University 2011.

[43] David Goodhew, Andrew Roberts and Michael Volland, *Fresh: An Introduction to Fresh Expressions of Church and Pioneer Ministry* (London: SCM, 2012), p. 41.

[44] See the statistics for stipendiary ministry and mission in Percy, *Anglicanism*, p. 46.

[45] Moynagh, *Church for Every Context*, pp. 158–9.

[46] See Richard Sudworth, 'Recovering the Difference that Makes a Difference: Fresh Ideas on an Older Theme' in Graham Cray, Ian Mobsby and Aaron Kennedy (eds), *Ancient Faith, Future Mission: Fresh Expressions of Church and the Kingdom of God* (Norwich: Canterbury Press, 2012), pp. 30–34.

will remain so.[47] In this way new initiatives complement rather than subvert traditional parish mission and challenge the parish to reach out to those 40 per cent of the population who are still drawn to existing traditional parish models of church.[48] Hence parishes which provide creative and accessible worship, good occasional office ministry, a tradition of communal hospitality and friendship and opportunities for nurturing faith and discipleship do flourish, as examples from the Isle of Dogs in East London, Wimbourne Minster's civic role and the renewed interest in cathedrals display. Patient and yet adventurous mission properly remains at the heart of parish ministry. Yet the key challenge today is how to resource such a parochial model of hospitable engagement through congregational giving at a time when the numbers of stipendiary clergy are rapidly reducing through retirements and when socio-economic changes have undermined the sort of localism within which parish life was traditionally rooted. Contemporary congregations, like all forms of social organisation in English society, are smaller than in the past and aging so a further challenge is to grow committed congregations so that the resources of people and money are available to continue in God's mission to England in ways faithful to the Anglican calling. Anglican mission like that of Jesus in the Gospels, seeks to offer blessing to the crowds who are not yet ready for discipleship but also to form committed disciples. At best fresh expressions and inherited models of church seek to do this in partnership rather than in competition.

Fresh Friendship with the Nation?

So should there also be a fresh relationship with the nation?[49] We have already noted John Milbank's statement that 'England remains as a political body, a body within an ecclesiastical body'.[50] As in Europe, so in England, it was the church which first mapped out the political terrain. The first place was sacred place and this suggests that, although questions about the character of establishment may change, England remains an ecclesiastical idea. Despite the

---

[47]   Cray et al., *Ancient Faith*, pp. 76, 183–208.

[48]   Paul Bayes and Tim Sledge with John Holbrook, Mark Rylands and Martin Seeley, *Mission-Shaped Parish: Traditional Church in a Changing Context* (London: Church House Publishing, 2006).

[49]   For a more formal exposition of the case for disestablishing the Church of England see Colin Buchanan, *Cut the Connection: Disestablishment and the Church of England* (London: DLT, 1994).

[50]   Milbank, *The Future of Love*, p. 273.

noise of secularists and historically ignorant Christians Christendom remains a latent reality particularly at grass roots as a sort of National Spiritual Service.[51] If Christendom has waned, it has not involved a tidy break into sacred and secular. Instead the picture is more nuanced, particularly at ground level. Indeed as we saw in Chapter 4, Bernice Martin argues that 'a distinctive aspect of Anglican congregational life is the way it manifests itself in the mundane local networks of social relationships and associational sympathies, and their subsequent realization are to be found in the networks of face-to-face relationships as exemplified in the local life of a parish.'[52] Christianity is deeply embedded in the weft and warp of English society. This was the force of Rowan Williams and Daniel Hardy's thinking about church as we saw in Chapters 8 and 10. It reflects Alan Billings's plea that the parish church is not crushed in the rush for more intense congregationalism. The latter may appear larger but may actually only grow through transfer from other congregations. Intense congregationalism may also make it difficult for genuine explorers since it often represents more closed understandings of Christianity.[53] Yet the character of the relationship between church and nation can change in surprising ways, as Ann Morisy argues.[54] Noting that many churches have been quietly re-established as welfare providers resourced by government funding initiatives, she raises concerns about the seductions of this re-establishment since money calls the tune and limits the church's freedom of action. Mission to the nation cannot simply be about meeting needs as defined by the regeneration industry. Such engagement must enhance the work of the Gospel. Otherwise churches will be secularised from within, hollowed out to become state-managed voluntary organisations or interest groups competing with others for a role in society on the terms of those in power. In contrast churches should be clearly Christian communities which cascade grace and embody venturesome love in society. Parishes are particularly fruitful contexts for this since they can represent 'bridging capital' and 'brave social capital'. They also enable stories to be told and shared which generate hope and enable people to sense the presence of God. In this they are community chaplains continuing the historic role of the parish church in English society. Parishes and Fresh Expressions can therefore challenge the increasingly dystopic character of English society populated with what the sociologist

---

[51]   Percy, *Anglicanism*, p. 113.

[52]   Quoted in Matthew Guest, Karin Tusting and Linda Woodhead, *Congregational Studies in the UK: Christianity in a Post-Christian Context* (Aldershot: Ashgate, 2005), p. 60.

[53]   Billings, *Lost Church*, pp.103–9.

[54]   Ann Morisy, *Journeying Out: A New Approach to Christian Mission* (Moorhouse: Harnsbury, 2004).

Zygmunt Bauman calls, 'decadent vagabonds'. These 'vagabonds' are spectators rather than participants in life, have no sense of their moral traditions and are motivated simply by the mantra 'I am, I want, I will'.[55] In contrast Christian mission must be embodied as reflective practice and conversation rather than simply proclamation and forming people of character and Christian virtue. In the face of new atheist challenges and popular cynicism, established religions need to cultivate the practices of patient attention and practical love. This will involve sustaining virtuous behaviour and selfless mission and pastoral care. Graced actions and the tangibly positive effect of religious practice will make the difference.

Kenneth Leech argues that 'the church is faced now, as always, with the false polarities of ghetto or surrender, of the heroic sect surrounded by impenetrable walls or the shapeless pseudo-community of the unclear and the vague'.[56] Yet Anglicanism is properly a conversation between pastoral and academic theology and socio-political struggle.[57] It nurtures hopeful commitment in difficult situations, rooted in the open, ongoing argument of tradition rather than acting as custodian to dull and uninspiring churches which stand for nothing. Its tradition forces the church to confront destructive capitalism at a local level, to work with others to identify the common good and to be engaged with those on the fringes of society since Christ is found more in the rough and tumble of urban ministry rather than in abstract academic contexts.[58] This is about integrating prayer and prophecy in order to reflect something of God's voice back to the Church. Like John the Baptist, Leech is a voice crying out in the wilderness of society and church convinced that following Christ is about becoming a distinctive community associated with those most marginalised by the powers that seek to rule society. For Leech the church has to be sacramentally engaged in the micro politics of ground level communities since God's activity is found in the material realities of their lives. This is about practical holiness in which worship is the critical lens through which the world is seen and the character of God discovered. Transformation is from below, which is not about 'posh' clergy condescending to live amongst the poor or Christians in the suburbs rolling out their view of Church growth into contexts unknown to them. Instead, following the practice of liberation theologians, Christians should inhabit the undesirable

---

[55]   Ann Morisy, *Bewildered and Troubled: Enacting Hope in Troubled Times* (London: Continuum, 2009), pp. 9–10.

[56]   Kenneth Leech, *The Sky is Red: Discerning the Signs of the Times* (London: Darton, Longman & Todd, 1997), p. 3.

[57]   Leech, *The Sky is Red*, p. 58.

[58]   Leech, *The Sky is Red*, pp. 212–3.

places of our society in order to listen to and work with these communities and so represent and share the Gospel. This is a challenge to a church which he believes has sold its soul for the pottage of Establishment. Church must take its bearings from a God whose concern is with the powerless of society rather than the powerful.[59]

Leech argues that the core mission of Anglicans should be focused on the mundane which works in partnership with others who share similar commitments as a form of friendship which has affinities with Luke Bretherton's view of hospitality.[60] Hospitable mission involves taking a principled position consonant with the traditions of one's faith community whilst being open to others around it.[61] It contrasts with the more competitive approach of identity Christian politics and avoids the dangers of co-option by new establishment welfare provision and the commodification of Christianity by a society that sees it as simply another life style option.[62] In the new post-secular world, all traditions have to become self-reflexive and aware of others.[63] They must engage creatively with each other rather than trying to ignore or defeat each other. In such circumstances the church must not simply rely upon its inherited status or power but instead should seek wherever possible to work on areas of common concern with other groups.[64] This hospitable approach listens deeply to the word of God and then improvises in a faithful and exemplary way. It is rooted in the crucial Christian practice of worship which contests the totalising of politics, resists the instrumentalising of the church and provides a way of reading the world. It involves a double listening to God and neighbour which can interpret the world trustfully and form faithful political action. [65] Worship therefore constitutes the church as a social and public body and contests any notion that the church is formed by the market or the state. It trains Christians to see the world in relation to God and neighbour through the hallowing of God's name. Such insight flags up themes of gift, judgement, promise and sanctuary which

---

[59] For a fuller discussion of Kenneth Leech's work see David Bunch and Angus Ritchie (eds), *Prayer and Prophecy: The Essential Kenneth Leech* (London: DLT, 2009).

[60] Luke Bretherton, *Hospitality as Holiness: Christian Witness Amid Moral Diversity* (Farnham: Ashgate, 2006), p. 1.

[61] Bretherton, *Hospitality as Holiness*, p. 109.

[62] Luke Bretherton, *Christianity and Contemporary Politics: The Conditions and Possibilities of Faithful Witness* (Chichester: Wiley-Blackwell, 2010), pp. 1–2, 31, 41–5, 48, 53–7.

[63] Bretherton, *Christianity and Contemporary Politics*, p. 13.

[64] Bretherton, *Christianity and Contemporary Politics*, p. 17.

[65] Bretherton, *Christianity and Contemporary Politics*, pp. 97–103.

guide Christian practice in the ordinary challenges of life.[66] For Bretherton 'the public work of the church is ... to be an agent of healing and repair within the political, economic and social order, contradicting the prideful, violent and exclusionary logics at work in the saeculum and opening it out to its fulfillment in Christ'.[67]

Conclusion

So is there a place for Anglican 'fresh friendship' with contemporary English society? From the above the clear consensus is that a more imaginative and hospitable engagement is needed rather than a defensive traditionalism or reactionary innovation. Nevertheless improvisations must embody the historic Anglican calling to be a church for and of England rather than for the elites or sub-cultures of England. Otherwise they will indeed simply become a mirror image of the dominant culture around it or a Trojan horse for a different mission tradition less sympathetic to English society. As John Drane argues, the challenge for the church is not to be relevant but to be incarnational.[68] Anglican history suggests that neither an isolationist confessional approach nor one which capitulates unreflectively to contemporary mores is adequate. The relationship of the ecclesiastical to the socio-political in England suggests that conversational mission is more faithful to Anglican conviction and hospitality. It respects the past and the practices of the church as Spirit infused, but accepts contingency as part of the created condition. This requires a renegotiation of the tradition in an improvising rather than innovatory way. It is about expressing the friendship of God in the vernacular and ensuring that the rumour of God is kept alive. It is about faithful presence in English society.[69]

---

[66] Bretherton, *Christianity and Contemporary Politics*, pp. 143–53.

[67] Bretherton, *Christianity and Contemporary Politics*, p. 210.

[68] John Drane, *After McDonaldization: Mission, Ministry and Christian Discipleship in an Age of Uncertainty* (London: Darton, Longman and Todd, 2008), p. 87.

[69] On the theme of Christian communities as faithful presence see Davison Hunter, *To Change the World: The Irony, Tragedy and Possibility of Christianity in the late Modern World* (Oxford: OUP, 2010).

Conclusion
Sharing Friendship: English Anglican Mission Today

Stanley Hauerwas asserts that 'the reality of a God who moves in history is consistently shown to be dependent upon the existence of a people whose lives bespeak the truth of his sovereignty and provision'.[1] Anglican practice is one way of embodying this reality expressed in friendship for the stranger. Such friendship involves going out of oneself. Its end or goal emerges through following in the wake of Christ's act of divine kenotic, or self-emptying, friendship. In this way Christ's friendship contrasts with the image of classical friendship represented in Aristotle's magnanimous man who shares his 'friendship' on his own terms.[2] This magnanimous man (and the gender specific designation is intentional here given the relative powers of men and women in ancient society) holds out the hand of 'friendship' from a place of unassailable power. This is friendship as will rather than grace. It is about imposing power rather than about liberating power. It is about self-centred control rather than other-centred commitment. In contrast Jesus calls his disciples friends instead of servants because, by divesting himself of all that separates, he has joined them and pitched his tent among them.[3]

Anglican mission in England is about pitching Christian tents among the diverse communities of English society. Originally the church came to England as a missionary movement. Missionaries leave the securities of their own culture and make their home among those they are called to share the Gospel with. They pitch their tents in communities in which they are strangers. English Anglicans need to re-discover this heritage and see the 'strange' areas of the country, the 'Bethlehems' and 'Galilees', as primary areas for mission. In so doing the temptation to look to 'successful' congregations and assume that their way can be replicated and franchised out should be avoided since this approach is neither incarnational nor contextually sensitive. It flattens out distinctiveness

---

[1]   Stanley Hauerwas, *Learning to Speak Christian* (London: SCM, 2011), p. 47.

[2]   On Aristotle's magnanimous man see Stanley Hauerwas and Charles Pinches, *Christians Among the Virtues: Theological Conversations with Ancient and Modern Ethics* (Notre Dame: University of Notre Dame Press, 1997), pp. 21.

[3]   John 1:14.

and standardises people often in the image of those who seem to be successful. In these cases talk about mission draws its inspiration from 'home' rather than from the 'foreign land' of the mission context. It is about mission to those we think are like us because we don't really know them. Such mission talk can also suggest swift solutions. Yet the missionaries I met as a child in Africa were people committed to the long haul. They spent time learning the language and culture of their new communities since to see transformation required patience and time. They realised that mission to strangers requires that we have a lot to learn before we can engage. As mentioned in Chapter 5, Anglicans discover their particular mission calling through practising worship and discipleship in context rather than by developing ideal mission theories or relying on portable techniques. There is no blue print for the future nor are there abstract models of church which can be rolled out or put into practice. Rather Anglicans are formed through worship to see how God is asking them to improvise upon the Gospel in the contexts they inhabit.

Improvising on Anglican Friendship

Three stories of ordinary parishes in the Diocese of Sheffield illustrate the improvising character of Anglican mission in one of the more challenging parts of England.[4] The first is a working class urban parish in Doncaster which emphasises the central role of worship in forming and disposing a Christian community to share in God's mission of sharing friendship. The congregation lives and acts from its worship and is able to be hospitable to its varied parish community because of the experience of God's hospitality discovered through such worship. Occasional office ministry is at the heart of this mission but it is also characterised by gatherings for public remembrance, social events and openness to those on the fringes of society. Scarecrow Saints and Stations of the Cross trails around the parish, community carol singing in the park and pubs and the co-creating of signs of Christ's passion by local community groups and the congregation represent imaginative and communal improvisations upon the Gospel. They represent artistic improvisations upon the story of grace which the community is encouraged to embrace. This way of mission follows the Gospel mission narratives in Matthew chapter 10 and Luke chapter 9, where the response

---

4   Material from this section is also to be found in Jeff Astley and Leslie Francis, *Exploring Ordinary Theology: Everyday Christian Believing and the Church* (Farnham: Ashgate, 2013*)*, pp. 189–97.

of the host community to the evangelists indicates something of their response to God. Similarly in Matthew chapter 18 the use of the child, the powerless member of the family, is an analogy for discipleship in the Kingdom of God and the church's relationship with the world underwrites this way of mission. The Christian community is to be among people as a relatively impotent community. It is to trust and depend upon the grace of God to form it into an appropriate Gospel sign which invites a response from its host society. That response will expose that society's response to the Gospel. The church cannot control mission since it is God's work. Instead the church's role is imaginatively to embody and improvise upon the Gospel where it is.

The second is a mining village to the north of Doncaster and is a particularly creative example of faithful commitment and improvising in mission. Some years ago local children asked if they could cook the tea of the vicar. As a result appropriately supervised meals, initiated by and prepared with local children, helped the congregation and wider parish understand the character of God's hospitality. Indeed the local un-churched children reversed social norms and taught the adult congregation that God's mission involves mutual blessing, the imparting of life, the healing and restoring of relationships and the dynamic of generosity at the heart of Eucharist. This led to further mission improvisations such as the community cinema, the Street Supper, building a Community Centre and engagement with the local Pit Club. Yet given the painful history of the parish, these improvisations have had to take account of the deep sense of bereavement and betrayal felt by this community following the mining disputes of the mid-1980s. Mission in such a sensitive situation required the congregation to listen deeply to the community's story and be responsive to its hospitality. For the vicar it meant being committed to the parish for a long time.

The third is an outreach initiative in an inner city multi-ethnic parish in Sheffield. The challenge here has been to see what is happening in the parish and interpret its meaning for mission. Once again it has been important to pay attention to the context and discover an appropriate rather than an abstract vision of mission for the community. This has involved using parish audits, long term commitment to local people and finding appropriate ways to reach out to the most marginal of the parish. In this case outreach has been through women's ministry to other vulnerable women in the parish. As a result of these initiatives fresh insights from Luke chapter 4 have emerged about ground-level mission. These speak of liberation from imprisonment, oppression and blindness and the importance of practising acceptance and respect. Sharing divine friendship with deeply wounded and vulnerable estranged people has integrated worship and mission. Worship is seen as mission since worship has enabled them to see what is before them in the love and friendship of God and to act in appropriate ways.

To support such improvisations has required flexibility, imagination and indeed improvisation by the diocese as well. Anglican mission privileges the periphery over the centre. Indeed it could be said that the centre is the periphery. Thus the mission centres are the parishes and other initiatives spread across the diocese. The Diocese of Sheffield has improvised upon the Anglican liturgy to produce *DOXA: A Discipleship Course* and developed a course, *Worship 4 Today*, to train those who lead worship in a way which is both faithful to Anglican inheritance and yet open to what is emerging. A Parish Development Project was piloted which works with the grain and history of parishes in order to see change as rooted in a deeper story. A School of Ministry ensures that initial ministry education is both collaborative and mission focused, whilst the present Diocesan Bishop, Steven Croft, has been central to the development of the Fresh Expressions Movement and has promoted a vision of nurturing sustainable and adventurous Anglican communities in every area of the diocese, particularly where circumstances are hard. This has also meant challenging those called to ordained ministry to see the vulnerable edges as the primary contexts for mission rather than opting for the more established areas. It requires a culture of shared ministry in which lay and ordained work together and congregations are the agents of mission. It necessitates an expansion in the range of publicly recognised ministries in order to release and distribute the energy for mission, deepen Christian wisdom and foster collegial forms of leadership. Yet there are many congregations which have capable people of Christian character who can be challenged to offer themselves for self-supporting ministry, lay and ordained. Similarly, enriching the wisdom of the community through discipleship development is vital to the life and witness of the church. As Anglicans grasp the depth and wonder of the Christian story embodied in Anglican practice, confidence, capacity and capability will grow with consequent impact in all the communities of this country.

Argentine Anglican Friendship

Sheffield Diocese is twinned with the Diocese of Argentina. There are lots of good reasons for a diocese to have a link with Argentina. The Igaçu Falls, site of the famous film, *The Mission*; Tierra del Fuego and the Magdalene Straits with their fierce South Atlantic beauty; Mendoza olives and wine; landscapes that pan into the horizon for mile upon mile and the great upheaval of the Andes in the west. Sadly none of these were the reason why the Dioceses of Argentina and Sheffield formed a partnership. Instead it was the shadow of the Falklands/Malvinas War of 1981 which lay behind their partnership. Both Sheffield and Buenos Aires lost service personnel in the Falklands/Malvinas conflict and it was this shared suffering which prompted suggestions for a link. In addition major differences between the two dioceses offered opportunities for mutual understanding, engagement and appreciation. Numerically the Diocese of Argentina is much smaller than the Diocese of Sheffield, its resource base is much more fragile and its relationship to the host society is very different from that in England. The Anglican Argentine church began as a chaplaincy church for the English who built the railways and engaged in commerce. Consequently a number of the church buildings are built beside railway lines. Yet the diocese is very small, with about 12 active clergy, six stipendiary and six self-supporting, including the Archbishop and an ex-patriot mission partner. It has 14 parishes, mainly in the city and province of Buenos Aires, where one third of the country's population live, though Cordoba, Rosario and Mendoza have relatively robust congregations. In part the size of the church reflects the limitations on proselytising imposed upon them by the Roman Catholic Church until the second half of the twentieth century. The Diocese of Argentina therefore represents an interesting comparative case study about how Anglicans in diverse contexts improvise in ways which share a family resemblance.

Three in particular stand out. The first is situated in the north west of the Province of Buenos Aires and has a modest adult congregation of about 50. Traditionally it was one of the more conservative and affluent English-speaking congregations but latterly, in concert with the rest of the diocese, it has embraced Spanish as its liturgical language. Indeed the parish priest, a former Roman Catholic priest, is the first cleric whose mother tongue is Spanish and his background has also added a more sacramental dimension to the church's worship and thinking. Although the language change has been painful, it has enabled the congregation to engage in imaginative and culturally sensitive mission to the local population beyond the old English-speaking community. For example, they have a School of Music for disadvantaged youngsters with professional teachers paid for by the church and instruments purchased using money from the Argentine Diocesan Association based in Sheffield. They also run a School of Carpentry on the same lines, training young people to become competent artisans. In addition there is a toy recycling project which fixes old toys and sends them to disadvantaged children in the north of the country, a men's football project which includes quiet days for prayer and a counselling service for local people staffed by professionals who offer their services at a cost far below the market rate.

The second parish is located in the midst of the financial sector of the city of Buenos Aires. Squeezed between high-rise office blocks, its relatively small size and apparent impotence reflect both the challenges and opportunities that Anglican mission faces in urban Argentina. Most of the surrounding population are office workers who leave the city centre in the evening. Those who remain are the poor who live in informal housing hidden under freeways and some more affluent urban residents who live in some nearby new housing. The parish's vision is to reach out to these three constituencies as well as to nourish the discipleship of the existing congregation as a Spanish-speaking Argentine Anglican church for all people. They are trying to engage the culture through the arts, debates on contemporary issues and in conversation with influential people. They also want to offer hospitality and help to street-dwellers and reach out evangelistically to new residential areas in the neighbourhood as well as to the working communities in the centre of Buenos Aires in partnership with others from the diocese. In all of this they aim to express an Anglicanism which is catholic, charismatic and open to ecumenical initiatives.

The third parish lies very close to one of the main railway lines which carry commuters from the suburbs and peri-urban areas into the city centre of Buenos Aires. The congregation numbers about 200 or more and has a significant youth ministry aided by the fact that many young people remain home based whilst at university and beyond. The parish priest has been in post for 16 years and has sought to encourage a form of worship and a style of leadership which reflects the liberty of a liturgical and ordered church in contrast to the authoritarianism of many local Pentecostal sects. The sign of an ordered, intergenerational, Spanish-speaking church, with an open Bible, lively worship, deep fellowship and an accountable, approachable ministry, is also proving attractive to those disenchanted by local Roman Catholicism. Here is a church where the people and priest work together rather than one where the priest or pastor acts as a unilateral authority or where anarchic individualistic intuition reigns. The congregation see their mission configured around social action, marriage renewal and youth work. Their outreach to displaced people through their Social Action Project began some years ago when the church realised that the children of these folk were begging around the station. The project aims to teach basic skills to the mothers, such as sewing and knitting, and to use painting as a means of building up their confidence and creativity. The younger children are occupied with creative activities as well as being fed. The church also offers financial incentives to the teenagers to stay in education and gain qualifications that will enable them to obtain longer-term, stable employment. Their marriage renewal ministry is expressed through a Spanish medium Marriage Encounter course, which is advertised locally and has attracted considerable numbers of couples, many of whom have become part of the church. The personal quality of the fellowship experienced in these groups and in congregational life acts as a draw to those who feel alienated by the formalism they experience in the Roman Catholic Church and the anonymity of large collectivist Pentecostal gatherings. A local variant of 'Back to Church Sunday' called 'Come to Church' has also helped in this regard. In addition to the social concern and marriage ministry there is considerable work done among young people. Interestingly these young people are very committed to the Anglican Communion since international Anglicanism embeds them in a larger Christian world, gives them a more deeply rooted sense of discipleship and enables them to visit other parts of the world within the Communion.

The way Anglicans in Argentina are improvising in mission reveals some interesting themes with affinities to English Anglican mission. The mission at the first church is rooted in the conviction that truth and beauty reflect God's character encountered in worship and life. Consequently music and craft offer a taste of this character, whilst affordable counselling helps people to face themselves truthfully in the love of God. This approach is a hermeneutical rather than an abstract approach to mission, a listening to and interpreting of the signs of God's activity around the area and joining in. Furthermore the costly commitment to worship in the vernacular embodies an incarnational understanding of God, whilst the Anglican way of worship integrating liturgy and liberty offers a distinctive way of encountering God in contrast to the perceived formalism of much Roman Catholic worship and the somewhat anarchic yet authoritarian Pentecostal spirituality surrounding it. The city centre parish focuses upon hospitable Anglican worship with an open Bible, shared ministry and an acceptance of diversity. It seeks to be a 'catholic' church by engaging people of very different backgrounds and spiritualities through conversational mission. In addition it embodies a narrative and hermeneutical mission, which looks to integrate and interpret the contemporary story of city centre Buenos Aires within the Anglican story of hospitable outreach. The third parish illustrates how witness is crucial to evangelism. The character of the community and the way its life and worship express the story of God's grace in Christ are fundamental to the ongoing credibility of the church in that context. Since the Anglican Argentine church is not the established church, its impact depends upon the contemporary witness of its members' lives. Likewise their mission involves interpreting their context and responding to this with hospitable friendship. Again this is hermeneutical, incarnational mission, which involves sharing God's friendship with those they find themselves among. In addition Anglican inclusiveness enables them to work in partnership with other Christian groups. They can thereby be a bridge between such groups when the latter find it more difficult to recognise one another.

Sharing Friendship in Practice

The stories of these congregations in South Yorkshire and in Argentina exemplify Anglican friendship at its best. Here we see mission and evangelism as being about a faithful and public witness to the stranger-seeking Gospel, an embodied witness in the lives and performance of ordinary congregations, an example of the beauty of holiness engaging their host communities.[5] Their practices and habits enrich their imagination enabling them to improvise in ways appropriate to their very different contexts. The stories reveal that both English and Argentine Anglican worship embodies the liturgical liberty of common worship. In Argentina this enables those who find Roman Catholic formalism and Pentecostal anarchy stifling or overwhelming to find a spiritual home in the Anglican tradition. In England it has enabled the Church of England to maintain very diverse traditions within a single polity. In both cases worship is characterised by a 'both-and' rather than 'either-or' approach. Anglican worship involves priest and people together. Scripture and sacrament are both treasured. There is shape and also Spirit in worship. Worship is therefore common in the sense that it is a mutually shared and accountable experience rather than being controlled simply by the clergy. In this way worship reflects the love of God reaching out to an estranged human community and inviting that community to be friends as they worship God together. The quality of Anglican congregational life in both countries is a distinctive feature of Anglican mission. People are drawn to these Anglican congregations because they are actively welcomed and personally known. This is a mission of hospitality and friendship. The Marriage Encounter ministry and ministry among youth show how the quality of relationships help folk to sense that they are part of a Christian community rather than the sort of liturgical or congregational collective they have experienced in their Roman Catholic or Pentecostal background. A similar theme emerged in one of the English parishes as common meals built community. Furthermore in Argentina the Anglican Church is an open community willing to engage with

---

5   I draw here upon themes in Stone, *Evangelism after Christendom*.

different views and discuss matters of faith. Consequently this fosters a relatively mature and stable discipleship even though it may be less spectacular than in the Pentecostal gatherings. Newcomers are also surprised by the accountability and accessibility of the clergy. In addition one young man said he was attracted to the Anglican Church by its sense of tradition and its worldwide, historic character. It is this slow, embedded, deep discipleship which characterises Anglican growth at its best.

Communicating with people in their vernacular is at the heart of Anglican mission. Spanish is now the primary language of the Anglican Church in Argentina and represents a commitment to be Argentine Anglicans rather than Anglicans who happen to live in Argentina. The change has been costly, particularly for older Anglicans, but it has enabled the church to embody the critical Anglican practice of pastoral mission; that is, mission which engages host communities in their vernacular languages and cultures. The English-speaking congregations have also had to re-learn how to share faith in the vernacular. The stories told above display an Anglican mission which pays attention to the locality and, through prayer and careful listening, discerns what God is inviting the church to be and do in that context as an expression of God's compassion. In this way it also reflects an amicable mission committed to long term friendship with local communities. In both England and Argentina, the Anglican Church has relatively limited power. Consequently mission is about being a tactical rather than a strategic player in society.[6] The church is a sign rather than a statement about grace which is seen in the variety of ways the parishes of the diocese are engaged with those around them as a sign of the friendship of God in Christ. In Argentina such friendship is rooted in accessible and liturgical forms of worship which are recognisable to and respected by those with a Roman Catholic background and yet are also ones which allow for the informality and passion of Pentecostal worship in a Latin context. It is witnessed in the painful process of becoming a Spanish-speaking church and in the sacrificial offering of time and resources to the needy. It is seen in the determination to remain connected to its Anglican heritage. In all of this Anglicans in Argentina today are discovering their distinctive identity as an indigenous Anglican church whose distinctive mission is to share friendship in Latin America. In South Yorkshire the Anglican Church is learning that it must prayerfully seek ways to improvise upon its inherited practices in order to engage contemporary people, whether this is by finding new ways to eat together, to symbolise the faith through art or

---

6   M. De Certeau, *The Practice of Everyday Life* (Berkeley: University of California Press, 1988), pp. 35–6.

to express hospitality to the vulnerable on the streets of Sheffield. This is a new way of sharing friendship in the vernacular.

Conclusion

In this book I have been arguing that the character of Anglicanism in England involves sharing friendship, friendship which reflects the way of Jesus to engage with those on the fringes, the margins, the *paroikio* (parishioners/strangers). This is the calling of the Church of England and is reflected in its commitments to common worship, to congregational life, to a shared history and to a pastoral approach to mission. This story of friendship for the stranger was a gift from North Africa and a story shared across the Anglican Communion. Such friendship requires that Anglicans, like Christ, divest themselves of powers which separate them from ordinary people and are willing to share what they are and have with them wherever they find themselves. It is kenotic friendship, friendship which seeks to befriend strangers or those who have become estranged. It embraces the strange world we inhabit as an occasion to explore the bright mystery of God's grace. It is friendship most explicitly seen in congregations and dioceses which embody the range of traditions and cultures of their contexts. It is ecclesial friendship committed to being among vulnerable communities, friendship which can only fulfil this vocation because God by his Spirit refuses to be apart from them.

This story informs the reflections of some of our best Anglican theologians and thinkers, as I have tried to demonstrate in the second section of the book. They reflect on the practice and performance of the church in order to see what the outworking of the story of Jesus means today. This intellectual work is also a part of Anglican mission. It is a way of giving voice to the richness of practice and helping practitioners to sense the depths of their story and its profound challenges. It is indicative of the argumentative and political character of Anglican discernment as the ways of God are found through robust conversation within and beyond the church. Yet the test of this friendship is the same as that of the Parable of the Sheep and the Goats in Matthew chapter 25:31–end. There Christ in glory judges the performance of those ranged before him. What characterises this judgement is the phrase 'in so far as you did it to the least of these my brethren, you did it to me'(v. 40). The parable seems to invite all people to care for the needy. However this phrase is used in the Gospel of Matthew to refer to his disciples and the phrase 'all the nations' (v. 32) is a Jewish reference to the Gentiles or those outside the community of Israel. Hence it implies that the world is judged by how it responds to the disciples when they are utterly vulnerable and powerless, that is walking the way of the cross. This is therefore a challenge to Christians to become vulnerable and to walk the way of the cross as a form of evangelism. Only thus will the face of Christ be set before the world.

Anglicans, like many Christians in contemporary England, can feel anxious about the future. Survivalism is a potent driver but it undermines the Gospel since it focuses on self-perceived needs rather than upon the mystery of Christ in our midst. Like John the Baptist, Anglicans need to recover confidence that the one they long for, God's gift as lamb, is actually in their midst, even though they don't always realise who and where he is.[7] God has not deserted his people but is inviting them to trust deeply and passionately in his commitment to be with his people to the end of time.[8] The desert is where Christians are formed through being stripped down and forced to confront their anxieties in ways they cannot avoid. It is where the Lord woos his people and also disciplines them. It is on the edge where Christians learn to trust and see truthfully.[9] It is where the interior journey is deepened since they cannot flee from themselves. It is where images of God and the self grow painfully yet together. It is where intimacy and depth replace superficiality and complacency. It is where truth is faced before God, a truth asking disciples who are they really for and what is their deepest desire. Deserts divest Christians of utopias and dreams yet also take them to a place of openness where they discover themselves to be in the presence of love itself, the ground of all Christian mission. Anglicans are nomads who wander and yet discover God's way which roots them in the long story of grace and invites them to walk trustfully into the unknown future. This is a journey which no human agency can control. Instead the undercover nature of God leads as a reassuring presence and providence inviting people to befriend all that comes to them as a gift, the occasion by which vocation is clarified.[10] For Anglicans this is a call to the difficult places, to serving among communities which seem strange and threatening. It is at the heart of parochial ministry and should be the driver for any fresh expressions initiatives. This is why it is vital to pay attention to ordinary Christian communities and to dioceses such as Sheffield and Argentina, all in challenging contexts. These fragile and often uncomfortable contexts act as beacons and barometers of faithful Anglican practice. They resist any temptation to see religion as a brand. They are a sharp reality check

---

[7] John 1: 26.

[8] Matthew 28: 20.

[9] John B. Thomson, *Church on Edge? Practising Christian Ministry Today* (London: DLT, 2004).

[10] I am grateful to Graham Pigott for helping me to grasp and clarify these insights.

asking whether mission is about authentic pilgrimage and spiritual process or simply marketed imagination. Their attempts to improvise show others how to follow Christ in contemporary mission precisely because they are in the midst of emptiness.

Sharing friendship with strangers embodies the character of Anglican Christian mission in England as it has emerged over the centuries through its commitment to common worship, community life, its history and the pastoral character of its mission. This is a mission which must be performed and theologically rooted if it is to be faithful to this calling. It is about being located among ordinary people in ways that enable them to display their response to the grace of God. It is about embracing the fundamental Anglican vocation to be a church in the ordinary rather than a church of the spectacular. As such, it often involves significant disempowerment of those called to share in this mission in order that a friendship can be established that embodies the sort of self-giving friendship Christ displayed. It involves embracing the way of humility outlined by Christ in the paschal process of his *kenosis* or self-emptying. Only then can Anglicans be free for God's mission. As W.H. Vanstone argues, the *kenosis* of God is seen in Jesus, who becomes the pattern for the way the church lives and the way society can recognise where the church is present.[11] Since mission happens in particular contexts there can be no abstract blueprint for mission. Instead Christian communities have to improvise within the contexts they find themselves in as communities of Christian practice.[12] The stories which are told in this chapter exemplify contemporary Anglicans improvising upon their tradition in the light of the Scriptures in order to find new ways of sharing this friendship in very different and demanding contexts. In these ordinary stories of Christian friendship is hope for the church. To use the language of Stanley Hauerwas, in such performances, the character of the Anglican community is displayed.

---

[11]   W.H. Vanstone, *Love's Endeavour, Love's Expense: The Response of Being and the Love of God* (London: DLT, 1977).

[12]   Walter Brueggemann, *Theology of the Old Testament: Testimony, Dispute, Advocacy* (Minneapolis, Fortress Press, 1997), p. 701.

Select Bibliography

Andrews, Christopher, *The Defence of the Realm* (London: Penguin, 2010).

Andrews, Dave, *Compassionate Community Work* (Carlisle: Piquant Editions Ltd, 2006).

Astley, Jeff, *Ordinary Theology: Looking, Listening and Learning in Theology* (Aldershot: Ashgate, 2002).

Astley, Jeff and Leslie J. Francis, *Exploring Ordinary Theology: Everyday Christian Believing and the Church* (Farnham: Ashgate, 2013).

Avis, Paul, *Ecumenical Theology and the Elusiveness of Doctrine* (London: SPCK, 1986).

_____ *Anglicanism and the Christian Church: Theological Resources in Historical Perspective* (Edinburgh: T & T Clark, 1989).

_____ *Christians In Communion* (London: Mowbray, 1990).

_____ *The Anglican Understanding of the Church: An Introduction* (London: SPCK, 2000).

_____ *Church, State and Establishment* (London: SPCK, 2001).

_____ *A Ministry Shaped by Mission* (London: Continuum, 2005).

Avis, Paul (ed.), *Public Faith? The State of Religious Belief and Practice in Britain* (London: SPCK, 2003).

Barley, Lynda, *Churchgoing Today* (London: Church House Publishing, 2006).

Barton, Stephen C. (ed.), *Where Shall Wisdom be Found? Wisdom in the Bible, the Church and the Contemporary World* (Edinburgh: T&T Clark, 1999).

Bayes, Paul and Tim Sledge with John Holbrook, Mark Rylands and Martin Seeley, *Mission-Shaped Parish: Traditional Church in a Changing Context* (London: Church House Publishing, 2006).

Bede, *Ecclesiastical History of the English Speaking People*, III/ 4 (London: J.M. Dent & Sons, 1912).

Berry, Philippa and Andrew Wernick (eds), *Shadow of Spirit: Postmodernism and Religion* (London and New York: Routledge, 1993).

Billings, Alan, *Making God Possible: The Task of Ordained Ministry Present and Future* (London: SPCK, 2010).

_____ *Lost Church: Why We Must Find it Again* (London: SPCK, 2012).

Birdwell, Jonathan and Martin Littler, *Faithful Citizens* (London: Demos, 2012).

Boesak, Alan, *Farewell to Innocence: A Social-Ethical Study of Black Theology and Black Power* (Johannesburg: Ravan Press, 1977).

_____ *Black and Reformed: Apartheid, Liberation and the Calvinist Tradition* (Johannesburg: Skotaville, 1986).

Bosch, David, *Transforming Mission* (Maryknoll: Orbis, 1992).

Braun, Willi, *Feasting and Social Rhetoric in Luke 14* (Cambridge: Cambridge University Press, 1995).

Bretherton, Luke, *Hospitality as Holiness: Christian Witness Amid Moral Diversity* (Farnham: Ashgate, 2006).

_____ *Christianity and Contemporary Politics: The Conditions and Possibilities of Faithful Witness* (Chichester: Wiley-Blackwell, 2010).

Brown, Colin (ed.), *The New International Dictionary of New Testament Theology*, vol. 3 (Exeter, Paternoster, 1978).

Brown, Callum, *Religion and Society in Twentieth Century Britain* (London: Pearson Longman, 2006).

_____ *The Death of Christian Britain: Understanding Secularism 1800–2000*, 2nd edn, (Abingdon: Routledge, 2009).

Brown, David, *Discipleship and Imagination: Christian Tradition and Truth* (Oxford: Oxford University Press, 2000).

Buchanan, Colin, *Cut the Connection: Disestablishment and the Church of England* (London: Darton, Longman and Todd, 1994).

Brueggemann, Walter, *Theology of the Old Testament: Testimony, Dispute, Advocacy* (Minneapolis, Fortress Press, 1997).

Bunch, David and Angus Ritchie (eds), *Prayer and Prophecy: The Essential Kenneth Leech* (London: Darton, Longman and Todd, 2009).

Burridge, Richard A., *Imitating Jesus: An Inclusive Approach to New Testament Ethics* (Grand Rapids, Michigan: Eerdmans, 2007).

Cameron, Helen et al. (eds), *Studying Local Churches: A Handbook* (London: SCM, 2005).

Cameron, Helen, *Resourcing Mission: Practical Theology for Changing Churches* (London: SCM, 2010).

Campbell, Gordon, *Bible: The Story of the King James Version 1611–2011* (Oxford: Oxford University Press, 2010).

Carey, George, 'Parties in the Church of England' in *Theology* 91 (1988), pp. 266–73.

Carmichael, Liz, *Friendship: Interpreting Christian Love* (T & T Clark: London, 2004).

Chadwick, N. and M. Dillon, *The Celtic Realms*, 3rd edn (London, 1974).

Chapman, Mark, *Anglican Theology* (London: T&T Clark International, 2012).

Collingwood, R.G., *The Idea of History* (Oxford: Oxford University Press, 1978).

Cray, Graham et al., *Mission Shaped Church* (London: Church House Publishing, 2004).

Cray, Graham, Ian Mobsby and Aaron Kennedy (eds), *Ancient Faith, Future Mission: Fresh Expressions of Church and the Kingdom of God* (Norwich: Canterbury Press, 2012).

Croft, Steven, *Transforming Christian Communities: Re-imagining the Church for the 21st Century* (London: Darton, Longman and Todd, 2002).

Croft, Steven (ed.), *The Future of the Parish System: Shaping the Church of England for the 21st Century* (London: Church House Publishing, 2006).

_____ *Mission Shaped Questions: Defining Issues for Today's Church* (London: Church House Publishing, 2008).

Croft, Steven and Ian Mobsby (eds), *Fresh Expressions in the Sacramental Tradition* (Norwich: Canterbury Press, 2009).

Crystal, David, *Begat: The King James Bible and the English Language* (Oxford: Oxford University Press, 2010).

Davie, Grace, *Religion in Britain since 1945: Believing without Belonging* (Oxford: Oxford University Press, 1994).

_____ *Religion in Modern Europe: A Memory Mutates* (Oxford: Oxford University Press, 2000).

_____ *Europe: The Exceptional Case: Parameters of Faith in the Modern World* (London: Darton, Longman and Todd, 2002).

_____ *The Sociology of Religion* (London: Sage, 2007).

Davie, Grace, Paul Heelas and Linda Woodhead (eds), *Predicting Religion: Christian, Secular and Alternative Futures* (Aldershot: Ashgate, 2003).

Davison, Andrew and Alison Milbank, *For the Parish: A Critique of Fresh Expressions* (London: SCM, 2010).

Dawn, Maggie, *Like the Wideness of the Sea: Women Bishops and the Church of England* (London: Darton, Longman and Todd, 2013).

Deanesly, Margaret, *A History of the Medieval Church 590–1500* (Oxford: Oxford University Press, 1972).

De Certeau, M., *The Practice of Everyday Life* (Berkeley: University of California Press, 1988).

De Gruchy, John W., 'South African Theology Comes of Age', *Religious Studies Review* 17/3 (July 1991), pp. 197–229.

De Gruchy, John and C. Villa Vicencio (eds), *Apartheid is a Heresy* (Cape Town: David Philip, 1983).

Dormor, Duncan, Jack McDonald and Jeremy Caddick, *Anglicanism: The Answer to Modernity* (London: Continuum, 2003).

Drane, John, *After McDonaldization: Mission, Ministry and Christian Discipleship in an Age of Uncertainty* (London: Darton, Longman and Todd, 2008).

Eusebius of Caesarea, *The History of the Church*, trans. G.A. Williamson (London: Penguin, 1965).

Finney, John, *Recovering the Past: Celtic and Roman Mission* (London: DLT, 1996).

Ford, David F. (ed.), *The Modern Theologians: An Introduction to Christian Theology in the Twentieth Century*, 2 vols (Oxford: Blackwell, 1989).

Ford, David F., *Self and Salvation: Being Transformed* (Cambridge: Cambridge University Press, 1999).

_____ *Christian Wisdom: Desiring God and Learning Love* (Cambridge: Cambridge University Press, 2007).

_____ *The Future of Theology* (Chichester: Wiley-Blackwell, 2011).

Ford, David and Dennis Stamps (eds), *Essentials of Christian Community* (Edinburgh: T&T Clark, 1996).

Gadamer, Hans Georg, *Truth and Method*, 2nd edn (London: Sheed & Ward, 1993).

Gibbs, Eddie and Ian Coffrey, *Church Next: Quantum Changes in Christian Ministry* (Leicester: IVP, 2001).

Gibbs, Eddie and Ryan K. Bolger, *Emerging Churches: Creating Christian Community in Postmodern Cultures* (London: SPCK, 2006).

Giddens, Anthony, *Modernity and Self-Identity: Self and Society in the Late Modern Age* (Cambridge: Polity Press, 1991).

Gill, Robin, *The Myth of the Empty Church* (London: SPCK, 1993).

_____ *Churchgoing and Christian Ethics* (Cambridge: Cambridge University Press, 1999).

Goba, Bonganjalo, *An Agenda for Black Theology* (Johannesburg: Skotaville, 1988).

Goodhew, David, Andrew Roberts and Michael Volland, *Fresh: An Introduction to Fresh Expressions of Church and Pioneer Ministry* (London: SCM, 2012).

Gorringe, Timothy J., *Furthering Humanity: A Theology of Culture* (Aldershot: Ashgate, 2004).

Gray, John, *Enlightenment's Wake: Politics and Culture at the Close of the Modern Age* (Abingdon: Routledge, 1995).

Green, Garett, *Theology, Hermeneutics and Imagination: The Crisis of Interpretation at the End of Modernity* (Cambridge: Cambridge University Press, 2000).

Gregory Jones, L. and Kevin R. Armstrong, *Resurrecting Excellence: Shaping Faithful Christian Ministry* (Michigan: Eerdmans, 2006).

Grundy, Malcolm, *Understanding Congregations: A New Shape for the Local Church* (London: Mowbray,1998).

_____ *Leadership and Oversight: New Models for Episcopal Ministry* (London: Mowbray, 2011).

Guest, Matthew, Karin Tusting and Linda Woodhead, *Congregational Studies in the UK: Christianity in a Post-Christian Context* (Aldershot: Ashgate, 2005).

Habgood, John, 'Where we get our civic ideas from', Review of Oliver O'Donovan, *The Ways of Judgment* in *The Church Times* (17 February 2006), p. 23.

Hardy, Daniel W., 'Today's Word for Today: Gerhard Ebeling', *Expository Times* 93 (Dec 1981), pp. 68–72.

_____ *God's Ways with the World* (Edinburgh: T & T Clark, 1996).

_____ *Finding the Church* (London: SCM, 2001).

Hardy, Daniel W. and Ford, David F., *Jubilate, Theology in Praise* (London: Darton, Longman &Todd, 1984), republished as Daniel W. and Ford, David F., *Living in Praise – Worshipping and Knowing God* (London: Darton, Longman and Todd, 2005).

Hardy, Daniel W. with Deborah Hardy Ford, Peter Ochs and David Ford, *Wording a Radiance: Parting Conversations on God and the Church* (London: SCM, 2010).

Hastings, Adrian (ed.), *A World History of Christianity* (London: Cassell, 1999).

Hauerwas, Stanley M., 'Forgiveness and Political Community', *Worldview* 23/1–2 (January–February 1980), pp. 1–2, 15–16.

_____ *Vision and Virtue: Essays in Christian Ethical Reflection* (Notre Dame: University of Notre Dame Press, 1981).

_____ *A Community of Character: Toward a Constructive Christian Social Ethic*, 4th edn (Notre Dame: University of Notre Dame Press, 1986).

_____ *The Peaceable Kingdom: A Primer in Christian Ethics*, 3rd edn (Notre Dame: University of Notre Dame Press, 1986).

_____ *Christian Existence Today: Essays on Church, World and Living in Between* (North Carolina: The Labyrinth Press, 1988).

_____ *Against the Nations: War and Survival in a Liberal Society* (Notre Dame: University of Notre Dame Press, 1992).

_____ *Dispatches from the Front: Theological Engagements with the Secular* (Durham: Duke University Press, 1994).

_____ *In Good Company: The Church as Polis* (Notre Dame: University of Notre Dame Press, 1995).

_____ *Wilderness Wanderings: Probing Twentieth Century Theology and Philosophy* (Colorado: Westview Press, 1997).

_____ *Sanctify Them in the Truth: Holiness Exemplified* (Edinburgh: T&T Clark, 1998).

_____ *A Better Hope: Resources for a Church Confronting Capitalism, Democracy and Postmodernity* (Michigan: Brazos Press, 2000).

_____ 'Many Hands Working: A Response to Charles Mathewes', *Anglican Theological Review* 82/2 (Spring 2000), pp. 343–60.

_____ *With the Grain of the Universe: The Church's Witness and Natural Theology* (London: SCM, 2001).

_____ *Performing the Faith: Bonhoeffer and the Practice of Nonviolence* (London: SPCK, 2004).

_____ *The State of the University: Academic Knowledges and the Knowledge of God* (Oxford: Blackwell, 2007).

_____ *Learning to Speak Christian* (London: SCM, 2011).

_____ *War and the American Difference: Theological Reflections on Violence and National Identity* (Grand Rapids MI; Baker Academic, 2011).

_____ *Approaching the End: Eschatological Reflections on Church, Politics and Life* (Grand Rapids MI/Cambridge UK: Eerdmans, 2013).

Hauerwas, Stanley, Nancy Murphy and Mark Nation (eds), *Theology without Foundations: Religious Practice and the Future of Theological Truth* (Nashville: Abingdon, 1994).

Hauerwas, Stanley, and Charles Pinches, *Christians Among the Virtues: Theological Conversations with Ancient and Modern Ethics* (Notre Dame: University of Notre Dame Press, 1997).

Hauerwas, Stanley, and Samuel Wells (eds), *The Blackwell Companion to Christian Ethics* (Oxford: Blackwell, 2006).

Hellas, Paul and Linda Woodhead et al., *The Spiritual Revolution: Why Religion is Giving Way to Spirituality*, (Oxford: Blackwell, 2005).

Hengel, Martin, *The Charismatic Leader and His Followers* (Edinburgh: T&T Clark, 1981).

Herbert, David, *Religion and Civil Society: Re-thinking Public Religion in the Contemporary World* (Aldershot: Ashgate, 2000).

Higton, Mike, *Difficult Gospel: The Theology of Rowan Williams* (London: SCM, 2004).

Hollinghurst, Steve, *Mission Shaped Evangelism* (Norwich: Canterbury Press, 2010).

Hull, John (ed.), *New Directions in Religious Education* (Lewes: The Falmer Press, 1982).

Hunter, Davison, *To Change the World: The Irony, Tragedy and Possibility of Christianity in the late Modern World* (Oxford: Oxford University Press, 2010).

Impey, Richard, *How to Develop Your Local Church: Working with the Wisdom of the Congregation* (London: SPCK, 2010).

Inge, John, *A Christian Theology of Place* (Aldershot: Ashgate, 2003).

Insole, Christopher J., 'The Truth Behind Practices: Wittgenstein, Robinson Crusoe and Ecclesiology' in *Studies in Christian Ethics* 20.3 (2007), pp. 364–82.

Jackson, Bob, *Hope for the Church: Contemporary Strategies for Growth* (London: Church House Publishing, 2002).

_____ *The Road to Growth: Towards a Thriving Church* (London: Church House Publishing, 2005).

Jenkins, Timothy, *Religion in English Everyday Life: An Ethnographic Approach* (Oxford: Berghahn Books, 1999).

_____ *An Experiment in Providence: How Faith Engages with the World* (London: SPCK, 2006).

Jones, L. Gregory and Kevin R Armstrong, *Resurrecting Excellence: Faithful Christian Ministry* (Michigan: Eerdmans, 2006).

Kallenberg Brad J., *Ethics as Grammar: Changing the Postmodern Subject* (Notre Dame: University of Notre Dame Press, 2001).

Kittel, G. and Friedrich, G., *Theological Dictionary of the New Testament* vol. 4 (Grand Rapids: Eerdmans, 1967).

Leech, Kenneth, *The Sky is Red: Discerning the Signs of the Times* (London: Darton, Longman & Todd, 1997).

Lindbeck, George A., *The Nature of Doctrine, Religion in a Post Liberal Age* (Philadelphia: Westminster Press, 1984).

Longenecker, Richard N. (ed.), *Patterns of Discipleship in the New Testament* (Cambridge: Eerdmans, 1996).

Loughlin, Gerald, *Telling God's Story: Bible, Church and Narrative Theology* (Cambridge: Cambridge University Press, 1996).

Lyotard, Jean-Francois, *The Postmodern Condition: A Report on Knowledge*, trans. G. Bennington and B. Massumi (Minneapolis: University of Minnesota Press, 1984).

MacCulloch, Diarmaid, *A History of Christianity* (London: Allen Lane, 2009).

Maimela, Simon, *Proclaim Freedom to My People: Essays in Religion and Politics* (Johannesburg: Skotaville, 1987).

Martin, David, *On Secularisation: towards a Revised General Theory* (Aldershot: Ashgate, 2005).

_____ *The Future of Christianity: Reflections of Violence and Democracy, Religion and Secularisation* (Farnham: Ashgate, 2011).

Mayne, Michael, *The Enduring Melody* (London: Darton, Longman and Todd, 2006).

Mayr-Harting, Henry, *The Coming of Christianity to Anglo-Saxon England* (London: Batsford, 1972).

McGrath, Alister E., *A Scientific Theology*, 3 vols (Edinburgh: T&T Clark, 2001–2003).

Meeks, Wayne A., *The First Urban Christians The Social World of the Apostle Paul* (New Haven and London: Yale University Press, 2003).

Milbank, John, *Theology and Social Theory: Beyond Secular Reason* (Oxford: Blackwell, 1990).

_____ *The Word Made Strange: Theology, Language, Culture* (Oxford: Blackwell,1997).

_____ *Being Reconciled: Ontology and Pardon* (London: Routledge, 2003).

_____ *The Future of Love: Essays in Political Theology* (London: SCM, 2009).

_____ 'The Church is the Site of the True Society', *The Church Times* (16 December 2011), pp. 12, 14.

Milbank, John, Catherine Pickstock and Graham Ward (eds), *Radical Orthodoxy* (London: Routledge, 1999).

Moltmann-Wendel, Elizabeth, *Rediscovering Friendship* (London: SCM, 2000).

Moore, Basil (ed.), *Black Theology: The South African Voice* (London: Hurst & Co, 1973).

Morris, Jeremy (ed.), *Faith and Freedom: Exploring Radical Orthodoxy* (Affirming Catholicism; Third Millennium, 2003).

Morisy, Ann, *Journeying Out: A New Approach to Christian Mission* (Moorhouse: Harnsbury, 2004).

_____ *Bewildered and Troubled: Enacting Hope in Troubled Times* (London: Continuum, 2009).

Mosala, Itumaleng J., *Biblical Hermeneutics and Black Theology in South Africa* (Michigan: Eerdmans, 1989).

Mosala, Itumaleng J. and Buti Thlagale, *The Unquestionable Right to be Free: Essays in Black Theology* (Johannesburg: Skotaville, 1986).

Moynagh, Michael, *emergingchurch.intro* (Oxford: Monarch Books, 2004).

Moynagh, Michael, with Philip Harrold, *Church for Every Context: An Introduction to Theology and Practice* (London: SCM, 2012).

Myers, Benjamin, *Christ the Stranger: The Theology of Rowan Williams* (London: T&T Clark International, 2012).

Norwood, Robin, *Women Who Love Too Much* (London: Arrow Books, 2004).

Nouwen, Henry J.M., *Reaching Out: The Three Movements of the Spiritual Life* (London: Collins, 1976).

O'Donovan, Oliver, *Resurrection and the Moral Order: An Outline for Evangelical Ethics*, 2nd edn, (Leicester: Apollos, 1994).

_____ *The Desire of the Nations: Rediscovering the Roots of Political Theology* (Cambridge: Cambridge University Press, 1996).

_____ 'Response to Respondents: Behold the Lamb!', *Studies in Christian Ethics* 11/ 2 (1998), pp. 91–110.

_____ *The Ways of Judgment* (Cambridge UK: Eerdmans, 2005).

Patterson, Susan, *Realist Christian Theology in a Postmodern Age* (Cambridge: Cambridge University Press, 1999).

Pecknold, C.C., *Transforming Postliberal Theology: George Lindbeck, Pragmatism and Scripture* (London: T & T Clark, 2005).

Percy, Martyn, *Clergy: Origin of Species* (London; Continuum, 2006).

_____ *Shaping the Church: The Promise of Implicit Theology* (Farnham: Ashgate, 2010).

_____ *The Ecclesial Canopy: Faith, Hope and Charity* (Farnham: Ashgate, 2012).

_____ *Anglicanism: Confidence, Commitment and Communion* (Farnham: Ashgate, 2013).

Pickstock, Catherine, *After Writing: On the Liturgical Consummation of Philosophy* (Oxford: Blackwell, 1998).

Pohl, Christine D., *Making Room: Recovering hospitality as a Christian Tradition* (Grand Rapids, Cambridge MI: Eerdmans, 1999).

Pollard, N., F. Kronenburg and D. Sakellariou (eds), *A Political Practice of Occupational Therapy* (Churchill Livingstone, 2008).

Pollard, Sam, 'Spirit-Dependent Discipleship and Contextual Mission: Establishing Stanley Hauerwas as a Resource for Contemporary Missiological Debate' unpublished MSS, Bristol University 2011.

Porter, Stanley E., and Matthew Malcolm (eds), *Horizons in Hermeneutics: A Festschrift in Honor of Anthony C. Thiselton* (Grand Rapids Michigan/ Cambridge UK: Eerdmans, 2013).

Radcliffe, Timothy, *I Call You Friends* (London: Continuum, 2001).

Radner, Ephraim and Philip Turner, *The Fate of Communion: The Agony of Anglicanism and the Future of a Global Church* (Cambridge: Eerdmans, 2006).

Redfern, Alastair, *Being Anglican* (London: DLT, 2000).

Rooms, Nigel, *The Faith of the English: Integrating Christ and Culture* (London: SPCK, 2011).

Sacks, Jonathan, *The Great Partnership: God, Science and the Search for Meaning* (London: Hodder & Stoughton Ltd, 2011).

Santer, Mark (ed.), *Approaches to Authority, Community and the Unity of the Church* (London: SPCK, 1982).

Scruton, Roger, *A Political Philosophy: Arguments for Conservatism* (London: Continuum, 2006).

_____ *Our Church: A Personal History of the Church of England* (London: Atlantic Books, 2012).

Setiloane, Gabriel M., *African Theology: An Introduction* (Johannesburg: Skotaville, 1986).

Shakespeare, Steven, 'The New Romantics: a Critique of Radical Orthodoxy', *Theology* 103 (2000), pp. 163–77.

Shanks, Andrew, *God and Modernity: A New and Better Way to do Theology* (London: Routledge, 2000).

Sheldrake, Philip, *Spaces for the Sacred: Place, Memory and Identity* (Baltimore, Maryland: The John Hopkins University Press, 2001).

Shier-Jones, Angela, *Pioneer Ministry and Fresh Expressions of Church* (London: SPCK, 2009).

Shortt, Rupert, *Rowan's Rule: The Biography of the Archbishop* (London: Hodder & Stoughton, 2009).

Smith, Dennis E., 'Meal Customs: Greco-Roman Meal Customs' in D. Freedman (ed.), *The Anchor Bible Dictionary* (New Haven & London: Yale University Press, 2007).

Stout, Jeffrey, *Democracy and Tradition* (Princetown: Princetown University Press, 2004).

Stone, Bryan, *Evangelism after Christendom: The Theology and Practice of Christian Witness* (Grand Rapids, Michigan: Brazos Press, 2010).

Sykes, Stephen, *Unashamed Anglicanism* (London: Darton, Longman and Todd, 1995).

Taylor, Charles, *A Secular Age* (London: Belknap Harvard, 2007).

Taylor, John V., *The Go between God* (London: SCM, 1972).

Thiessen Nation, Mark and Samuel Wells, *Faithfulness and Fortitude: In Conversation with Stanley Hauerwas* (Edinburgh: T&T Clark, 2000).

Thiselton, Anthony C., *The Two Horizons: New Testament Hermeneutics and Philosophical Description with special reference to Heidegger, Bultmann, Gadamer and Wittgenstein* (Exeter: Paternoster, 1980).

_____ *New Horizons in Hermeneutics: The Theory and Practice of Transforming Biblical Reading* (London: Harper Collins, 1992).

_____ *Interpreting God and the Postmodern Self: On Meaning, Manipulation and Promise* (Edinburgh: T&T Clark, 1995).

_____ 'Human Being, Relationality and Time in Hebrews, 1 Corinthians and Western Traditions', *Ex Audito* 13 (1997), pp. 76–95.

_____ *The Hermeneutics of Doctrine* (Cambridge UK: Eerdmans, 2007).

Thompson, E.A., 'The Origin of Christianity in Scotland', *Scottish Historical Review* 37 (1958).

Thomson, John B., 'Protestant Theology: South Africa' in Alister E.McGrath (ed.), *The Blackwell Encyclopedia of Modern Christian Thought* (Oxford: Basil Blackwell, 1993), pp. 520–24.

_____ *The Ecclesiology of Stanley Hauerwas: A Christian Theology of Liberation* (Aldershot: Ashgate, 2003).

_____ *Church on Edge? Practising Christian Ministry Today* (London: Darton, Longman and Todd, 2004).

_____ *DOXA: A Discipleship Course* (London: Darton, Longman and Todd, 2007).

_____ *Living Holiness: Stanley Hauerwas and the Church* (London: Epworth, 2010).

Torrance, Thomas F. (ed.), *Belief in Science and in Christian Life: The Relevance of Michael Polanyi's Thought for Christian Faith and Life* (Edinburgh: Handsel Press, 1980).

Turnbull, Michael and Donald McFadyen, *The State of the Church and the Church of the State: Re-Imagining the Church of England for our World Today* (London: Darton, Longman and Todd, 2012).

Vanier, Jean, *Community and Growth* (London: Darton, Longman and Todd, 1979).

Vanstone, W.H., *Love's Endeavour, Love's Expense: The Response of Being and the Love of God* (London: Darton, Longman and Todd, 1977).

Wallis, Ian, *Holy Saturday Faith: Rediscovering the Legacy of Jesus* (London: SPCK, 2000).

Walls, Andrew and Cathy Ross (eds), *Mission in the 21st Century: Exploring the Five Marks of Global Mission* (London: Darton, Longman and Todd, 2008).

Walton, Roger, *The Reflective Disciple* (London: Epworth, 2009).

Wansbrough, Henry (ed.), *Jesus and the Oral Gospel* (Sheffield: JSOT Press, 1991).

Ward, Graham, *Cities of God* (London: Routledge, 2000).

_____ *The Politics of Discipleship: Becoming Postmaterial Citizens* (London: SCM, 2009).

Ward, Kevin, *A History of Global Anglicanism* (Cambridge: Cambridge University Press, 2007).

Ward, Kevin and Emma Wild-Wood, *The East African Revival: History and Legacies* (Farnham: Ashgate, 2012).

Ward, Pete, *Gods Behaving Badly: Media, Religion and Celebrity Culture* (London: SCM, 2011).

Weder, H, 'Disciple, Discipleship', in D.N. Freedman (ed.), *The Anchor Bible Dictionary* vol. 2 (New York: Doubleday, 1992), pp. 207–10.

Wells, Samuel, 'The Disarming Virtue of Stanley Hauerwas', *Scottish Journal of Theology* 52/1 (1999), pp. 82–88.

_____ *Improvisation: The Drama of Christian Ethics* (London: SPCK, 2004).

_____ *God's Companions: Reimagining Christian Ethics* (Blackwells: Oxford, 2006).

_____ *Be Not Afraid: Facing Fear with Faith* (Grand Rapids, Michigan: Brazos, 2011).

Wells, Samuel and Sarah Coakley (eds), *Praying for England: Priestly Presence in Contemporary Culture* (London: Continuum, 2008).

Wells, Samuel and Ben Quash, *Introducing Christian Ethics* (Oxford: Wiley-Blackwell, 2010).

Wells, Samuel, and Marcia A. Owen, *Living Without Enemies: Being Present in the Midst of Violence* (Downers Grove, Illinois: IVP Books, 2011).

Williams, Rowan, *The Wound of Knowledge: Christian Spirituality from the New Testament to John of the Cross* (London: Darton, Longman and Todd, 1979).

_____ *Arius: Heresy and Tradition* (London: Darton, Longman and Todd, 1987).

_____ 'The Body's Grace' (Lesbian and Gay Christian Movement, 1989), pp. 2–8.

_____ *Open to Judgement* (London: Darton, Longman and Todd, 1994).

_____ *The Truce of God* (Glasgow: Collins, 1983).

_____ *Christ on Trial: How the Gospel Unsettles our Judgement* (London: Fount, 2000).

_____ *Lost Icons: Reflections on Cultural Bereavement* (Edinburgh: T & T Clark, 2000).

_____ *On Christian Theology* (Oxford: Blackwell, 2000).

_____ *Ponder these Things: Praying with Icons of the Virgin* (Norwich: Canterbury Press, 2003).

_____ *The Dwelling of the Light: Praying with Icons of Christ* (Norwich: Canterbury Press, 2003).

_____ *Silence and Honey Cakes: The Wisdom of the Desert* (Oxford: Lion, 2003).

_____ *Anglican Identities* (London: Darton, Longman and Todd, 2004).

_____ *Grace and Necessity: Reflections on Art and Love* (Harrisburg PA: Morehouse, 2005).

_____ *Why Study the Past? The Quest for the Historical Church* (London: Darton, Longman and Todd, 2005).

_____ *Faith in the Public Square* (London: Bloomsbury, 2012).

Williams, Rowan and Larry Elliott (eds), *Crisis and Recovery: Ethics, Economics and Justice* (Basingstoke, Palgrave MacMillan, 2010).

Willimon, William H. and Stanley Hauerwas, with Scott C. Sage, *Lord Teach Us: The Lord's Prayer and the Christian Life* (Nashville: Abingdon Press, 1996).

Woodhead, Linda, 'The Quiet Revolution in UK Faith', *Church Times* (10 Feb 2012), p.12.

The House of Bishops Working Group on Human Sexuality (London: Church House Publishing, 2013).

The Kairos Document: Challenge to the Church, 2nd edn., (Johannesburg: Skotaville, 1986).

The Road to Damascus: Kairos and Conversion (Johannesburg: Skotaville, 1989).

Index